REMAINS

Historical and Literary

CONNECTED WITH THE PALATINE COUNTIES OF

Lancaster and Chester

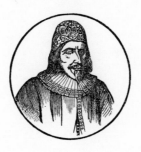

VOLUME XXIV—THIRD SERIES

MANCHESTER:

Printed for the Chetham Society

1976

THE ENCOURAGEMENT
OF THE FINE ARTS
IN LANCASHIRE
1760–1860

by

C. P. DARCY, Ph.D.

MANCHESTER
Printed for the Chetham Society
1976

© 1976 The Chetham Society
Published for the Society by
Manchester University Press
Oxford Road
Manchester M13 9PL

ISBN 0 7190 1330 5

PRINTED IN GREAT BRITAIN
BY BUTLER AND TANNER LTD, FROME AND LONDON

CONTENTS

                                                              PAGE

INTRODUCTION: The State of Patronage in Lancashire in 1760   1

CHAPTER
    I   General Causes of the Movement   7
    II   Early Manifestations of Patronage in Liverpool   20
    III Mature Plans for Liverpool   42
    IV   Liverpool's Rival   63
    V   Art Unions in Lancashire   80
    VI   Other Manifestations   95
    VII Lancashire Collections   122
    VIII The Influence of the Provinces   156

APPENDIX   163
BIBLIOGRAPHY   165
INDEX   175

ACKNOWLEDGEMENTS

I am glad to be able to acknowledge here my obligation to Jacques Barzun, James L. Clifford, Peter Gay, and John D. Rosenberg for their useful suggestions. I owe a large debt of gratitude to R. K. Webb and W. H. Chaloner for their sturdy help and productive criticism. My wife has been an active participant throughout the development of this dissertation and I am particularly grateful for her understanding and patience.

I am also indebted to Harvard University Press for permission to quote from *The Diary of Benjamin Robert Haydon*.

The following libraries have kindly granted permission to use and quote from manuscript materials in their collections:

Liverpool City Libraries
Manchester Public Libraries
The Pierpont Morgan Library
University of Liverpool Library

INTRODUCTION

THE STATE OF PATRONAGE IN LANCASHIRE IN 1760

The Industrial Revolution in England thrust forward merchants and manufacturers who challenged the political power of the aristocracy and gentry and vied with them in wealth. Some of these 'new men' of fortune began to aspire to a cultured way of life. Often, the town house or country mansion, filled with books and paintings, was not enough. Culture, for these men, meant art schools, concert halls, public libraries, church schools, and new churches: municipal enlightenment. This study focuses on those 'new men' who encouraged art and artists in an area of England transformed by the Industrial Revolution. The period associated with the Industrial Revolution in England in this study is defined as between 1760 and 1860. John Smeaton, the engineer, was certain that, 'Before or about the year 1760, a new era in all the arts and sciences, learned and polite, commenced in this country. Everything which contributes to the comfort, the beauty, and the prosperity of a country moved forward in improvement, so rapidly, and so obviously as to mark the period with particular distinction.'[1]

Nowhere were changes more rapid than in Lancashire, the focal point of this study. The adoption of the term 'the provinces' at the end of the eighteenth century reflected a growing awareness in influential circles in London of the significant changes taking place. Up to this time, England outside of London had usually been described as 'the country', but now this old term, with its rural overtones, was becoming inappropriate to describe fast-growing urban complexes such as Liverpool and Manchester.[2] These communities were no longer parochial in the way that villages and small country towns in other areas were; they were centres of intellectual activity with learned societies, newspapers, and theatres, supported by the commercial, industrial, and professional middle classes. The expansion of this group, or rather series of groups, was one of the most important social developments in Great Britain and on the Continent during this period.[3]

In Lancashire 'before or about the year 1760', the aristocracy[4]

[1] *Reports of the Late John Smeaton F.R.S.* (London, 1837), I, ix.
[2] Donald Read, *The English Provinces, c. 1760–1960* (London, 1964), p. 1.
[3] M. S. Anderson, *Eighteenth Century Europe 1713–1789* (London, 1966), p. 60.
[4] In England there was no nobility in the strict sense. On the Continent, nobility was usually a status; the legal rights enjoyed by this class were distinct and visible. The nearest analogy in England was the class of families possessing titles recognised

and gentry, rather than the middle classes, were the chief patrons of the arts. The wealthier had visited Italy, the land of marvels, the antique shop of Europe, and returned, more sophisticated and urbane than when they went forth, laden with works of art, which were often placed in stately country houses. Henry Blundell of Ince, a member of an old Lancashire Catholic family, is a perfect example of this type of patron. He began collecting paintings in the sixties, favouring the fashionable Italian baroque masters and Romanizing Dutchmen. In 1777, the *annus mirabilis* in Blundell's career as a collector, he bought a number of pictures in Italy from Thomas Jenkins, the English banker and dealer in Rome, and a 'Magdalene' from Mr. Byers, another dealer. In Florence, he bought several pictures from the extraordinary Englishman, Ignazio Enrico Hugford, painter, teacher, collector, faker, and one of the first dealers in Italian primitives.[1] In the same year, he ordered a 'Vesuvius in Eruption' from Volari, while a group of paintings by Labruzzi were snapped up for him by John Thorpe, a Jesuit priest turned dealer, who also acted as Blundell's agent in the purchase of both marbles and pictures.[2] Blundell, like most pilgrims of the Grand Tour, strengthened his taste and collection with the aid of these Anglo-Roman expatriates who devoted themselves to the British aristocracy's passions for sightseeing and for art.

Blundell and other travellers brought back statuary, bronzes and pictures ranging from antique Greek marbles to eighteenth-century Italian paintings. Henry Blundell's collection of classical sculpture vied in quantity, if not in quality, with that of his friend Charles Townley.[3] Over five hundred works, chiefly Roman copies of Greek originals, were arranged by Blundell in two specially built galleries at Ince: the large Rotunda, a miniature Pantheon of Rome, and the Garden Temple.[4] His collection of paintings not only contained Old Masters, but also illustrated the patronage Englishmen gave to fashionable Italian artists. Blundell possessed two Canalettos, a Giaquinto, and works by Nogari, Sebastiano Ricci, Vanvitelli, and

---

by law, but having hardly any other legal privileges. H. J. Habakkuk, 'England', *The European Nobility in the Eighteenth Century*, ed. Albert Goodwin (New York, 1967), p. 1; C. B. A. Behrens, *The Ancien Régime* (London, 1967), pp. 46–62; G. E. Mingay, *English Landed Society in the Eighteenth Century* (London, 1963), and F. M. L. Thompson, *English Landed Society in the Nineteenth Century* (London, 1963). Alexis de Tocqueville emphasised that the English aristocracy was founded not on birth but on wealth. *Journeys to England and Ireland* (London, 1958), p. 59.

[1] An interesting portrait of Hugford is found in John Fleming, *Robert Adam and His Circle* (Cambridge, 1962), pp. 276–8.

[2] *Pictures From Ince Blundell Hall* (Liverpool. 1960), p. 6.

[3] Charles Townley possessed the ancient seat, Towneley Hall, near Burnley in Lancashire, though the marbles and terra-cotta reliefs that surround him in the well-known painting by Zoffany were placed at 7 Park Street, Westminster. After his death, the collection was purchased by the British Museum.

[4] *An Account of the Statues, Busts, Bass-Relieves, Cinerary Urns and Other Ancient Marbles and Paintings at Ince. Collected by H. B.* (Liverpool, 1803).

Zuccarelli.[1] Other English collectors had magnificent examples of the works of Guardi, Piranesi, Batoni, Rosalba, and Panini.[2] This passion for Italian works, whether antique or modern, forced English painters and architects to make their own pilgrimages to Rome, for they stood little chance of making a living in England in the eighteenth century unless they could parade a recognizable virtuosity to the returned travellers.[3] Blundell commissioned Reynolds to paint a portrait of his first wife and purchased from Richard Wilson three Italian landscapes. Both artists were heirs of the Italian tradition.

The education of a Lancashire artist, Hamlet Winstanley, reveals how Italian influences touched the provinces. His first patron, John Finch, rector of Winwick, helped him to gain an Italian finish by sending him to the academy of Sir Godfrey Kneller in London. According to a contemporary memoir written either by Hamlet or his brother Peter, James Stanley, the tenth Earl of Derby, sent him to Rome in 1723:

> To compleat his study in painting, as perfect as possible to be attained and in order thereto his lordship got letters of credit, and recommendation for Mr. Winstanley, to a certain cardinal at Rome, to whom his lordship sent a present of a large whole piece of the best black broad cloth that London could produce, with a prospect to introduce Mr. Winstanley into what favors he had occasion for, to view all the principal paintings, statues and curiosities of Rome, and to copy some curious pictures (that could not be purchased by money) which Lord Derby had desire of, and he employed him while he stayed at Rome and at Venice awhile, in all but two years, for he came home in 1725.[4]

The Earl, engaged in much building at Knowsey between 1722 and 1732,[5] needed many paintings for his decorative schemes. Sketches of Rome's treasures and studies of antique figures helped Winstanley give an Italian air to his portraits of the aristocracy and gentlemen of the North.

In the towns of Lancashire, the taste for art was slight in 1760. Matthew Gregson, a publisher's agent for the sale of prints in his early years, later a decorator for merchants and manufacturers taking their first steps as connoisseurs, and now better known as an antiquarian and author of local history, in 1824 asked William

[1] *Ibid.*, pp. 211–73.
[2] Frederick Antal, *Hogarth and His Place in European Art.* (New York, 1962), ch. III.
[3] Artists' sketchbooks and drawings were often points of reference and recollection. The sketchbook of Richard Wilson has recently been published. *An Italian Sketchbook*, ed. Denys Sutton (London, 1968).
[4] 'Hamlet Winstanley', *Dictionary of National Biography*, XXI, 678.
[5] Now that the present Lord Derby has pulled down most of the Victorian and Edwardian additions, the present house is very much as it was in the middle of the eighteenth century. For a vivid portrait of the family in the nineteenth and twentieth centuries see Randolph S. Churchill, *Lord Derby, 'King of Lancashire'* (London, 1959).

Roscoe, the outstanding cultural leader in Lancashire for half a century, to recall the first chapter in the history of community patronage of art in Liverpool. 'I should wish some record of this period drawn up, for evidence in times to come . . . to mark the first dawn of taste—when a print of 2s. value could not find a purchaser in Liverpool nor was there a painting worth three pounds . . .'[1] Introductory paragraphs would describe a print society organised 'to purchase all the books and prints extant, to circulate them from house to house in rotation weekly, to collect the whole monthly, to meet and spend a pleasant evening over them; again to pass them around; at the end of the year to sell them amongst subscribers only, and make fresh purchases again for the ensuing year. By this means the best and most expensive works have been in the possession of the Society and now remain divided amongst them.'[2] Next he described a raffle for a print. 'John Gore the vendor paid 5s. to the expenses of the evening—and I the winner of that wonderful print paid the other 5s.—the Royal Academy of Zoffany . . .'[3] Increased wealth in the community brought more sophisticated methods. 'A short while after this time I paid £18 for a print for your Brother-in-Law Dan Daulby Esq.—and I paid 63s. for a portfolio to carry it in safe to Liverpool. The print was the Burgomaster Six by Rembrant. . . .'[4] The proposed chapters of Gregson's work would be a history of the further progress of patronage.

The following chapters fill in the Gregson outline with much material on the character of individual and group patronage in Lancashire in a period of great intellectual, economic, and political change. Particular emphasis is placed on the history of co-operative endeavours. Following the pioneer efforts of London painters and patrons, leading citizens in Lancashire pooled their energies in group enterprises having a two-fold purpose: to create and diffuse a taste for the fine arts among the people through the study and exhibition of the works of art, in order to enlighten men and women, and to offer professional training to young artists, in order to encourage the growth of national art. Throughout the period (1760–1860), the idea grew and spread that public co-operative enterprises devoted to the cause of art, particularly English art, were necessary, useful, and valuable to the provinces as well as to London and that their development was the responsibility of men of wealth, position and leadership.[5] Until the eighteen thirties a definite mercantile

---

[1] Matthew Gregson, Liverpool, 1824. Letter to William Roscoe, Roscoe Papers, Liverpool Record Office.
[2] *Ibid.*   [3] *Ibid.*   [4] *Ibid.*
[5] T. S. Ashton emphasises that in the eighteenth century the characteristic instrument of social purpose was not the individual or the state, but the club. 'The idea that, somehow or other, men had become self-centered, avaricious, and anti-social is the strangest of all the legends by which the story of the industrial revolution has been obscured.' *The Industrial Revolution 1760–1830* (London, 1964), p. 68.

and upper class bias pervaded provincial aesthetic enterprises. With the appearance of vigorous advocates of popular instruction such as Brougham and the growth of the Mechanics' Institute movement, art programmes became more democratic.[1]

[1] J. A. Roebuck, a leading member of the radical group, declared: 'My object has been through life to make the working man as exalted and civilised a creature as I could make him. I wanted to place before his mind a picture of civilised life such as I see in my own life . . . my household has been a civilized household. It has been a household in which thought, high and elevated ideas of literature, and grace and beauty, have always found everything that could recommend them . . . I wanted to make the working class like me.' *Life and Letters of John Arthur Roebuck . . . with Chapters of Autobiography*, ed. Robert Eadon Leader (London, 1897), p. 325.

CHAPTER I

GENERAL CAUSES OF THE MOVEMENT

I. THE ECONOMIC BACKGROUND

The economic growth of Lancashire coincided with that of the whole nation. From the beginning to the middle of the eighteenth century, the total volume of English foreign trade (imports, exports, and re-exports) doubled. By the mid-1780's it stood about 50 per cent higher than in 1750, and in the next fifteen years it doubled once again. In the mid-1840s foreign trade was more than three times as high as at the beginning of the nineteenth century.[1] This rapid growth was closely related to the development of the industrial segment of the economy. Phyllis Deane calculated that between 1688 and 1801 the total national income from mining, manufacturing, and building rose from 21 per cent to 23·6 per cent and from trade and transport from 12 per cent to 17·5 per cent, while the income from agriculture, forestry, and fishing fell from 40 per cent to 32·5 per cent.[2] In this period, the largest relative increase in the growth of national income took place in trade and transport, a fact that helps to explain the phenomenal growth of Liverpool, the great port of the Mersey. Although Manchester, the manufacturing centre of Lancashire, had become a boom town by 1801, the full effects of the Industrial Revolution developed only in the next four decades. By 1840 mining, manufacturing, and building moved from 23·6 per cent to 34·4 per cent; primary activities dropped from 32·5 per cent to 22·1 per cent; and trade and transport moved from 17·5 per cent to 18·4 per cent.[3] 'It has been estimated that Lancashire was the thirty-fifth wealthiest English county in 1693, third in 1803, fourth in 1814, and second in 1843.'[4] Whether in the eighteenth or in the nineteenth century, economic growth provided the stimulus for cultural growth in England.

The port of Liverpool, the first base for the development of urban culture in Lancashire, grew earlier and progressed faster through most of the eighteenth century than the rest of Lancashire.[5] The

[1] B. R. Mitchell with the collaboration of Phyllis Deane, *Abstract of British Historical Statistics* (Cambridge, 1962), pp. 279–83.
[2] Phyllis Deane and W. A. Cole, *British Economic Growth, 1688–1959, Trends and Structure* (Cambridge, 1932), p. 161.
[3] *Ibid.*, p. 166.
[4] Seymour Shapiro, *Capital and the Cotton Industry in the Industrial Revolution* (Ithaca, 1967), p. 151.
[5] Several studies illustrate economic change in Lancashire in this period. The growth of Liverpool is described in C. Northcote Parkinson, *The Rise of the Port of*

great fortunes of Liverpool were made in the colonial trade. Her merchants imported colonial produce, such as sugar, coffee, and cotton, which was often re-exported to Holland, to Hamburg, or to other Baltic ports. They bartered cargoes of light textiles, metal wares, beer, and spirits on the African shore for slaves. They also had the ability to develop saleable lines in the colonies: Irish linens, Lancashire cottons and earthenware, and the metal wares of the Birmingham region.[1] Liverpool not only trafficked in products from overseas and the hinterland but also developed her own specialities: ships built on the Mersey, tools, clocks[2] and watches, and earthenware. By 1760 there were a number of factories manufacturing earthenware and porcelain along Shaw's Brow, the largest, that of Richard Chaffers. Seth Pennington also operated a large factory, which was noted for its fine punch bowls in earthenware and porcelain. Much printing on chinaware was done in Liverpool by the firm of Sadler and Green, and porcelain was sent from considerable distances to Liverpool for decoration.[3]

In 1760, Samuel Derrick, the master of ceremonies at Bath, visited Liverpool and found many signs of refinement. Many houses were faced with stone in an elegant manner. The new Exchange, designed by the Woods of Bath, contained noble apartments in which the corporation transacted business and an assembly room that 'is grand, spacious, and finely illuminated; here is a meeting once a fortnight to dance and to play cards; where you will find some women elegantly accomplished and perfectly dressed.'[4] In the very neat theatre 'a company of London performers exhibit during the summer season and acquire a great deal of money . . .[5] About the

---

Liverpool (Liverpool, 1952). Port operations and problems of trade are detailed in *The Customs Letterbooks of the Port of Liverpool, 1711–1813*, edited by R. C. Jarvis (Manchester, 1954). The influence of the slave trade on the merchant community is vividly brought out in Averil Mackenzie-Grieve's *The Last Years of the English Slave Trade, 1750–1807* (London, 1941). The impact of cotton is the subject of an article by F. E. Hyde, B. B. Parkinson, and Sheila Marriner, 'The Cotton Broker and the Rise of the Liverpool Cotton Market', *Ec.H.R.*, 2nd ser., VIII (1955). The struggle to develop internal waterways and the effects of increased navigation are subjects of T. S. Willan's *The Navigation of the River Weaver during the Eighteenth Century* (Manchester, 1951). Aspects of industrialization are described in T. C. Barker and J. R. Harris, *A Merseyside Town in the Industrial Revolution: St. Helens, 1750–1900* (Liverpool, 1954).

[1] Ralph Davis, *The Rise of the English Shipping Industry* (London, 1962), ch. XIII.

[2] Among the best known clockmakers were the Finneys. Five members of the family worked in Liverpool, the earliest being Joseph who worked between 1734 and 1761 ,and the last, another Joseph who worked between 1770 and 1796. *Art at Auction: The Year at Sotheby's and Parke-Bernet: 1966–67* (London, 1967), p. 420.

[3] Knowles Boney, *Liverpool Porcelain of the Eighteenth Century and its Makers* (London, 1957).

[4] Quoted in Thomas Barnes, *History of the Commerce and Town of Liverpool* (London, 1852), I, 426.

[5] *Ibid.* In emulation of London, Liverpool also had a playhouse named Drury Lane, first opened in 1749 or 1750. Many of the London players went out into the provinces during the summer, and some found their way to Liverpool. *The Letters of David Garrick*, ed. David M. Little and George M. Kahrl (Cambridge, Mass.,

same time, an Irish gentleman found 'The Lion' 'one of the best ordinaries in England, as you've the nicest and most uncommon dishes at only 8d per piece.'[1] St. Paul's, consecrated in 1769, was the most magnificent church of the establishment, and chapels and churches of the various groups of dissenters were numerous.[2] The first local newspaper made its appearance in 1710. In 1775 there were two: Williamson's *Liverpool Advertiser and Mercantile Register* and *The General Advertiser.*

The development of the manufacture of cottons brought rapid growth to the hinterland beyond Liverpool in the last quarter of the eighteenth century. Many of the towns had their own particular processes or products, some specializing in combing, others concentrating on weaving. Manchester firms specialised in the lighter and more valuable products and laid particular emphasis on the finishing processes.[3]

Early in the eighteenth century, the merchants who organised the manufacture of cloth in Manchester and the surrounding region were called 'linen drapers'; only as the century progressed did they emerge as 'merchants' and 'manufacturers' specialising in particular products. As late as 1800, all the leading Manchester merchants were manufacturers without exception; i.e., they employed domestic workers over a wide area. They might also be dealers in various raw materials—cotton, wool, linen warps—and finishers, who bought unbleached fabrics, dyed them, and sold them in various markets. From the 1760s onwards, the larger firms concentrated on selling in the London and overseas markets, while the middling class of manufacturers made the home market the centre of its endeavours. Until 1800 Manchester was still largely a town of little dealers and manufacturers. By 1820, these men had increased greatly in wealth and economic importance and were advertising in the newspapers for commissions to finish goods either for the home trade or for the overseas markets. Their success stimulated the expansion of warehousing, particularly in the 1820's.[4]

As they accumulated profits from trade, some of the merchants invested in the new inventions, but many of the industrialists began

---

1963), II, 563. An interesting series of eighteenth-century playbills from Liverpool is in the Harvard Theatre Collection.

[1] An Irish Gentleman, *Journey Through England* (1751), p. 12.

[2] William Enfield, *An Essay Towards the History of Leverpool, drawn up from the papers left by the late Mr. George Perry, and from other materials since collected* (London 1774), p. 45.

[3] Asa Briggs, *The Age of Improvement* (London, 1959), p. 53.

[4] W. H. Chaloner, 'The Birth of Modern Manchester', *Manchester and Its Region* (Manchester, 1962), pp. 133-4. For a more detailed picture of facets of the textile industry see G. W. Armitage, *The Lancashire Cotton Industry from the Great Inventions to the Great Disaster* (Manchester, 1951); G. A. Turnbull, *A History of the Calico Printing Industry* (Altrincham, 1951); and A. and N. L. Clow, *The Chemical Revolution* (London, 1952).

as manufacturers of textile machinery. The successive issues of the Manchester and Salford directories disclose a steady increase in the number of engineering firms and textile machinery makers between 1781 and 1800. Often skilled joiners and turners and clockmakers transformed themselves into shuttle makers and loom makers. Some went very far, establishing large engineering firms or developing cotton spinning enterprises.[1] By 1795 there were at least six considerable foundries in Manchester and Salford. In this period 'the cumulative technical progress made by the engineers and machine builders of Lancashire was far more significant than the contributions of the hand full of inventors who figure in the text books'.[2]

Other manufacturers expanded:

> The making of paper at mills in the vicinity has been brought to great perfection, and now includes all kinds, from the strongest parcelling paper to the finest writing sorts, and that on which banker's bills were printed. The tinplate workers have found additional employment in furnishing many articles for spinning machines. . . . Harness makers have been much employed in making bands for carding machines, whereby the consumption of strong curried leather has been much increased.[3]

As trade and manufacturing increased in the eighteenth century, the foundations of provincial banking were laid. The manufacturers and traders of Lancashire could obtain fixed capital by borrowing from relatives or by ploughing back profits into their enterprises, but they needed circulating capital to purchase raw materials, to pay workers, and to maintain factory or workshop. They needed both cash and short-term credit. To meet their needs, however imperfectly and unsystematically, country bankers began operations. There were only a handful in 1750, but their number grew rapidly in the next half century. They were recruited from three main sources—merchants and industrialists whose main concern was to furnish a local means of payment; financial agents, like country attorneys who received money on trust and were familiar with the investment scene; and remitters of funds between London and provincial centres, such as collectors of government revenue.[4]

In Liverpool, pioneer bankers emerged from the community of drapers. In the directory of 1774, William Clarke was described as 'banker and linen draper', but by 1781 he had abandoned textiles and was concentrating on banking. William Roscoe had been ap-

[1] A. P. Wadsworth and J. de L. Mann, *The Cotton Trade and Industrial Lancashire* (Manchester, 1931), Ch. XIII and XIV.

[2] S. D. Chapman, *The Early Factory Masters: The Transition to the Factory System in the Midlands Textile Industry* (Newton Abbot, 1967), pp. 213–14.

[3] Dr. John Aikin, *A Description of the Country from Thirty to Forty Miles Round Manchester* (London, 1795), p. 178.

[4] 'Of fourteen banks of any importance listed for Liverpool, ten sprang from merchants' houses . . .', L. S. Pressnell, *Country Banking in the Industrial Revolution* (Oxford, 1956), p. 49.

prenticed to an attorney and had come into banking as a result of a request for his services when the affairs of William Clarke and Co. were in difficulties; but he, too, was connected with textiles in that he married a linen draper's daughter. Representing a specialisation and development of financial resources, the country banks were indispensable to economic progress. And, with good management and good fortune, the rewards of country banking could be very great. Leyland, Bullins & Co. of Liverpool and Jones, Loyd & Co. of Manchester were very substantial firms. In 1815, Leyland, Bullins had total assets of more than one million sterling and in 1836 almost three million.[1]

Both before and after the establishment of country banks, the manufacturer was assisted by merchant credit. The Liverpool merchant who imported cotton might enable a young manufacturer to set up for himself by giving him three months' credit, while an exporting merchant gave similar assistance by paying for the manufacturer's output week by week. By a continuous flow of capital inwards from commerce, many of the early industrial firms of Lancashire developed.

Of all the manufacturing centres of Lancashire, Manchester received the closest inspection. John Byng, a lover of country life, viewed the community with a critical eye in 1790. 'After breakfast I wander'd about this great, nasty manufacturing town; looking exactly like Spitalfields, and those environs: their exchange is an handsome building, just crowded into a low situation. . . .'[2] He found the town 'hourly increasing in building, and of the better sort; opposite to Lever Row is the grand new infirmary; and in Mosley Street now finishing, are chapels of prayer, and assembly rooms for dancing, well built, and bespeaking opulence and an increasing trade'.[3] Engels would have liked his parting shot: 'Who but a merchant cou'd live in such a hole; where the slave working and drinking a short life out, is eternally reeling before you from fatigue or drunkenness.'[4]

Much of the early building in Manchester took place when many of England's finest streets and terraces were inspired by the great tradition of Georgian architecture. Although there were a dozen or more dignified buildings in John Street and around Ardwick Green, town houses of the wealthy in King Street, a crescent at Salford, and a few terraces in Upper Brook Street, these were the efforts of builders who were not the equal of those of London and Edinburgh. The majority of commercial buildings were mediocre in style, cheaply and hurriedly built. The old cathedral remained the architectural

[1] Rondo Cameron, *Banking in the Early Stages of Industrialisation* (New York, 1967), pp. 26–7.
[2] John Byng (later fifth Viscount Torrington), *The Torrington Diaries* (London, 1954), p. 258.
[3] *Ibid.*   [4] *Ibid.*, p. 259.

B

triumph of the city. Venerable, too, was the home of the Grammar School, founded in 1519 and Chetham's Hospital, founded in 1653. St. Peter's, designed by James Wyatt, and the Cross Street Chapel were graceful Georgian churches. Beyond the town were two elegant neo-classic mansions: Platt Hall, with its dignified symmetrical facade, and Heaton Hall, another design of James Wyatt in the best Adam style.[1] The most elegant of Manchester's libraries, the Portico, was a building of the Ionic order in Runcorn stone, designed by Thomas Harrison, built at a cost of £8100 between 1802 and 1806.[2]

Joseph Farington, the artist, was much more tolerant of Manchester than Byng. A visitor in 1808, he found the Portico an important foundation for the cultural development of the town. 'A very spacious and handsome room, with a gallery above and a library. Strangers residing more than six miles from Manchester are admitted gratis. . . .'[3] Farington was also favourably impressed with the Commercial Room, a club for business men, and the assembly rooms, which were 'very spacious and handsome, with very large pier glasses, Chandeliers and Girondolas'.[4]

The pattern of development in most of the new towns was much the same. As the citizens grew in wealth and education, they came to demand not only a higher standard of cleanliness, with adequately paved, drained, and lighted streets, but they desired also such things as a spacious assembly hall, a subscription library, possibly a printing press with a local newspaper, certainly book shops, and often a literary and philosophical society.[5] Already, many merchants and manufacturers had become members of such London societies as the Royal Society of Arts; they participated by correspondence when at home and attended meetings during their occasional visits to London. Such organisations in the capital, however, were not adequate for the needs of a changing England. The increasing intellectual interests of a widely diffused middle class and the rigours of travel and communication combined to encourage the growth of small intellectual and cultural circles throughout the provinces. Although some of the leaders in these groups looked to London for models, many were consciously proud of their independence of

---

[1] Arthur T. Bolton, *The Architecture of Robert and James Adam* (London, 1922), 2 vols.

[2] Tinsley Pratt, *The Portico Library, Manchester: its history and associations (1802–1922)* (Manchester 1922); Rachel Horsfield, 'The Portico Library', Manchester', *Manchester Review*, Summer 1971, pp. 15–18.

[3] Joseph Farington, *The Farington Diary*, ed. James Greig (London, 1924), V, 107.

[4] *Ibid.*

[5] 'In spite of the multiplication of printed matter man feels an irrepressible impulse to communicate his thoughts by word of mouth. To satisfy needs which libraries are incapable of satisfying institutions of a novel type sprang up in the provinces.' Elie Halévy, *England in 1815*, Vol. I of *A History of the English People in the Nineteenth Century* (New York, 1949), pp. 561–2.

London and deliberately directed their attention toward other provincial groups like themselves. For many of them, the intellectual centre of their universe was not London, but Edinburgh or Glasgow.

To claim that every cotton spinner and every tobacco importer was an enthusiastic supporter of cultural endeavours would be an exaggeration. The majority of merchants and manufacturers was pouring a large part of their energies and profits into the expansion of their firms. Yet, they were at the same time creating the surplus wealth that made other, less material, activities possible, and attracting professional men, doctors, attorneys and teachers, men more capable of enjoying them, to the expanding provincial communities. And, though the trader and manufacturer might never get away from ledger or machine, wives and daughters and even sons were often attracted to the theatre, the concert hall, and the assembly room.[1] If these entrepreneurs were not ready to spend £50,000 on a great house, they were prepared to invest a few thousand pounds in a town house or a country villa.[2]

In Liverpool about 1760 the houses that faced upon the various streets were of great variety in size and style, for rich and poor lived side by side, and even the most opulent merchants lived above their cellar warehouses in Lord Street, Old Hall Street, and Duke Street. Towards the end of the century many wealthy men abandoned their old houses and sought more elegant surroundings. Rodney Street attracted such powerful merchants as John Gladstone, the father of the statesman. St. Anne Street, too, was fashionable, and about 1800 Mosslake Fields were laid out as well as Bedford Street, Chatham Street, and Abercromby and Falkner Squares. Country estates of merchants and bankers impressed themselves on the near countryside, at Everton Hill and Toxteth Park, and were found farther away in Allerton and Childwall. In 1801 a traveller approaching Liverpool observed, 'at a distance of five miles from the town, we perceived ourselves in its environs, elegant houses, the retreats of merchants rose on every side.'[3]

In the last quarter of the eighteenth century, as Manchester's streets filled with low brick dwellings interspersed with mills and warehouses, some successful businessmen, such as Thomas Walker, exchanged their residences on South Parade for big country houses for the summer months.[4] Others abandoned the town altogether, becoming estate owners and improving landlords. In this great era of domestic architecture, for each gentleman's seat in Lancashire

---

[1] Witt Bowden, *Industrial Society in England Towards the End of the Eighteenth Century.*

[2] Frank Jenkins, *Architect and Patron* (London, 1961), p. 82.

[3] Quoted in Dorothy Marshall, *English People in the Eighteenth Century* (London, 1956), p. 264.

[4] Frida Knight, *The Strange Case of Thomas Walker: Ten Years in the Life of a Manchester Radical* (London, 1957), p. 16.

that was built or altered by a fashionable architect,[1] a dozen more modest suburban dwellings were put up. These undertakings also gave employment to builders and decorators; there were consultations with artists and picture dealers.

II. OPPORTUNITIES FOR ENGLISH ARTISTS

In 1712, *The Spectator* had commented: 'No nation in the world delights so much in having their own, or Friend's or Relatives' Pictures, whether from their own National good-nature or having a love to Painting, and not being encouraged in the great article of Religious Pictures, which the Purity of our worship refuses the free use of . . .'[2] In 1760 portrait painting still offered the greatest opportunities to English artists, since the Protestant religion excluded many other types of subjects commonly enjoyed on the Continent. Aristocrats, country gentlemen, and great City merchants extended their patronage only to a very limited number of fashionable portrait painters. In London and the provinces, the middle class often favoured 'the conversation piece', which represented a number of persons, a family or a group of friends, with an air of informality. 'When the middle classes, often with large families, began to wish to have their portraits painted, a kind of picture that was inevitable evolved which was adopted to relatively small houses. For figures of this modest scale, a correspondingly modest price per head could legitimately be demanded, so that economic and social conditions combined to promote the vogue of the conversation piece.'[3] Arthur Devis was a most successful practitioner, and his patrons consisted almost entirely of businessmen, their wives, and children.[4]

Many artists were dissatisfied with their social status, which was equivalent to that of a craftsman, with their limited financial opportunities, and with the restrictions to portraiture. They vigorously asserted that an academy, after the model of the French Academy established by Louis XIV in France, 'not only would promote the intellectual and professional competence of its members, but would, above all, place the artist on a social level with his client and assure patronage.'[5] A real academy of arts on the continental model would have the two-fold function of giving instruction to art students and holding annual exhibitions for the display and sale of new works. Through the efforts of Sir Joshua Reynolds and other leading artists,

[1] Descriptions and engravings are found in John Bernard Burke, *A Visitation of the Seats and Arms of the Noblemen and Gentlemen of Great Britain* (London, 1852), 2. vols.
[2] Quoted in Thomas Ashcroft, *English Art and English Society* (London, 1936), p. 36.
[3] Arts Council of Great Britain, *Early Conversation Pieces of the Eighteenth Century*, Illustrated Catalogue (London, 1946), p. 3.
[4] Sydney H. Paviere, *The Devis Family of Painters* (Leigh-on-Sea, 1950), p. 35.
[5] Rudolph Wittkower, 'The Artist', *Man versus Society in 18th Century Britain*, ed. James L. Clifford (Cambridge, 1968), p. 83.

the Royal Academy was instituted under the patronage of George III in 1768 to provide systematic instruction, to promote annual exhibitions of pictures, and, above all, to give artists an improved status.[1]

The academy fulfilled these aims admirably. Annual exhibitions gave artists the opportunity of studying each other's works and provided them with a shop window in which to show their achievements, thus helping to free them from the older, narrower system of patronage and the tyranny of picture dealers. The Royal Academy was largely responsible for raising the status of artists above that of ordinary craftsmen. Invitations to its banquets were sought after, and members of the royal family, diplomats, and politicians attended these elaborate affairs, which were a far cry from the jesting evenings of the old artists' clubs. The schools gave students a good academic grounding and an opportunity to draw from models and casts.

The academy exhibitions opened up a much wider market, enabling artists to exhibit historical scenes, genre paintings, and landscapes with the hope of either finding purchasers or creating enough interest to justify the publication of engravings. Though certain artists complained loudly and constantly of the lack of patronage, especially for history pictures, the sheer quantity of paintings produced in the last quarter of the century is witness to the demand from the wealthy for pictures to complete the decoration of town and country houses. Thus, it is not incorrect to state that the forces that brought about the foundation of the academy were social as well as artistic, reflecting the continuing growth of a community of patrons in which aristocratic and middle-class elements were balanced.

Collecting English art became fashionable as the eighteenth century ended, with members of the aristocracy and of the upper middle class setting the example. Sir Thomas Bernard, the lawyer and philanthropist, gathered a collection 'which consists chiefly (or entirely) of the work of modern English artists. This gentleman, whose life is a series of active benevolences, is said to have annually set apart, during many years past, for the purchase of works of his own countrymen, such a sum as he esteemed proportional to his station and wealth.'[2] Sir George Beaumont gave intelligent support to Constable, Haydon, and Wilkie. Alexander Davidson, a banker, formed a Gallery of British Pictures, filled with works painted expressly for the collection by West, Tresham, Smirke, Devis, Wilkie, Copley, Northcote, and Westall. Sir Richard Colt Hoare possessed at

---

[1] The standard history now is Sidney C. Hutchison, *The History of the Royal Academy, 1768–1968* (London, 1968).

[2] Prince Hoare, *An Inquiry into the Cultivation and Present State of the Arts of Design in England* (London, 1806), p. 231.

Stourhead 'a collection of Paintings, by modern artists, which,' he informed the editor of the *Annals of the Fine Arts*, 'is respectable though by no means equal to that of my friend Sir John Leicester. To show that modern art has not been neglected,' he continued, 'it would not be amiss to mention other collections which are deposed about the metropolis and country.'[1]

Mr. Chamberly, near Southampton, has been a very great encourager. Sir John Swinburne also. He has a picture of Turner for which he paid £700—a very fine one by Callcott, and another by Mulready. . . . Mr. George Cary of Torr Abbey has many moderns. Of these last two, I could procure lists. . . . Lord Stafford, Lord Coventry and many others whom you may possibly know, have been patrons.[2]

The editor of the *Annals* made his own evaluations. He agreed that Sir John Leicester held first position as an encourager of English art, but pointed out that the Marquis of Stafford, Sir George Beaumont, and Lord Mulgrave were not far behind. Mr. Allnutt of Clapham Common possessed several English pictures. Lord Grosvenor had fine examples of the work of Hogarth, Wilson, and Gainsborough, and Mr. Wheeler of Gloucester Place possessed drawings by Heaphy, Hills, and others. The editor concluded that no list of patrons of the English school would be complete without the names of Hoare and Walter Fawkes, the Yorkshire magnate.[3]

The collections of Sir Richard Colt Hoare, Sir John Leicester, and Walter Fawkes reflected the fashionable new trends in English collecting. Both Sir Richard and Sir John enjoyed 'the grand romantic scenery of Wales',[4] and watercolours that captured impressions of that land. Sir Richard possessed many works of romantic sensibility such as Thomson's 'A Child and a Dead Pheasant', Northcote's 'The Dumb Alphabet', and 'A Boy and Gold Finch', and 'A Shepherdess and Lamb' by Woodforde.[5] Sir John gradually collected many fine examples of British art in a gallery at his London house in Hill Street where, from 1818, the public was admitted to view the collection. Walter Fawkes, an intimate friend and early patron of Turner, followed Sir John's example and exhibited a magnificent collection of landscapes in watercolours at his house in Grosvenor Square. The example set by these men quickened interest in English art and in collecting works of the English school of painting and sculpture.

In the late eighteenth century, perhaps an even greater patron

---

[1] *Annals of the Fine Arts* (London, 1817), II, 270.
[2] *Ibid.*
[3] *Ibid.*, p. 235.
[4] William Carey, *Some Memoirs of the Patronage and Progress of the Fine Arts, in England and Ireland, during the reigns of George the Second, George the Third, and his Present Majesty; with anecdotes of Lord de Tabley, of other Patrons, and eminent Artists, etc.* (London, 1826), p. 110.
[5] *Ibid.*

of the English school of art than these was the print maker. Print sellers in London and the provincial towns catered to every section of the community. Cottagers and craftsmen purchased crudely illustrated chapbooks at country fairs; prosperous farmers and innkeepers bought coloured mezzotints published by Carrington Bowles and other old-established city firms; while connoisseurs collected portfolios of expensive reproductions of the works of old and contemporary masters, caricatures, and literary illustrations. The print seller often provided income for a painter when all else failed. Northcote remembered that,

Deprived of all resources in the line of portrait painting, I betook myself from necessity to painting small historical and fancy subjects from the most popular authors of the day, as such subjects are sure of sale amongst the minor print dealers, being done in a short time, and for a small price. From those which I executed, there are prints taken such as Sterne's *Sentimental Journey*, the *Sorrows of Werther*, Gay's pastorals, etc. I did also small pictures, or rather sketches of the events of the moment, such as at the times were topics of general conversation. But all this was work against my will, work of necessity, . . . undertaken only for the lack of better commissions.[1]

The production of prints became a truly national endeavour with the successes of Alderman Boydell, who broke the foreign monopoly on prints and engravings. Before his triumphs, English prints and engravings were disdained, and thousands of pounds of foreign engravings were imported into England each year. Boydell turned the tide with his engravings of Wilson's 'Niobe' (c. 1760) and West's 'Death of General Wolfe' (1771), which Londoners and provincials purchased by the score. By 1785 the exports of English engravings were worth £200,000, and the imports of foreign engravings had sunk to about £1,000.[2]

What subjects were popular with the men of the North? Views of gentlemen's seats and gardens and landscapes were favourites with the gentry. Now, merchant and manufacturer encouraged the topographical artist to depict the wealth of England, her coal pits, quarries, and ironworks. The features and dress of the working population and its various occupations were also recorded by the deft pencils of such artists as Paul Sandby.[3] These men were also interested in the impressions that artists brought back from distant expeditions: the tour of Joseph Banks to Iceland, the voyages of Captain Cook, and the travels of Lord Macartney in China. In the houses of the wealthy, perhaps, were folios filled with illustrations of classical temples or Gothic churches.

---

[1] Stephen Gwynne, *Memorials of an Eighteenth Century Painter* (London, 1898), pp. 199–200.

[2] Thomas Balston, 'Alderman Boydell—Printseller', *History Today*, August, 1952, p. 547.

[3] Francis D. Klingender, *Art and the Industrial Revolution* (London, 1947), pp. 39–55.

The print seller continued to be an influential patron of the artist in the early nineteenth century, and artists of great reputation were richly rewarded. In 1817 Wilkie wrote:

The print from my picture of the Rent Day has just been published, and seems very much liked. We hope for a great sale, as 450 impressions were sold within the first six days after publication. I expect that the great sale will be in the country, and particularly in the agricultural districts. We have had a considerable demand from Norfolk, and I shall not be satisfied if there is not as great a demand for them in Fifeshire.[1]

The proofs of Wilkie's prints were usually four guineas each, while the ordinary impression was half that sum. A generation later, Landseer received generous sums for the engraving rights to his works. His paintings were extremely popular in middle-class households and, even when translated into black and white, made a forceful impact. Throughout his most productive years, Landseer derived half his income from copyrights. Henry Graves alone paid him about £60,000.[2]

Publishers kept a host of artists busy with illustrations for novels and independent works, such as those favourites with middle-class women, the annual and the keepsake.[3] Often these artists were underpaid. For example, in 1813, young William Collins sold the 'Pet Lamb' to a print publisher for a fee well above the 20 to 25 guineas that was usual for him, namely £145 10s. In view of the fact that the print, originally a magazine illustration, was re-issued in 15,000 impressions, the price was low. In 1821, John Martin had a similar experience. A small engraving of his Marcus Curtius picture, originally an illustration in the *Forget-me-not Annual*, was re-cut several times and sold 10,000 extra impressions.[4] Thackeray, denouncing as servitude the old dependence on individual patronage, declared that, thanks to engravings, the great public had now become the painter's true patron. This is exaggeration. The public was still limited. In 1843 Cunningham noted that publishers were shying away from large prints of a good class, for some had failed to attract buyers.[5]

In 1845, however, the development of electro-typing made larger editions of steel engravings possible without the loss of detail. The same year saw another important innovation. The duty on glass, which made framing a print eight times as expensive as on the

---

[1] Allan Cunningham, *The Life of David Wilkie* (London, 1843), I, 458.
[2] James A. Manson, *Sir Edwin Landseer* (London, 1902), p. 200.
[3] Some artists began and ended their careers with this work. Thomas Stothard contributed to the first volume of *Lady's Poetical Magazine* in 1781, and in the 1820s his work was found in *The Amulet*, *The Bijou* and other works of this type. A. C. Coxhead, *Thomas Stothard* (London, 1906), p. 33, and p. 55.
[4] G. R. Reitlinger, *The Economics of Taste* (London, 1961), p. 98.
[5] A. P. Oppé, 'Art', *Early Victorian England 1830–1865*, ed. G. M. Young (London, 1951), II, 122.

Continent, was abolished. The householder of the lower middle class hesitated to spend four guineas for a proof and two guineas for a frame, but a two-guinea proof in a five-shilling frame was an enticement to buy.

The triumphs of the English printmakers and the opening of the Royal Academy coincided with social changes long in the making. England's ascendancy in trade and industry had produced men of ambition and wealth,[1] proud of past cultural achievements, ready to support contemporary endeavours. This class responded to themes of national interest, modern problems of moral conduct, social criticism, and political and personal satire. Many academicians modified the aims of 'high art' to obtain the patronage of the middle classes in London and the provinces.[2]

[1] A heterogeneous bourgeoisie was developing 'whose multitudinous shadings of income, origin, education, and way of life are over-ridden by a common resistance to inclusion in, or confusion with, the working classes, and by an unquenchable social ambition.' David S. Landes, *The Unbound Prometheus: Technological Change and Industrial Development in Western Europe from 1750 to the Present* (Cambridge, 1969), p. 9.
[2] Wittkower, p. 82.

CHAPTER II

EARLY MANIFESTATIONS OF PATRONAGE IN LIVERPOOL

I. ACADEMIES IN THE LATE EIGHTEENTH AND EARLY NINETEENTH CENTURIES

In the eighteenth century, the new urban agglomerations of Lancashire lacked both the charms of the country and the dignity of great cities; they were without galleries, museums, academies, palaces: ornaments of a kind in which artists and lovers of art might learn lessons of value and find enjoyment. The great majority of the merchants and manufacturers had neither the opportunity nor, perhaps, the disposition to become educated in the manner of the aristocracy. Nevertheless, there were some among the merchants and manufacturers who became aware of their own cultural deficiencies, who felt that taste was lacking in their homes and towns and that it must be supplied, as a matter of principle.[1] The ideas of the Enlightenment became the guiding principles for these influential men, encouraging them to assume the responsibility for the moral, intellectual, and cultural well-being of their towns. For these men, the town or city[2] existed for the development of culture as well as capitalism. 'The eighteenth century developed out of its philosophy of Enlightenment the view of the city as virtue.'[3] Such *philosophes* as Voltaire and Adam Smith emphasised that cities laid the foundation for progress in both industry and culture. 'When [men] are secure of enjoying the fruits of this industry,' Smith wrote, 'they naturally exert it to better their condition and to acquire not only the necessities, but the conveniences and elegancies of life.'[4]

In Lancashire manifestations of progress appeared in the middle

[1] S. G. Checkland, 'English Provincial Cities', *Ec.H.R.*, 2nd ser., VI (1953).

[2] It was maintained by Coke and Blackstone that a city in England is an incorporated town which is or has been the see of a bishop. In the nineteenth century a number of boroughs were given the status of cities. Manchester, incorporated in 1838, was made the centre of a bishopric in 1847 and became a city in 1853. Liverpool was transformed into a city by Royal Charter when the new diocese of Liverpool was created in 1880. Asa Briggs, *Victorian Cities* (London, 1964), pp. 30–1. In this essay the word 'city' denotes an important town.

[3] Carl E. Schorske, 'The Idea of the City in European Thought', *The Historian and the City* (Cambridge, 1963), p. 96.

[4] *Ibid.*, p. 98. The view prevailed in the nineteenth century. 'That cities are both cause and consequence of a high *Cultur* can hardly be doubted.' Adna Ferrin Weber, *The Growth of Cities in the Nineteenth Century* (Ithaca, 1967), p. 441. This work was originally published in 1899 for Columbia University as Vol. XI of *Studies in History, Economics and Public Law*.

of the eighteenth century with the expansion of educational facilities of many kinds—schools, libraries, and the press. The increasing complexity of trade and manufactures brought forth demands for a higher degree of literacy. Throughout provincial England charity schools, grammar schools, and academies of higher education introduced increasing numbers of artisans' and shopkeepers' children to the world of books, periodicals and newspapers. The sons of successful merchants, bankers, and manufacturers, who were dissenters, attended these academies, organised as substitutes for the universities the dissenters could not attend. The dissenters' educational system fostered vigorous speculation and the development of philosophical doctrine, often of a frankly utilitarian kind. Alive to the needs of the dynamic commercial society, these academies offered courses in foreign languages, history, political theory, English literature, inductive logic, and, above all, science.[1]

Arthur and Benjamin Heywood, merchants and founders of an important Lancashire bank; Thomas Bentley, the partner of Josiah Wedgwood; and other prominent Lancashire businessmen supported one of the outstanding dissenting academies of the eighteenth century, that of Warrington, representing more fully than had previously appeared the principle of a well-rounded education to be shared by all, which had been outlined by reformers of the seventeenth century like Comenius[2] and Locke[3] as an alternative to the traditional scheme of classical and theological education inherited from the Middle Ages. Later, for a brief time (1783-7), business and professional men supported the Manchester College of Arts and Science, another centre of modern studies. The principal objective was 'to provide the means of instruction for the young men of the town between the time of their leaving a grammar school, and that of managing a business'.[4] The founder, Dr. Barnes, the minister of Cross Street Chapel, hoped that the college would attract those who wished to 'unite the intellectual and moral culture of the mind with the pursuits of fortune'.[5] Thus, businessmen who might acquire great wealth would have the power of enjoying it. This institution was a pioneer of the adult education movement.

One of the first gentlemen's subscription libraries in England was formed in Liverpool. In the early fifties, a group met at the house of William Everard, schoolmaster, mathematician, and later architect, to discuss literary topics, particularly the articles in the *Monthly*

---

[1] For a more complete discussion of the role of dissenting academies, see H. McLachlan, *English Education Under the Test Acts* (Manchester, 1931).

[2] *Great Didactic* (1632).

[3] *Thoughts on Education* (1693).

[4] John Yates, *A Funeral Discourse, occasioned by The Death of the Rev. Dr. Barnes, preached at Cross Street Meeting House in Manchester, On Sunday, 15th July, 1810* (Liverpool, 1810), p. 62.

[5] *Ibid.*

Review, while other men met at the Merchants' Coffee House and the Talbot Inn for the purpose of reading together the latest books and reviews. The Liverpool Library emerged out of the informal meetings of these reading societies.[1] Thomas Bentley, 'a man of excellent taste, improved understanding, and good disposition'[2] was one of the most enthusiastic supporters of the endeavour. The entrance fee was £1. 1s. and the annual subscription 5s., indications that the English subscription libraries were rather exclusive. The Liverpool Library provided its members with the best literature of the day: *belles-lettres*, history, natural history, and works on antiquities and travel. This foundation was a club as well as a library, with organised discussions that invigorated the intellectual life of the community. The preface to the second catalogue (1760) enumerated the advantages of membership. 'As many kinds of useful and polite knowledge cannot otherwise be acquired than by Reading, an attempt to furnish the public with an ample fund of amusement and improvement of this kind at the easiest Expense, can hardly fail of general approbation . . . the terms are moderate; and prospects of Advantage are obvious and extensive . . .'[3] This invitation did not go unanswered. From the initial 109 members, the catalogue of 1760 shows an increase to 140. By the end of the century this modest figure reached the astonishing total of 950.[4] What lends particular importance to the list of subscribers in the 1760 catalogue is the inscription of occupation or status against 103 of the 140 names. Of these, about fifty were merchants. There were also two brewers, two brokers, four attorneys, four drapers, a pottery manufacturer, a hosier, a chandler, a cabinet maker, a painter, a druggist, six surgeons, two doctors, a customs officer, two teachers, an innkeeper, and four gentlemen.[5]

Not satisfied with this foundation, the more scholarly men of Liverpool, such as William Roscoe and Dr. James Currie, joined together to found the Athenaeum in 1799, 'a Public Library of well-selected books in all the useful as well as ornamental branches of knowledge, in the learned languages and in some of the modern languages of Europe, as well as our own', in order to aid 'every person inclined to literary pursuits',[6] who found it difficult to pursue these studies in the provinces. In 1803 community leaders founded

---

[1] P. Macintyre, 'Historical Sketch of the Liverpool Library', *Transactions of the Historic Society of Lancashire and Cheshire*, IX (Liverpool, 1856–7).

[2] Eliza Meteyard, *The Life of Josiah Wedgwood* (London, 1865), I, p. 308.

[3] *A Catalogue of the Present Collection of Books in the Liverpool Library: To which is prefixed a Copy of the Laws and a List of the Subscribers* (Liverpool, 1760), pp. 3–4.

[4] Paul Kaufman, 'The Community Library: A Chapter in English Social History', *Transactions of the American Philosophical Society*, New Series, LVII (Philadelphia, 1967), p. 30.

[5] There were also subscription libraries in Warrington (1760), Lancaster (1768) and Rochdale (1770).

[6] Quoted in George T. Shaw, *History of the Athenaeum, Liverpool, 1798–1898* (Liverpool, 1898), p. 5.

a botanic garden. The hope was that in addition to gardens and pleasure grounds, there would be a library of natural history, but this library did not materialise. However, the proprietors did draw together valuable manuscripts and correspondence and developed a collection of plants.

Men of established social and economic position, merchants, manufacturers, bankers, and doctors, organised scientific societies and interested themselves in the natural history of the region. The beginning of the Scientific Revolution in the seventeenth century was principally centred in London and the Royal Society. By the end of the eighteenth century the movement had spread to the provinces and led to the formation of a number of philosophical societies. The Manchester Literary and Philosophical Society, founded in 1781, was the most important in Lancashire.[1] In Liverpool a society called the Liverpool Philosophical and Literary Society was formed in 1779 to discuss scientific and literary subjects, but it did not meet beyond 1783. Then in 1784 William Roscoe revived the society, but it again faltered at the end of the decade. In 1790 a small, rather informal literary club existed in the town. All these societies were the forerunners of the more substantial Literary and Philosophical Society established in 1812.[2]

A sympathetic attitude towards the arts existed in Liverpool in the 1760's, and it was the knowledge of this that induced Joseph Wright of Derby and other artists to seek patrons there. Wright spent the better part of three years at Liverpool (1768–71), boarding with Richard Tate, a merchant. He was well supplied with commissions for portraits from leading families, including the Heskeths and the Ashtons, and other prosperous merchant families.[3] Peter Romney, a younger brother of George Romney, who was also seeking commissions in the town, found the competition of Wright formidable. In a letter, dated from Liverpool 5th November 1769, he complained: 'I have about a dozen pictures in hand here, but what further encouragement I shall meet with I cannot judge. Mr. Wright, a famous painter from Derby, is here, who swallows up the business. He is indeed a true copier of nature; he is of a studious disposition, has a fine taste, and is, in short, qualified for a portrait painter of the first class; but he seems to want a certain force of feeling, and strength of conception necessary in history-painting.'[4]

In his account book, Wright lists twenty-eight names of sitters in Liverpool, but there were several portraits not included in it. Time and again, he encountered members of the hard-headed merchant class who were anxious to be commemorated 'and he saw his

---

[1] See Chap. VI.
[2] See Chap. VI.
[3] Benedict Nicolson, *Joseph Wright of Derby: Painter of Light* (London, 1968), I, 4.
[4] John Romney, *Memoirs of the Life and Works of George Romney* (London, 1830), p. 300.

chance for developing his bent for realism which had lurked at the heart of his earlier experiments. . . . Suddenly he found himself precipitated into a progressive mercantile community ruled by a slave-trading and ship-owning oligarchy . . . and in this atmosphere Wright's talents blossomed.'[1]

Among Wright's finest studies were those of Mrs. Sarah Clayton and of Mrs. John Ashton: 'He responded with his deepest feelings to people whose youth had been spent rising in the world and had no time left for the "douceur de vivre".'[2] Mrs. Clayton achieved success in the coal market centred in Liverpool during the 'monopoly' period of about 1757 to 1773. In 1745 she had inherited Parr Hall with its coal mine near St. Helens. By 1757, when the Sankey navigation reached Parr, she opened two new pits. With her two nephews, the Case brothers, she was in the forefront of the Liverpool industrial scene.[3] Apart from her business activities, Mrs. Clayton took an interest in painting and architecture. In her portrait[4] by Wright, she is shown holding an architectural plan. As early as 1749, she had recommended John Wood of Bath as the architect for the new exchange in Liverpool. She laid down Clayton Square in the 1750s and took up residence there just before Wright arrived in Liverpool.

The Ashtons were an old Liverpool family, but they were just emerging as one of the wealthiest trading families. John Ashton was a slave trader, projector of the Sankey canal, and a prosperous salt manufacturer. His son, Nicholas, was to make his fortune as a ship owner and organiser of privateering operations. He was anxious to enjoy the pleasures of life. The owner of four town houses, he acquired a country place, Woolton Hall, in 1772 which was rebuilt under the supervision of Robert Adam.[5] The friend of William Roscoe, high sheriff of Lancashire in 1770, an amateur painter, he gave vigorous support to the first art societies in Liverpool. In Wright's portrait of Mrs. John Ashton in the Fitzwilliam, one can see a member of the older generation, who has struggled for power and refinement.

Other local magnates sat to Wright. Fleetwood Hesketh was a member of a ship-owning family. Thomas Staniforth, a native of Yorkshire, married into a ship-owning family, the Goores. His father-in-law traded in Africa and was interested in the Greenland Fisheries. Staniforth trafficked in these areas and at the end of the eighteenth century joined a firm of wine merchants and was a partner in a bank. There is uncertainty about the backgrounds of

[1] Nicolson, p. 99.
[2] *Ibid.*, p. 34.
[3] *Ibid.*, p. 99.
[4] Now in Fitchburg, Mass., Art Museum.
[5] Stanley A. Harris, 'Robert Adam and Woolton Hall, Liverpool', *Transactions of the Historic Society of Lancashire and Cheshire*, CI (1950).

other sitters. Nicolson[1] emphasises that many of the names found in Wright's list of sitters in 1769 are found in a list of the 'Company of Merchants trading to Africa . . . belonging to Liverpool, June 24th, 1752.'[2] On both lists are Atherton, Lee, Hardman, Parr, Goore, and Tarlton.

In Liverpool, as the tempo of commercial development increased, local life did not fail to reveal ugly aspects of commercialism and 'to provoke an aesthetic and humanitarian protest. The violence to human rights involved in slavery, the press gang, privateering, the corrupt electoral system, and the relative cultural paucity, caused a few local men to speak out for the cultivation of non-material values. Their problem was the reconciliation of well-being, power and wealth.'[3] Men such as William Roscoe, though not repudiating their commercial heritage, worked diligently to bring beauty and culture to the town.

The establishment of the Royal Academy in 1768 soon produced a response in Lancashire. A group in Liverpool, 'who were desirous of promoting a taste for the fine arts,'[4] formed an art society in 1769 and took a room over the subscription library in John Street. Drawing masters and businessmen who had an interest in the improvement of product design, particularly those connected with the earthenware and watch trades, were in the lead. P. P. Burdett, a cartographer[5] and aquatint engraver[6] much employed at the potteries, was president of the society of twenty members. Surrounding him were Thomas Chubbard, a painter of portraits and landscapes, and Richard Caddick, portrait painter; John Wycke, a well-known watchmaker; Charles Eyes, a surveyor, and his brother John, a lawyer; Dr. Matthew Turner, a physician and friend of Josiah Wedgwood; and Michael Renwick, a doctor; John Barnes, master of the free Grammar School; Richard Tate, the friend of Wright; and William Everard, a founder of the first subscription library. The society held regular meetings in its room, which was furnished with prints and a few plaster casts.[7]

There was nothing original in this effort.[8] According to the classical tradition, a sound education in art for patron and artist

[1] p. 100.

[2] Elizabeth Dornan, *Documents Illustrative of the Slave Trade to America* (Washington, 1931), II, 496–8.

[3] S. G. Checkland, 'Economic Attitudes in Liverpool, 1793–1807', *Ec.H.R.*, 2nd ser., V (1952), p. 66.

[4] Enfield, p. 62.

[5] He produced maps of Derbyshire, Cheshire and Lancashire.

[6] An old but standard work on this subject is S. T. Prideaux, *Aquatint Engraving* (London, 1909).

[7] Joseph Mayer, *Early Exhibitions of Art in Liverpool* (Liverpool, 1876), pp. 3–4.

[8] There were over a hundred academies in Europe by 1790, a fact that illustrates the educational fervour of the age of Enlightenment. Arno Schonberger and Halldor Soehner, *The Rococo Age: Art and Civilization of the Eighteenth Century* (London, 1960), p. 25.

required primarily the study of a good collection of models from antiquity and paintings or copies of paintings from the Old Masters. The patron would gain greater appreciation of art, a desirable accomplishment of the gentleman.[1] For the artist and craftsman, the academy would introduce good principles, purified taste, and bring youth into contact with that philosophy of painting that never reached the workshop, as well as provide educational facilities such as models, casts, and other examples for copying. For most of the smaller academies of the eighteenth century, drawing was the main area of concentration, and it followed that the foundation of academic teaching was training in the use of the pencil. As in the Renaissance, the human body was the subject of almost every study, and these compositions were varied only by an occasional geometrical or architectural exercise. The novice spent a great deal of time copying eyes, ears, and limbs from engravings. Then he proceeded to copying from the round. From simple objects, he moved to elaborate casts from the antique. These studies were interspersed with lectures on anatomy and perspective. The final stage in academic training was the life class with its nude model, a pale reflection of the ideal classical form. Wright's painting 'Three Persons Viewing the Gladiator by Candlelight' gives us a glimpse of the activity within an academy. Here, three men are concerned with an idea. 'The nobility of the antique statue fills their minds, and justifies their earnestness. Its grace has lifted them above pettifogging everyday life, and from its contours their own features have borrowed refinement.'[2] Brief, however, were the opportunities for discussion and observation, for in 1770 patrons, artists and students ceased to attend the meetings of the society.

In 1773 patrons and artists revived the society. William Caddick the portrait painter, was the president of the society, which now boasted of fifty-nine members. The most important of these upheld the classical tradition, and the direction the institution took was to a large extent determined by their taste. 'A few gentlemen agreed to form a society last winter,' a member wrote, 'with a view of improving each other, as far as their situation would permit, in some of the more useful arts, particularly in such as have relations to painting—and of assisting youth in their studies, to the best of their power, without any pecuniary advantage.'[3] The drawing classes resumed, and there was a lecture programme. Everard spoke on problems of architecture; Dr. Turner, on anatomy; Burdett, on perspective; and Dr. Renwick, on chemistry and colours.

William Roscoe presented in poetic form a philosophical justification for the foundation, depicting artists as potential agents of

---

[1] Both Castiglione and Peacham had emphasised that a knowledge of the visual arts, and an ability to practice them, were achievements proper for gentlemen.
[2] Nicolson, p. 39.   [3] Mayer, p. 5.

morality and bulwarks of the honest state. One of the chief preoccu-
pations of late eighteenth century European art was the concern for
moral education. There was a movement away from a view of art
as a means of pleasurable sensation towards one of art as a medium
for moral improvement.[1] 'A new moralizing fervour penetrates the
arts, as if to castigate the sinful excesses of hedonistic style and subject that had dominated the Rococo. The origins of this didactic
mode may be traced back broadly to the growth of bourgeois
audiences . . .'[2] which were rational, utilitarian, realistic, desirous
for knowledge, critical, tolerant, sentimental and humanitarian. A
major source of these aesthetic ideas was the third Earl of Shaftesbury, who insisted that 'the knowledge and practice of the social
virtues, the familiarity and fervour of the moral graces are essential
to the character of a deserving artist and just favourite of the muses.'[3]
Sir Joshua Reynolds, in the ninth 'Discourse', delivered in 1780, also
assigned to the young artist a great moral task. The artist was to un-
fold the truths that lie hidden in nature, revealing the ideal beauty
of natural forms, and thereby making virtue attractive and vice
repellent. Such beauty 'if it does not lead directly to purity of
manners', he wrote, 'obviates at least their greatest depravation.'
By turning the mind from base appetite and leading it to the excellent, that 'which began by Taste', he contended, 'may conclude
in Virtue'.[4] In his poem and in later works Roscoe emphasised that
the study of the works of thoughtful artists would enrich personality
and bring greater harmony to the lives of businessmen.

A unique project of the society was an exhibition of art in 1774,
the first provincial exhibition of art in the kingdom. The prefatory
essay of the catalogue emphasised that art academies were necessary
for the cultural growth of the state and appealed to men of wealth,
position, and leadership to support the endeavour: 'To cultivate
the polite arts with success requires the utmost extent and exertion
of human abilities—even the united powers of many men are
necessary to insure a moderate progress in any of them, although
they are far from a state of perfection.'[5]

The organizers of the exhibition limited their selections to the
works of the members of the society, 'the productions of a small
private society, resident in a remote spot, to which the muses have
been lately invited.'[6] There were landscapes, engravings, models of
ships, miniatures, designs for furniture, portraits in oil, and Indian
ink and chalk studies. The works of such professionals as Caddick

[1] Wylie Sypher, *Rococo to Cubism in Art and Literature* (New York, 1960), Part One.
[2] Robert Rosenblum, *Transformations in Late Eighteenth Century Art* (Princeton, 1967), p. 50.
[3] Quoted in L. D. Ettlinger, 'The Role of the Artist in Society', *The Eighteenth Century: Europe in the Age of Enlightenment*, ed. Alfred Cobdan (London, 1969), p. 245.
[4] *Discourses on Art* (San Marino, 1959), p. 171.
[5] Mayer, p. 21.
[6] *Ibid.*, p. 22.

c

and Chubbard, portrait painters, and Burdett, the engraver, jostled with those of amateurs such as Roscoe and his brother-in-law, Daniel Daulby. The exhibition reflected the aims of the society: the improvement of the designs of local artists and craftsmen and the advancement of the taste of the local business and professional men who were their patrons. However, a group of artists and patrons looked upon the artist pre-eminently as a painter and sculptor producing works complete and understandable in themselves, suitable for the adornment of galleries and homes. They did not wish the academy to be the training centre of artists for industry, nor did they want the exhibits to be the showcase for industrial designs. They sought a higher social status for the artist than that of ingenious craftsman. These conservatives were encouraged to uphold the principles of high art by the President of the Royal Academy. In his 'First Discourse', Reynolds declared: 'An Institution like this has often been recommended upon considerations merely mercantile; but an Academy, founded upon such principles, can never effect even in its own narrow purposes. If it has an origin no higher, no taste can ever be formed in manufactures; but if the higher Arts of Design flourish, these inferior ends will be answered of course.'[1]

Matthew Gregson did not accept this pronouncement. He believed that the Liverpool Academy should sponsor a vigorous teaching programme of industrial design and exhibits in which the best designs of artisans were displayed. In the succeeding years, Gregson and his sympathisers were thwarted by their more powerful colleagues who, as disciples of Reynolds, were intent upon the development of the grand style of art. The exhibit of 1774 is thus significant for another reason. Gregson had attempted to link the development of the Academy with the industrial developments of the age by introducing designs for furniture and other articles. England stood on the threshold of mass production; yet design was often divorced from utility in the academies both in London and the provinces just when it was most important that the artisan and manufacturer be most sensitive to design. The French had greater foresight. In Paris a large industrial school was founded by Jean Jacques Bachelier, in 1762, and academies of design were set up in nearly every French town of any importance in succeeding years. In England industry was left to provide its own art,[2] and the great new industrial cities expanded without well organised schools of design.

After the explosion of activity in 1774 the members resumed their schedule of meetings. The society acquired additional casts executed

[1] Reynolds, p. 13.
[2] Through the collaboration of designers and producers, such as Flaxman, the artist, and Josiah Wedgwood, the potter, many branches of craft production were reorganised for mass production. See Neil McKendrick, 'Josiah Wedgwood and Factory Discipline', *The Historical Journal*, IV (1961), pp. 30–55.

by Flaxman; models received small sums. Then, quite suddenly, on 2nd November 1775, all property was sold to individual members for £11. 1s. 9d. and the society was dissolved. Roscoe later declared that the society's collapse was principally occasioned by the loss of a very ingenious and spirited member who went to Germany. He was probably referring to Burdett, who had entered the service of the Margrave of Baden in 1774. One must also remember, however, that these were months of economic depression. First the American and then the French wars gravely disturbed Liverpool's trade. Merchants and manufacturers are usually less munificent patrons of art in times of recession than in times of plenty.

Even against a clouded political and economic background, discussion and study of art continued. Former members of the academies such as William Everard, Charles Eyes, and Matthew Gregson, were members of Liverpool's first Philosophical and Literary Society, founded in 1779. 'At every meeting some philosophical or literary subject shall be considered . . .'[1]—and art found a place. On 26th March 1782 the members listened to and discussed a paper 'On Taste', and on 3rd and 9th April of the same year, William Everard discussed problems of architecture.

By 1781 Gregson, Daulby, and others were actively working for the revival of a society of arts, and steps were taken in 1783 to restore a civic form of patronage. The Liverpool businessman and half-amateur art dealer,[2] Thomas Taylor, informed his Manchester friend, John Leigh Philips, a successful cotton and silk manufacturer, of the progress of the undertaking: 'The number of painters now in town first gave rise to the present purpose, they must be eleven strong, Morland,[3] Tate,[4] Pack, Chubbard, Caddick, etc. Lectures are to be given as before on Anatomy and chemistry as far as it relates to colours by Dr. Turner who is a chief supporter of it. Lectures are also to be prepared by the professors and delivered in rotation and by the gentlemen on perspective, architecture, etc. . . .'[5]

The prospectus leads one to believe that Gregson and the advocates of training in industrial design played an influential role in

[1] Printed announcements of discussion subjects of the first Philosophical and Literary Society in Holt and Gregson Papers, Liverpool Record Office.

[2] Thomas Taylor was one of the founders of the Liverpool Athenaeum. An inhabitant of the town for thirty years, he 'frequently distinguished himself in the promotion of many public matters'. *Gentleman's Magazine*, LXX (1800), p. 935.

[3] Patrick McMorland, a miniaturist, and not the genre and animal painter, George Morland.

[4] William Tate, the brother of the merchant Richard Tate, was a portrait painter, a friend and pupil of Wright. He was a regular exhibitor at the Society of Artists in London from 1771 to 1775. He describes himself in the early catalogues as a 'pupil of Mr. Wright of Derby'.

[5] W. Barnard Faraday, 'Selections from the Correspondence of Lieutenant-Colonel John Leigh Philips, of Mayfield, Manchester, Part II', *Memoirs and Proceedings of the Manchester Literary and Philosophical Society*, XLIV (1900), p. 31.

the organisation of the educational programme.[1] But in the re-organized academy, not only did the patrons control affairs, but the principles of high art also dominated the principles of industrial design. Amateurs and professionals met in the evening to draw for a couple of hours and to discuss problems of art in a room fitted up with casts and engravings. Henry Blundell of Ince-Blundell, the learned connoisseur, was the president of the revived society; lectures were delivered on anatomy, chemistry, and the philosophy of art; and Christopher Pack, a pupil of Reynolds, had the direction of everything, 'and we are much indebted to him, he goes on very successfully in his painting'.[2] Like his master, Pack painted in and advocated the grand manner.

Further evidence that the views of the disciples of high art prevailed in the academy appears with the exhibition of 1784. Painting dominated everything, and it was evident that advocates of high art hoped that this exhibit would be compared to that of the Royal Academy, for the organizers had invited not only provincial artists but also London artists to show. Taylor was ecstatic. 'We shall have 9 or 10 Wrights, as many Sandbys and are likely to have the best picture that Zoffany ever painted, Garrick in Tancred, in short I believe seriously it will be as good an exhibition as the Royal Academy was.'[3] Later, he added: 'Tarleton (a portrait by Reynolds) has come and proves as hot as fire, and yet they don't all shrink from it. Pack has succeeded my hopes in Miss Philips, he has got a striking likeness, and has made it an elegant picture, his masterpiece. Tate has painted Mr. Richard Heywood the same size (half length) these are to be pitted against each other on each side, Sir Joshua. I am pleased this business has caused such emulation.'[4]

Although the introduction to the catalogue talks of the unity of beauty and utility, and artisans acquiring taste and a practical knowledge of design, the catalogue lists no examples of applied art. Drawings were sketches of landscape or other picturesque subjects, not examples of industrial design such as Matthew Gregson believed were all-important. The needs for high art were served, and the exhibit gave further encouragement to the national school of painting.

Lancashire artists were well represented. Caddick sent three portraits; Chubbard, five portraits and seven landscapes; Patrick McMorland, a bevy of miniatures, sea-pieces and landscapes; Christopher Pack, nine portraits and two landscapes; William Tate, ten portraits; and John Williamson, portraits and landscapes. Although the successful artist of Liverpool, in the economic sense, was

[1] Mayer, p. 32.
[2] Faraday, p. 34.
[3] *Ibid.*, p. 38.
[4] *Ibid.*

the portraitist, certain London artists, with a more diversified market, were not hemmed in by the specifications of portraiture. From Henry Fuseli came 'The Dispute Between Hotspur, Glendower, Mortimer and Worcester, about the division of England'; from Thomas Hearne and Thomas and Paul Sandby, antiquarian views; from Thomas Stothard, 'Old Robin Gray' and its companion, scenes of simple life that were soon to be everywhere in the Romantic Age; and several magnificent studies from Joseph Wright of Derby. Among the honorary exhibitors were William Roscoe, Daniel Daulby, and Richard Tate.

This exhibition of 1784, a shrewd blending of London and provincial talent, pleased patrons and public. Roscoe was particularly grateful to the president of the Royal Academy, who later assured Roscoe of his continued support: 'I am very glad to hear of the success of your exhibition. I shall always wish to contribute to it to the best of my power.'[1] Reynolds 'was not a good teacher to his own pupils, but he possessed a grand overriding desire to help the young artist. "If all those whom I have endeavoured to help forward by lending them pictures and telling them their faults," he once wrote to William Roscoe, "should do me the honour of calling themselves my scholars, I should have the greatest school that ever Painter had." '[2] Taylor believed that the permanency of the society could not be questioned. At the end of 1784, he wrote: 'The number of members and students is double what they were last year and the places are commonly filled up every night. We have a handsome sum in hand from the Exhibitions and last year's subscription.'[3]

The lectures continued. In 1785, Roscoe spoke 'On the history of Art', describing the achievements of the great masters of the past and on occasion praising a modern artist such as Fuseli: 'On the Knowledge of the Use of Prints', and 'On the History and Progress of the Art of Engraving'. No one was a more enthusiastic collector of prints than Roscoe, and this interest continued throughout his life. In his lectures on prints and engravings, he presented an organised body of knowledge in a way that would appeal to the amateur, and by emphasising the moral and historical lessons to be learnt from a study of these works, he attracted those who were responsive to utilitarian principles.

The society mounted a second exhibition in 1787. In the catalogue, there is no mention of the society encouraging applied art. The patrons were primarily interested in providing a showcase for the works of Lancashire and London artists.[4] Those who sought

---

[1] Sir Joshua Reynolds, London, 2nd October 1784, letter to William Roscoe, Roscoe Papers 3112, Liverpool Record Office.
[2] Derek Hudson, *Sir Joshua Reynolds* (London, 1958), p. 238.
[3] Faraday, p. 40.
[4] *The Exhibition of the Society for Promoting Painting and Design in Liverpool, The Second* (Liverpool, 1787), p. 4.

wider recognition and monetary rewards were numerous. Henry
Fuseli sent a 'Hamlet', the 'Adieu of Theseus and Ariadne', and the
'Death of Cardinal Beaufort'; Thomas Gainsborough, a 'Village
Girl With Milk', and 'Cottage Children'; Sir Joshua Reynolds, the
'Death of Dido'; Francis Wheatley, the 'Cruel Father and the Kind
Father'; Angelica Kauffmann Zucchi, a 'Scene From the Tempest';
and Joseph Wright, 'Julia, the Daughter of Augustus, and supposed
mistress of Ovid, deploring her exile by Moonlight, in a cavern of
the Island to which she was banished.' Chubbard, Peter Holland,
W. Jackson, Patrick McMorland, Joseph Parry, William Tate, and
John Williamson, with numerous portraits and landscapes, were
the most prominent of the Lancashire contributors.

The contributions of the London artists reveal some of the themes
of English art during the late eighteenth century. Fuseli's paintings
based upon scenes from Shakespeare and early British history are
but two examples inspired by these stimuli. The Gainsborough is
significant because the artist had combined unsophisticated beauty
with the simplicity of common life. 'It was in the new spirit of the
times, for a writer in the *Gentleman's Magazine* for 1780 (p. 76)
writes, ". . . and you will find artists who know nothing of Greek
and Latin, and can hardly talk English, paint a beggar-boy or
gypsey-girl with the propriety of Poussin and Rubens." The "aristocratic" critic did not like the new experiment, but the Academies
of the 1780's were soon abounding in pictures of this genre . . .'[1]
Wheatley exhibited a work of the sentimental bourgeois genre which
was becoming more and more popular. In all his works of this kind,
he was careful to emphasise the proper relations of father and son
and upper and lower classes.[2] The Wright was but one example of
his many studies of caverns in moonlight, the eruptions of Vesuvius
and St. Peter's illuminated by fireworks, for the play of light was
always his absorbing interest. In Lancashire and Derbyshire, surrounded by a society devoted to experiments in science, Wright
found patrons receptive to his studies of different kinds of reflected
light.

This was the last exhibit of the society, and Thomas Taylor was
quite wrong about the permanency of the institution. In a few years
it was no more. Daniel Daulby gave a thoughtful analysis of its
failure.

The Society is again dormant, [he wrote to John Holt] not for want of subscribers to support it. The subscriptions would be ample, the assistants and
students would be sufficiently numerous to carry it on, and a triennial
Exhibition would again be honored with the works of the first painters. The
two last have increased the taste of the town for the arts, and many excellent
pictures which were sent to the Exhibition without any particular interested

---

[1] Ellis Waterhouse, *Painting in Britain: 1530 to 1790* (Baltimore, 1962) p. 180.
[2] *Ibid.*, p. 221.

view (but merely to promote a general taste for the arts) have been purchased and remain in the town. It is, however, much to be regretted that
in a mercantile town like Liverpool, it is extremely difficult to meet with
gentlemen who have leisure to conduct such a society; to the want of such
gentlemen may be attributed the present suspension of the society for the
promoting of the arts.[1]

The founders of the first academy in Liverpool intended that
study and exhibitions should improve the designs of local artists and
craftsmen and assist business and professional men in developing a
taste for art. During the successive reorganisations of the academy,
the proponents of a programme of applied art were more and more
pushed to the side by the advocates of high art, who wished to give
vigorous support to the English school of art. The two exhibitions at
the academy in the eighties were similar to those of the Royal
Academy but on a smaller scale. The wealthy and educated of
Liverpool had an opportunity to see portraits, landscapes, studies
from literature and history, and scenes of contemporary life, while
artists had the opportunity to vie for the excess capital of the merchants and manufacturers of Lancashire.

II. THE ACADEMY OF 1810

In 1810, artists and civic leaders re-established the Liverpool
Academy under favourable economic circumstances. In the midst
of the Napoleonic Wars, Liverpool was thriving; each year her
docks extended farther on each side of the Mersey to handle increasing trade, particularly that in raw cotton and cotton cloth.[2]
William Carey, art critic and art dealer, surveying the Liverpool
scene in 1811, was impressed with the physical growth of the city.
He noted that in the last twenty-five years the King's and Queen's
Docks had been constructed and piers and embankments raised to
improve the harbour.

That fine edifice, the Exchange, with its noble square of adjoining offices,
have been erected, and the valuable institution, the Botanic Garden founded.
Two hospitals and twelve public schools, independent of those of the Metho-
dist persuasion, have been built, and many charitable societies established
and maintained; all by public contributions. Seven news-rooms and three
Libraries, some buildings of superior order, have been raised. In the centre,
the narrow and inconvenient avenues have been opened and rebuilt upon a
commanding scale.[3]

The political and economic leaders of Liverpool, members of

---

[1] J. A. Picton, *Memorials of Liverpool* (London, 1875), p. 211.
[2] J. Steven Watson, *The Reign of George III, 1760–1815* (Oxford, 1960), pp.
509–10.
[3] William Carey, *Cursory Thoughts on the Present State of the Fine Arts; occasioned by
the founding of the Liverpool Academy; respectfully Addressed to Thomas Walker, Esq. of
Leeds, President of the Northern Society for the Encouragement of Arts* (Liverpool, 1810),
p. 3.

building and memorial committees, now were in the habit of offering commissions to prominent architects and sculptors. Liverpool
was perhaps first in the field with plans for a memorial to Lord
Nelson.[1] William Roscoe played a leading part in the project, and
such firms as Lloyds and the West India Association contributed
generously to the cost, which reached £9,000. The design, created
by M. C. Wyatt, was executed in bronze by Richard Westma-
cott, R.A.[2]

Carey believed that the successful organisation of the Northern
Society at Leeds for the support of English art hastened the reestablishment of the Liverpool Academy. The first exhibition of the
Northern Society, containing many outstanding works, received the
blessing of the President of the Royal Academy, Benjamin West,[3]
and all supporters of the English school of art. Farington, the artist
and diarist, tells a somewhat different story about the resumption
of the Liverpool academy's activities. In January 1811 he wrote:
'Gandy [the architect] called to speak about the Academy Election.
He said he had been settled at Liverpool one year and a half, and
had been well employed, having built much There. . . . He said
whilst He was at Liverpool He called the artists who are there
together, and proposed to them to open an Exhibition in that town,
which had been done. . . .'[4] Carey, however, emphasised that
Roscoe's influence was most important for the undertaking.

During the first thirty years of the nineteenth century, William
Roscoe was the most important single influence guiding art patronage in Liverpool. He led a conservative society, wealthy and consciously aristocratic, with town houses and suburban retreats and
the Wellington Assembly Rooms, founded in 1814, where six or
seven balls were given each year, to which only families of 'position
and standing' were admitted.[5] Reserved, dignified, Roscoe influenced the leading families, not because of his own great wealth,
but because of his taste and knowledge that came not from the
experiences of the Grand Tour or study at Oxford or Cambridge,
but from the intelligent study of literature and history.

[1] Sculptors commemorated many warriors and naval captains during the war
years. For the earliest commissions see C. F. Banks, *Annals of Thomas Banks* (Cambridge, 1938).

[2] *Liverpool Mercury*, 22nd October 1813.

[3] He composed an open letter to the Northern Society in which he emphasised
the moral and economic benefits of such a foundation. Children and adults would
find many truths in the canvases and the taste of artisan and manufacturer would
be improved. The letter is found in *The Artist*, ed. by Prince Hoare (London, 1810),
II, no. 5.

[4] Farington, III, 227. Joseph Michael Gandy studied in Italy and upon his
return to England worked as a draughtsman for Sir John Soane. He was attracted
to Liverpool in 1809 and entered into a short-lived partnership. In 1811 he returned to London. H. M. Colvin, *A Biographical Dictionary of English Architects 1660–
1840* (London, 1954), p. 223.

[5] For a more complete view see *The Gladstone Diaries*, Vol. I, *1825–1832*, Vol. II,
1833–1839, ed. M. R. D. Foot (Oxford, 1968).

Roscoe gained an international reputation as an historian almost overnight with the publication in 1796 of his *Life of Lorenzo de Medici, called the Magnificent*. The work was one banker's tribute to another. The subject was quite new, and Roscoe was praised particularly for procuring copies of manuscripts from Italy and for making the work both readable and an addition to learning.[1] Essentially, Roscoe attempted to write a *Kulturgeschichte* of the Renaissance era.[2] He conceived of the whole cultural revival in Italy as centering on the Medici family, in fact, as being to a large extent the product of the family's intelligent direction and liberal patronage.[3] Later he completed his cultural survey of the most memorable achievements of the Renaissance with the *Life and Pontificate of Leo the Tenth*.

Roscoe glorified the commercial spirit as the nurse of liberty and the arts and included an apotheosis of the Medici as courageous, liberal-minded innovators. With great detail, the Liverpool historian described the patronage of Cosimo and Lorenzo, in part to stimulate the same spirit in his fellow citizens. For example, he carefully described how Lorenzo, dissatisfied with the progress of art in Florence, purchased ancient statues and busts and deposited them in the garden of San Marco and how he retained talented instructors such as Bertoldi and gave sincere encouragement to young artists like Michelangelo.[4] Because he believed in academies and the academic principles, it was only natural that Roscoe's analysis of the Florentine academy's influence would be exaggerated. 'To this institution, more than any other circumstance, we may without hesitation, describe the sudden and astonishing proficiency which towards the close of the fifteenth century, was evidently made in the arts, and which commencing at Florence, extended itself in concentric circles to the rest of Europe.'[5] Roscoe, like Reynolds,

---

[1] For the place of this work in English historical writing, see Thomas Preston Peardon, *The Transition in English Historical Writing 1760–1830* (New York, 1933), p. 254.

[2] Dr. Joseph Warton and several of his friends had contemplated such a project earlier in the eighteenth century. They planned 'to give a history of the revival of letters, not only in Italy, but in all the principal countries of Europe; and . . . the history of English Poetry by Mr. Thomas Warton was only a part of this great design. When we advert to the various and excellent critical productions of these liberal and learned brothers, and consider that among the names of their coadjutors would probably have been found those of West, of Walpole, of Mason, and of Gray, we cannot sufficiently lament the want of public encouragement, which was, in all probability, the chief cause that prevented the noble and extensive undertaking from being carried into complete execution.' William Roscoe, *The Life and Pontificate of Leo the Tenth* (London, 1846), I, xiii.

[3] Wallace K. Ferguson, *The Renaissance in Historical Thought* (Boston, 1948), p. 164.

[4] William Roscoe, *Life of Lorenzo de Medici, called the Magnificent* (London, 1846), pp. 273–4. Roscoe was particularly enthusiastic in his praise of Michelangelo. At the end of the eighteenth century Michelangelo's work was more highly regarded than the more classically inspired paintings of Raphael. In the first half of the century, the opposite was true. David G. Irwin, *English Neoclassic Art: Studies in Inspiration and Taste* (New York, 1966), p. 105.

[5] *Ibid.*, p. 274.

believed that well endowed and properly organised academies had a notable mission; they were to bring a country such as England into pre-eminence among the great civilised nations of the world; they were to develop artists in the antique mould of Raphael and Michelangelo, and so act upon the nation that 'the present age may vie in arts with that of Leo the Tenth; and that the dignity of the dying art (to make use of an expression of Pliny) may be revived under the reign of George III'.[1]

Carey, Roscoe, and other enthusiasts believed that these academies should be regional for the most effective development of English art: 'The institution of three or four Provincial Academies in England, must prove a means of introducing British Art to a more general and intimate acquaintance with the public. A strong local interest would group up round and feel a pride in supporting them. So long as the collective display of genius is confined to the Capitol, there is little chance that the love of British Art will become national.'[2]

Fashionable patrons, encouraged by Roscoe, and artists, impressed by the signs of enthusiasm in Leeds, London, and Lancashire for English art, thus joined together. When they met in April of 1810, the artists first announced they would hold an annual exhibition to encourage art and to raise the funds necessary for the establishment of an academy of painting, sculpture, and architecture; then they adopted the 'laws of the Royal Academy of London as the groundwork for the regulation of the institution'.[3] Henry Blundell was elected Patron and there were seventeen members, two honorary members, and four associates. Roscoe was the treasurer, Dr. Thomas Stewart Traill, lecturer on anatomy, W. Strachan, lecturer on chemistry, and somewhat later Thomas Rickman became the lecturer on architecture. Thomas Winstanley, the leading auctioneer of the community, lent to the artists his Gothic rooms and gallery in Marble Street for the first exhibition of 1810. Succeeding exhibitions were held in 1811, 1812, 1813, and 1814. After the Academy ceased to meet in 1814, there were no further Academy exhibitions, although Winstanley, independently, in 1815, mounted an exhibition that included many works of the English school.

London artists sent their works to these exhibitions as they had done in 1784 and 1787. In 1810, the President of the Royal Academy, West, lent 'The Harmony of Affection over Creation'; T. C. Hofland, the landscape painter, sought a purchaser for his 'Knaresborough Castle' as did Henry Howard for 'Sabrina Revived by the Nereids' and 'Hero and Leander'. The Daniell brothers offered

[1] Reynolds, p. 21.
[2] Carey, p. 39.
[3] H. Smithers, *Liverpool* (Liverpool, 1825), p. 339.

exotica, impressions of the lush jungles and strange temples of India. James Ward presented native ware in romantic garb: a prize ox, a drunkard and a gleaner. Richard Westall explored literature and ancient history. The results were 'The Trial of Constance' from *Marmion*, 'A Bacchante Sleeping', and 'The Lover, [from Shakespeare] penning a sonnet to his mistress'. The sources of Samuel Woodforde's work were equally varied. The Bible inspired 'Ruth Gleaning', the love of the country 'A Village Maid', and Byronic romance, 'Abra, the Georgian Shepherdess'. J. M. W. Turner offered 'Fishermen hauling a Whitstable Hoy'. Liverpool's resident portrait painters and sculptors submitted numerous examples of their work, and Charles Towne and Daniel Williamson sought purchasers for their studies of nature. Gandy reported to Farington that the exhibition was financially rewarding to the provincial artists if not to those of the capital. 'The profits were sufficient to defray the expenses and leave a surplus of £200. . . . Several pictures painted by artists at Liverpool were sold but he (Gandy) believed not any of those sent from London though the number was considerable. . . .'[1] Gandy believed that the exhibition hastened the advancement of reputations. He mentioned as an example 'Williamson a young landscape painter, aged 18 or 20, who had many commissions and is superior to Burns and other landscape painters.'[2]

In 1811 the Liverpool Academy borrowed more of the trappings of London, holding a banquet before the opening of the second exhibition. This was an occasion for rejoicing, for, through the efforts of Roscoe, the Academy had recently obtained the patronage of the Prince Regent, and after the recent death of Henry Blundell it had received £1,600 to be used towards the building of a permanent home for the association. In his address to the artists and patrons, Roscoe emphasised that increasing wealth, interest in the fine arts, and the presence of well-trained artists in the community gave strength to the Academy. He envisioned a future time when the Liverpool Academy would be known throughout the world. Then turning to what he considered to be the realities of the current mode of patronage, he emphasised that the artists of Liverpool could depend on the schools of the Academy for their education, but then they must stand independently, not soliciting the patrons of art as a matter of favour. 'No artists ought to expect as a bounty that which ought to be the reward of talent alone. No person ought to be expected to purchase a work of art for any other reason than because he approves of it. To act otherwise was in fact an injury to the artist, who was thus led to content himself with mediocrity instead of aiming at excellence. . . .'[3] Roscoe ended with a strong appeal to the

[1] Farington, III, 227.   [2] *Ibid.*
[3] *Liverpool Mercury*, 16th August 1811, p. 51.

artists to rely on the liberal and impartial patronage of the public. This was a patronage quite different from that of the ruling princes of Renaissance Italy.

In 1811 Liverpool had an opportunity once again of viewing works of leading English artists. The President of the Royal Academy showed his serious desire to extend patronage by submitting another neo-classical study, 'Iris communicating Jove's commands to King Priam'. J. M. W. Turner sent a 'View of Tabley, the seat of Sir John Leicester'. James Ward offered 'Ashbourne Mill'; Sir Thomas Lawrence, a portrait of Benjamin West; and Peter deWint, Louis Francia, and Thomas Heaphy, fashionable and romantic watercolours. The Liverpool artists were also well represented at this exhibition. In 1812, 1813, and 1814 patrons and artists again had opportunities to view similar surveys of contemporary art in which the major themes were nature, the past, literature, contemporary events, and studies of emotions. The works of Turner, De Wint and Ward, shown at the Liverpool Academy in this period, particularly reflected the new tastes and ideas that were beginning to pervade English thinking about art. Reynolds had repeatedly asked the artist to go forth and examine nature, but he placed greater emphasis on the contemplation of Old Masters. More and more, with the influence of Alison and the Associationists, the writings of the Rev. William Gilpin and Uvedale Price on the picturesque, and the stress that Wordsworth and other Romantic poets placed on the close relationship between man and nature, the English were attracted to artists who emphasised in their works nature and instinct rather than formal training. And, beyond the more elemental aspects of nature, were the Orient and the Middle Ages, exotic stimuli for artists.[1] From time to time, architects submitted drawings that reflected of the taste of the times. In 1813 Thomas Rickman offered examples of Gothic architecture and W. Atkinson, a 'Design for a Villa proposed to be built near Manchester'.

A catalogue of 1814 records prices for exhibited works. William Etty requested four guineas for his 'Sleeping Nymph in Danger' and five guineas four 'Susanna and the Elders'. William Collins wanted ten guineas for a study of a boy and eight guineas for 'The Fishing Place'. Samuel Williamson asked ten guineas for 'Landscape—Welsh Scenery'. John Glover valued his 'View at Matlock' at fifty guineas, and James Ward wanted twenty-five guineas for 'The Death of the Goldfinch'. None of these prices was outrageous, and the artists, many of them just beginning their careers, seemed aware of the climate of the market place. Of course, Benjamin Robert

---

[1] For an introduction to the many themes of Romantic art and the many interpretations of these themes, see A. K. Thorlby, *The Romantic Movement* (New York, 1966), pp. 136-8. An interesting sampling is *Romantic Art in Britain: Paintings and Drawings, 1760–1860* (Philadelphia, 1968).

Haydon demanded four hundred and sixty guineas for his 'Macbeth Approaching to Murder Duncan', but then, Haydon never did understand the laws of the market place.

The catalogue of the exhibition of 1812 informed the public 'it is the intention of the Liverpool Academy to open, as soon as possible a School of Design for the instruction of Pupils in the art of Drawing from models and from the Life. . . .'[1] and Thomas Harrison exhibited a 'Design for the intended Liverpool Academy of Arts'. The artists envisioned casts, engravings, and studies from life, as well as lectures on anatomy and perspective. The principles of high art would prevail, while no serious attempt would be made to communicate with the industrial community. Matthew Gregson showed his dissatisfaction with the philosophy that guided the organisers of the Academy's school when, in 1813, he addressed a letter to the trustees of the Blue Coat Hospital and to the directors of the charity schools in the area. He emphasised that good taste and industrial design are related, that English manufacturers would not be dependent on foreign designs if they supported programmes in the applied arts: 'What additional value does the introduction of a tasty design give to a piece of Lancashire Calico printed as an article for Furniture, or Drapery, for Dress when the Design is really tasty and the subject appropriate! yet it costs no more in printing, when the Design is made, than the most ordinary Drawing. . . .'[2] The members of the Liverpool Academy, however, had no great desire to jeopardise their economic and social position by admitting craftsmen and the problems of applied art, while the majority of the patrons followed the laws of fashion and were content to support an educational programme for painters and annual exhibitions that emphasised the principles of high art.

Members of the Liverpool Academy who attracted loyal patrons in Lancashire in these years were J. W. Faulkner and Thomas Hargreaves, miniaturists; John Turmeau, miniaturist and portrait painter, and John Williamson, the portraitist, who contributed his skills to the earlier art societies. His elder son, Daniel, composed rather undistinguished landscapes, but his younger son, Samuel, was adept in this field. William Henry Burns also found favour with his landscapes, and Charles Towne, who appeared in Liverpool about 1806, gained praise for his landscapes with cattle and his portraits of animals. Architects used the exhibitions of these years for their own advancement. John Bird and John Foster, jun., in their architectural drawings, were true to neo-classic principles, while Thomas Rickman's designs increased the interest in Gothic architecture.

[1] *The Exhibition of the Liverpool Academy* (Liverpool, 1812), p. 14.
[2] Matthew Gregson, *To the Trustees of the Blue Coat Hospital, and Ladies and Gentlemen Subscribers to that excellent Charity; also To the Governors, Committee, and Directors of the various other Charity Schools in Liverpool* (Liverpool, 1813), p. 2.

The sculptor George Bullock found favour with his portrait busts, in 1810 displaying eight studies including those of Henry Blundell, William Roscoe, and the Duke of Gloucester. In the same year, John Gibson, young and ambitious, offered a delicate 'Psyche' and the more robust 'Alexander preserving the works of Homer'.

The work of Gibson particularly appealed to elegant, conservative Liverpool. Roscoe welcomed young Gibson to his estate, Allerton, and introduced him to his collection of engravings, paintings, and Renaissance bronzes and taught him to respect the simplicity of statement and ideal beauty of the Greek and Florentine achievements. 'The works of the ancients,' said Roscoe, 'will teach you how to select the scattered beauties displayed in nature. The Greek statue is Nature in the abstract; therefore, when we contemplate these sublime works, we feel elevated.'[1] During the post-war recession Gibson, seeking wider fame and patronage, set out for Italy with the blessings of Roscoe and Fuseli, taking with him £50 collected by his Liverpool friends. At Rome, his drawings at once attracted Canova's attention, and the great sculptor took him into his studio and treated him as one of his favourite pupils. At Rome he remained until his death in 1866,[2] gaining an international reputation. For the men of Liverpool and for other patrons, he carved statues of a clean, simple line: a famous example, Huskisson, clad in a toga with one arm bare, in St James' cemetery in Liverpool. Here, too, in John Foster's Ionic funerary chapel above the gorge are his sculptural studies of William Hammerton, Emily Robinson, and William Earle: 'Nowhere can the rhythms and idealisation of English neo-classicism be more surely experienced.'[3] 'In you,' wrote Lord Lytton in his dedicatory epistle to *Zanoni* (1846), 'we behold the three great and long undetected principles of Grecian art, simplicity, calm, and concentration.'[4] Gibson had first learned these principles in the Academy, the homes of generous patrons and the artists' studios of Regency Liverpool.

For Gibson and other English artists, the academies that flourished at brief intervals in Liverpool in the late eighteenth and early nineteenth centuries were important because of the intellectual and economic stimuli they offered. For the business and professional men and their families, the exhibitions, sponsored by the academies, were an important influence for the moulding of taste. Visitors could examine the fashionable portraits of Reynolds and Lawrence;

---

[1] Lady Eastlake, *Life of John Gibson* (London, 1870), p. 34.

[2] From time to time he received English visitors. 'In the afternoon went to Gibson's, the sculptor. He is very simple and intelligent, and appears devoted to his art.' Entry of 1830. C. C. F. Greville, *A Journal of the Reigns of King George IV and King William IV* (London, 1874), I, 383.

[3] T. S. R. Boase, *English Art, 1800–1870* (Oxford, 1959), p. 144. Margaret Whinney, *Sculpture in Britain 1530–1830* (Baltimore, 1964), p. 227.

[4] Edward Bulwer Lytton, *Zanoni*, Vol. III of *Novels of Sir Edward Bulwer Lytton* (Boston, 1893), p. vi.

imaginative studies based on English history, German epics, and Greek tragedy by Fuseli; moral essays by Wheatley; and beautiful and romantic landscapes by Turner and deWint. The men of the North also had ample opportunity for judging the works of Lancashire artists and, in the end, for evaluating the progress of the national school of art.

CHAPTER III

MATURE PLANS FOR LIVERPOOL

I. THE ACADEMY AND THE LIVERPOOL INSTITUTION

In the early nineteenth century, adult education flourished in a wide variety of forms in Lancashire, but the characteristic feature of the period was the tremendous interest in the teaching of science. This interest had developed in the form of scientific societies in the eighteenth century and received impetus as a result of the increasing importance of applied science in the Industrial Revolution.

The interest in science and learning, in general, grew as the wealth of merchants and manufacturers increased. Technological interest induced men of wealth to endow many new scientific societies, both specialist and non-specialist, in the early nineteenth century. The study of science was also pursued in a more general cultural context, in societies that were enlarged versions of the Manchester Literary and Philosophical Society, with the reading of papers on scientific and literary subjects, the formation of a library and the equipment of a laboratory. One of the most widely known and influential was the Royal Institution in London, founded in 1799. The institution gained fame through its public lectures, which were delivered by such scientists and literary figures as Humphry Davy, Michael Faraday, and Sydney Smith. In the Institution's laboratory, significant research in chemistry and electricity was conducted by Davy and Faraday.[1]

The Liverpool Royal Institution, which was in the early nineteenth century one of the major provincial foundations devoted to the diffusion of learning, was in part modelled after the London institution. The Institution was founded by the same group of men who were so important in the history of the Athenaeum, the Lyceum, to which the Liverpool Library was transformed, the Botanic Garden, and the Literary and Philosophical Society. In the creation of all these institutions, Roscoe had played an important role, and the general plan of the Royal Institution itself reflects his cosmopolitan interests in art, literature, science, and education. If the original idea of the Institution was not his own, he supervised its development, becoming Chairman of the General Committee in 1814 and the first President in 1822. Dr. Thomas Stewart Traill, a graduate in medicine from the university of Edinburgh, who practiced in Liverpool, assisted Roscoe effectively, as he did in the reestablishment of the

[1] Thomas Kelly, *A History of Adult Education in Great Britain* (Liverpool, 1962) pp. 113-14.

Literary and Philosophical Society and the founding of the Mechanics' Institution.

On 28th February 1814, thirty-six business and professional men met at the Liverpool Arms Hotel to discuss the possibilities of establishing lectureships in literary and scientific subjects and the probable costs. As a result, the first public meeting was held in March, Benjamin Arthur Heywood,[1] a member of the well-known family of Lancashire bankers, acting as chairman. It was resolved that a society 'for promoting the increase and diffusion of Literature, Science, and Arts'[2] be established in Liverpool. A building was to be erected containing scientific equipment and a museum and a permanent fund of not less than £20,000 raised in shares of £100 and £50. By June, when the building and endowment fund reached £20,000 a general committee was formed to oversee development.

In August, a detailed plan of the institution appeared that defined areas of support as: 'academical schools', public lectures, cultural societies already in existence, collections of books, specimens of art, and examples of natural history, and a scientific laboratory. However, it was not until three years later that the Committee was able to make a further report. The failure of the banking firm of Roscoe, Clarke, and Roscoe, custodians of the institute's funds, brought difficulties and turned the chief advocate of the scheme away from this public endeavour for some time. On 17th July 1817, the committee reported that it had raised £22,100 by subscription and had obtained a property on Colquitt Street, and that the building would contain a periodical room for the proprietors, a lecture room, committee rooms, a meeting room, a library, and a museum, an exhibition room for the Academy of Arts when it resumed, and rooms for a drawing school. On the roof would be an observatory and there would be a laboratory at the back of the main building. Soon professors were appointed in a variety of subjects, an extensive programme of morning and evening lectures was arranged, a library, a natural history museum, and an art gallery were formed. Classical and mathematical schools were started for boys. In addition, the Institution provided a meeting place for other cultural organizations such as the Literary and Philosophical Society and the Philomathic Society.

---

[1] Benjamin Arthur Heywood supported cultural institutions in both Liverpool and Manchester. He moved to Manchester at the end of the eighteenth century. 'In 1812 he became tenant under Benjamin Gaskell, of Clifton Hall, the substantial old red-brick building in the Agecroft Valley. . . . In 1825 he removed to Claremont, Pendleton, in earlier times the residence of Mrs. Ford, mother of the celebrated Colonel Ford, whose name so often appears in the history of the Manchester Volunteers.' Leo H. Grindon, *Manchester Banks and Bankers: Historical, Biographical and Anecdotal* (2nd ed.; Manchester, 1878), p. 82.

[2] *Resolutions, Reports, and By-Laws of the Liverpool Royal Institution, March, 1814– March, 1822* (Liverpool, 1822), p. 4. (Hereafter referred to as *L.R.I. Resolutions*, etc.)

D

These enterprises met with varying success. The boys' school (the two schools were soon formed into one) proved very valuable[1] and continued until 1892, when the competition of new schools led to its closing. The museum of natural history was popular with the members as well as with the general public, especially on those days when the public was admitted without charge. How successful was the Institution as a patron of English art? Let us spend the rest of the chapter examining that question.

The Institution became the guardian of the Liverpool Academy. In 1817 the Institution proposed that the five trustees of the Blundell fund turn this sum over to it in consideration of exhibition space and rooms in the Institution building for the use of the Academy. When, however, the Academy ceased to hold meetings in 1814, it was arranged that five members of the committee for the Institution would join with the five Blundell trustees to draw up a plan for an academy of painting, drawing, and sculpture. The funds of the Academy, whether obtained from private contributions or annual exhibitions, were to be distinct from the funds of the Institution. The Institution, in return for providing accommodation for the Academy, was to receive the whole of the Blundell bequest, estimated with accumulated interest to amount to £1,800, which would be appropriated to the building fund of the Institution itself. In all other respects, the new Academy, although occupying permanent quarters in the Institution building, was to be a wholly independent body.

The exact date on which the new Academy came into being is uncertain, but in the report of 14th March 1820 (page 20), the names of 18 academicians are given, and in the Institution's by-laws, adopted on 27th February 1822, it is mentioned with the Literary and Philosophical Society as one of the societies with which the committee of the Royal Institution was empowered to make arrangements designed to promote the objects of the institution, and accommodation had been allotted to it by August 1822. A grant, the amount of which it is not stated, was made to the Academy in December, 1822, for the instruction of pupils, presumably in the school of design. In his address to the members of the Institution of February, 1824, Benjamin Arthur Heywood stated that the School of Design was being superintended by members of the Academy.[2]

The artists of Liverpool once again took as their model the Royal Academy. There were fourteen members, four associates, and seven honorary members. The programme of the Academy was twofold: first, the support of the School of Design where artists and members

---

[1] Throughout England middle-class schools, both day and boarding, enjoyed a remarkable expansion after the 1820s, with day proprietary schools coming before the wave of boarding schools. F. Musgrove, 'Middle-Class Education and Employment in the Nineteenth Century', *Ec.H.R.*, 2nd ser., XII (1959), p. 100.

[2] Henry A. Ormerod, *The Liverpool Royal Institution: A Record and a Retrospect* (Liverpool, 1953), pp. 76–7.

of the Institution could study; and second, the establishment of a gallery, where the works of the artists could be admired, criticised, and they hoped, purchased. The academic system introduced into the school of design was based on the principles of high art as modified in the neo-classical age. David and his followers had challenged the disciples of the ideal, emphasising that it was right and good to go to certain periods of history such as Republican Rome and Periclean Athens, to find pure examples. Neo-classicism was a tendency towards archaeology rather than towards ideal form, a turning back to the historical past, which in England had already produced an interest in Gothic architecture.

The Institution quickly amassed a series of casts to aid the artists and the students of the schools. In 1818 A. Littledale, a merchant and connoisseur, informed Roscoe that he had received from Paris casts of the 'Apollo Belvedere', 'Venus de Milo', and 'Gladiator', 'Diana and the Fawn', and the 'Battle of the Amazons' and that he wished to present them to the Liverpool Royal Institution. Many other casts, examples of the achievements of the ancients, were purchased.

John Foster, jun., architect and now president of the Academy, encouraged the neo-classic tendency in the school of design. A student of classical archaeology, with Dr. Charles R. Cockerell he had explored Greek sites and had the thrill of discovering sculptures from the pediment of Athena's temple at Aegina in 1811. In 1823 he drew up a catalogue of the cast collection in the Liverpool Institution, which by that date included reproductions of the Elgin marbles, a gift from George IV. Like Cockerell and Benjamin Robert Haydon, he believed that the Greeks had made anatomical dissections of animals to obtain their information and to make their works follow the rationale of nature, yet had combined their observations with refined compositional principles and an enthusiastic grasp of the animal's power. He remarked that the heads of the horses in one of the Parthenon group were 'full of animation and display the great anatomical skill of the artist'.[1] Like so many other instructors of the period, Foster believed that casts of the Elgin marbles were invaluable aids to the student and mature artist who would master the neo-classical repertoire.

One of the results of the close connection of the Academy with the Royal Institution was an attempt to provide lectures on the fine arts and architecture, which would be of interest to the proprietors and general public as well as to the art students. The latter, traditionally, listened to lectures on anatomy and perspective. Now they were to receive further stimulus. The title of Professor of Ancient and Modern Architecture was conferred on John Foster in 1824.

---

[1] *Catalogue of the Casts in the Statute Gallery of the Liverpool Royal Institution* (Liverpool, 1823) p.7

Although he was a firm supporter of the school of design, he was unable to organize public lectures at that time. The first recorded architectural course was a curious medley entitled 'Sketches of History as Connected with the Progress of Architecture', presented by George Wood, F.S.A., and was unlikely to have benefited the student of the Academy, but it may have stimulated the general public. More rewarding, perhaps, for student and general public were Wolstenholme Parr's seven lectures in 1822 on Raphael's pictures in the Vatican and a series in the following year on the other painters of the Italian Renaissance: 'On the picture of the School of Athens, he made a profound display of classical erudition, delivered in concise language, on the physical and ethical systems of opinions which distinguished the philosophies of Greece, painted by Raphael in that wonderful picture.'[1] No further lectures on art and architecture, however, are recorded until 1828, when Arthur Perigal, a portrait and landscape painter, was invited to lecture on the fine arts. Benjamin A. Heywood hoped that 'lectures upon architecture, delivered by men learned in the art, might have influence not only in directing the public taste to the pure fountains of ancient superiority, but also enabling the living artist to vary and modify those perfect examples to modern uses'.[2] In the twenties, however, neither the students of the Academy nor the general public were introduced to a well-organised survey of the arts. The lecture programme was for the most part self-supporting, financed by the subscriptions of the general public, that usually preferred to spend its money on courses of a scientific nature. The founders of the Institution outlined a magnificent educational task, but the capital of the proprietors was always inadequate for a really large conception, and in consequence they were never able to pay a proper teaching faculty, which they needed if their programme was to develop vigorously in all areas of the arts and sciences.

Roscoe and his friends were concerned that Liverpool's artists and patrons had had no opportunities to evaluate English art through local exhibitions since 1814. In 1823, the president of the Institution, Benjamin A. Heywood, emphasised how important frequent exhibitions were for the provincial artist and particularly for the provincial patron.

It is, however, neither solely nor principally for the benefits that would be rendered to the artists that we have reason to lament the want of such a display; its advantage would be general, and probably its greatest use would be to instruct and improve the taste of the spectators, and to lead by the opportunity of comparison to the just appreciation of the works of art, and not only to display excellence, but to beget the taste which may value it. By

---

[1] *The Kaleidoscope* (Liverpool), 16th July 1822, p. 13.
[2] *Addresses delivered at the Meetings of the Proprietors of the Liverpool Royal Institution, on the 17th February 1822 and 13th February 1824* (Liverpool, 1824), pp. 56–7.

the means of exhibitions, works of a great artist produce an observable area in the public judgment, for it is the artist, not the patron, who establishes the fashion which for a time becomes irresistible. The prevailing taste is not dictated by the patron, but imposed upon him, by the uncommon skill of particular genius. . . .[1]

Once the Academy was re-established, several inquiries were made and letters were written to the newspapers on the subject of the next exhibition of contemporary art. On 4th August 1821, a letter appeared in the *Liverpool Mercury* regretting that a proposed exhibition was not held, because only 200 pictures were promised, and pointing out that the Royal Academy had only 136 pictures in its first exhibition. The artists dug in and in 1822 opened an exhibition. The majority of the works were from the studios of Lancashire artists. Richard Westall was one of the few London artists who contributed. The critic of the *Kaleidoscope* considered the exhibition 'decidedly inferior to those of the Liverpool Academy at the News-rooms . . .'[2] Liverpool artists, sensitive to such criticisms, were further disheartened when the proprietors of the Institution announced that they would next sponsor an exhibition of Old Masters, foregoing in 1823 an exhibition of contemporary art. It was natural that the proprietors, upholders of the eighteenth-century classical tradition, might wish to organise such an exhibition to further the education of artists and the general public. They were not, however, turning away from the English school.

In the catalogue for the exhibition, Wright of Derby and the collectors of his work are praised.[3] After 'A Child with her Mother's muff and cloak' by Reynolds, the compiler of the catalogue, perhaps the dealer Winstanley, reminded the collectors of Liverpool that such works were gilt-edged investments. 'Look at the large sums given for the pictures of the late Marchioness of Thurmond, and at the recent sale of Mr. Watson Taylor's collection. . . .'[4]

This was rather cold comfort for Liverpool artists who had expected to benefit from a second annual exhibition. Their answer was the organisation of an exhibition of contemporary art at the Lyceum. In the 'Advertisement' of their catalogue, the artists remarked that the proprietary attitude of some of the members of the Institution towards the Academy had alienated artists, and made them long for independence. And there were differences of opinion over the advisability of annual exhibitions. Some proprietors doubted whether 'works of Art could . . . be produced in so short a period as twelve months, with sufficient merit to deserve public attention and,

---

[1] *L.R.I. Resolutions, etc.*, pp. 20–1.
[2] 6th August 1822, p. 40.
[3] *Catalogue of the Paintings, the works of the Old Masters of the Various Schools, and of Deceased British Artists, Contributed by the Proprietors of Most of the Principal Collections in Liverpool and the Neighbourhood* (Liverpool, 1823), p. 30.
[4] *Ibid.*, p. 32.

therefore, that a proportional annual increase of interest could . . .
possibly be effected'.[1] However, the artists believed that a growing,
dynamic Liverpool was anxious to possess the same cultural advantages as her rivals in the North and Midlands. Dynamism within the
artistic community would grow as public support grew. 'When an
annual display is afforded to the Artists, there can exist little doubt
of its leading to a favourable result: Liverpool cannot be less dis-
cerning in this respect than neighbouring towns possessing not a
tithe of its consequences.'[2]

To the exhibition at the Lyceum, Augustus Callcott sent from
London a landscape and Richard Westall, 'Johanna, the Mother
of the Emperor Charles V, watching the body of her Husband', but
the majority of the works came from the artists of Lancashire.
Sales were slow in these prosperous times. The *Liverpool Mercury* reported: 'At Leeds this season there was taste enough for the purchase
of £900 worth of pictures. At Liverpool . . . only three pictures were
sold. From which statement it clearly appears that there are here
too many of those pretended well-wishers and would-be thought
patrons.'[3] This report conflicts with a later one in the *Kaleidoscope*.
That paper's correspondent found an upswing in sales before the
close of the exhibition. 'This patronage will raise the spirits of the
artists, and as long as they are content with moderate prices, that
patronage will no doubt be progressive now that the opulent amateurs are ashamed of what has been done at Leeds and other places.'[4]
The 'amateurs', however, did not buy in 1824 and 1825, when exhibitions were held once again at the Institution. In 1825 a correspondent of the *Mercury* regretted that 'there had been sold one [picture
ten days ago, and only one;—Mr. Donaldson's painting of vege-
tables. Only one picture for the second town of the Kingdom! So
much for Liverpool taste and so much for Liverpool liberality.'[5]

In 1826, no exhibition was held 'owing to the exhibitons of 1824
and 1825 having been a mutual disappointment to the public and
the Academy'. Times were bad, for the frenzied economic activity of
1825, the first cyclical boom of the modern type, was no more. By
the summer of 1825 speculation had gone too far, and a bout of
liquidation and failures occurred, beginning in the United States
and spreading to Liverpool, Manchester, and London. 'For some
seven years after 1825 the economy, though it made progress in the
sense of a continued increase in output due to greater efficiency, and
perhaps to greater effort, was not able to reach full employment.'[6]

---

[1] *Catalogue of Paintings and Drawings, by Living Artists, Exhibited at the Lyceum, Bold Street, Liverpool* (Liverpool, 1823), p. 3.   [2] *Ibid.*
[3] *The Liverpool Mercury*, 19th September 1823, p. 91.
[4] *Kaleidoscope*, 30th September 1823, p. 98.
[5] *Liverpool Mercury*, 7th October 1825, p. 106.
[6] S. G. Checkland, *The Rise of Industrial Society in England 1815–1885* (London, 1964), p. 14.

The artists realised that they needed more generous, constant, and enthusiastic support from the educated and wealthy and more contributions from London studios in order to create and maintain interest in the exhibitions. The wealthy saw they would have to be generous in bad times and in good, if the community was to have a vigorous art programme. 1827 was a turning point, when extraordinary efforts brought a new day for English art in Liverpool. First, on Friday, 24th August, there was a dinner at the Institution to mark the opening of the exhibition. On that occasion, speaker after speaker praised the rightness of the effort. Winstanley, the dealer, emphasised the soundness of investments in English art, citing the large sums paid for English works at the sale of the late Lord de Tabley's collection. Winstanley also noted that the Mayor and the members of the Common Council of Liverpool were seriously considering ways by which they could support art.[1] No doubt these municipal leaders now realised the full implication of the failures of the previous exhibitions and were determined that Liverpool's name would not again be slurred. Leading citizens not only viewed but they also purchased. Two hundred and seventy pictures were exhibited and the names of Copley Fielding, Henry Howard, Samuel Austin, Charles Barber, Henry Pickersgill, and the Williams family were prominent in the catalogue. Fielding and Pickersgill were two of the London contributors. The former, a painter in watercolours, found a wide market for his impressions of Wales, the Lakes and the sea. The speed with which he executed his works easily allowed him to send examples of his output to all the chief exhibits. Pickersgill, a portrait painter, wished to show Liverpool that he could be counted on for a distinguished study of eminent men, suitable for home, club, or civic office.

On 31st August the correspondent of *The Mercury* noted: 'We are glad to learn that the attendance at the Exhibition is considerably more numerous than it has been on former occasions, being upwards of 150 daily including subscribers; and the sales of pictures have been effected to a very respectable amount. . . .'[2]

In 1828, at the second banquet, John Gladstone,[3] merchant, town booster and father of W. E. Gladstone, presided at the banquet, and nearly one hundred gentlemen, including the Mayor and members of the Common Council, were present. During the toasting, Gladstone singled out the Mayor and the Common Council 'for the public spirit and liberal conduct generally evinced by them, and in particular, for having given three premiums of twenty guineas each,

---

[1] *Liverpool Mercury*, 24th August 1827, p. 271.
[2] *Ibid.*, 31st August 1827, pp. 279–80.
[3] For the story of his fortune see S. G. Checkland, *The Gladstones: a family biography, 1764–1851* (Cambridge, 1971).

for the best specimens in painting, drawing, and sculpture'.[1] Then he plunged into an analysis of the past and present state of art patronage in the community. Rightly, he emphasised first the importance of Liverpool's economic growth for present and future cultural development.

She has made the name of her merchants known and respected in every quarter, nay, in every corner of the world. She had even rivalled the metropolis of the British Empire in her most difficult undertakings. Though the metropolis had been protected by monopoly and other exclusive commercial advantages, yet Liverpool now treads close on her heels in general commerce, and in some of its branches, has even outstripped her. (Loud cheers.)[2]

Gladstone was confident that, if Liverpool could triumph in the economic realm she could excel in cultural endeavours as well. It was a question of these hundred or so gentlemen giving their support to the Academy's exhibits and programmes. 'Might they not see her infants schools of art arising in importance, and equalling if not rivalling the metropolis itself in the production of the fine arts?' (Loud cheers)[3] Gladstone next praised the abilities of the members of the Academy. There could be a Liverpool school as well as an English school of art. 'That they had the materials was shown from the specimens of genius and talent around them; genius which only required to be fostered and cherished to confer honour on its patrons and on the artists themselves.'[4] No one was more optimistic about the economic future of the Academy and the exhibitions. 'The pictures sold last year were more numerous, and at more liberal prices, than those sold at any previous anniversary.'[5]

A correspondent for *The Albion* noted that Gladstone had, prior to the dinner, made a wise psychological move, when at the private view he had selected an important work. Later he purchased several other paintings,[6] setting an example for other gentlemen to follow. A significant group of wealthy men now regularly came to the aid of the artists and in the succeeding years not only were the exhibitions popular social events, but Liverpool's expenditures for art could be compared favourably to those of other provincial cities.

Many London artists showed, encouraged by the reports of brisk sales. In 1828, Richard Westall sent from London 'Fireside' and 'Children', two sketches, and Henry Howard, 'A Young Florentine of the Fifteenth Century leaning on her Mandolin'. Westall, who painted chiefly in watercolours, had in his studio rustic scenes and historical subjects ready for buyers and was quite ready to send works to the provincial exhibitions. Howard had a stock of fancy

---

[1] *The Liverpool Mercury*, 15th August 1828, p. 262.
[2] *Ibid.*   [3] *Ibid.*
[4] *Ibid.*   [5] *Ibid.*
[6] Clipping from *The Albion* (Liverpool, 1828) in Liverpool Academy Catalogues, 1822–30 in L.R.I. Collection at University of Liverpool.

pictures suitable for the drawing rooms of merchants and manufacturers. In 1824, he had sent to Liverpool 'Venus Placing the
Quiver on Cupid's Back'; in 1827, 'Manfred and the Witch of the
Alps'; in 1829, 'A Greek Girl'; and in 1830, 'Hylas carried off by
the Naiads-Theocritus'.[1] Both artists painted for the market, a
market in which the middle classes more and more asserted their
likes and dislikes.

At the general meeting in 1829, Dr. T. S. Traill, then president
of the Liverpool Institution, reviewed the progress of the Academy
and the exhibitions. He reported that sales had reached £489 in
1827, but the zeal of Gladstone and other men of wealth made that
figure insignificant next to that of 1828: 'the amount of the sale in
the room had actually reached £846, a decisive proof of an increasing love of the fine arts among our opulent merchants'.[2]
Everyone present was optimistic about the current exhibition. Sir
Thomas Lawrence, the President of the Royal Academy, led the
list of contributors with his study of Southey, painted for Robert
Peel and lent by the statesman.[3] To Dr. Traill, the patronage of the
Common Council of Liverpool was of great significance, for it was
'the only instance of a purely disinterested encouragement of the
fine arts hitherto shown of any similar body in Great Britain'.[4]

Indeed, the corporation's gestures became quite magnificent; in
1830, it voted the sum of 100 guineas for prizes. At the annual
Academy banquet in that year, Winstanley emphasised that this
grant would not only benefit local artists, but the example of Liverpool would also stimulate the development of municipal patronage
in other cities.

In 1830 Winstanley was both complimentary and critical. Liverpool was vigorously supporting the exhibitions, yet Liverpool could
not become complaisant. Manchester had, perhaps, already forged
ahead of Liverpool as a patron of the English school of art. Civic
rivalry had spurred the men of Manchester to found the Manchester
Institution, for the promotion of literature, science and the arts;
and the arts were well served, declared Winstanley.

When we look at Manchester as regards the patronage and support of the
arts in comparison with Liverpool, we should also look at her situation; on

---

[1] Howard, though far below Turner as an artist, was his superior in education
and the two artists often got into hot disputes. Howard, for example, maintained
that artists should paint for the public. Turner believed that artists should paint
only for judges, but in truth he did not paint for 'judges' or 'general public'. Jack
Lindsay, *J. M. W. Turner* (New York, 1966), p. 134.
[2] *Address delivered in February, 1828, at the General meeting of the Members of the
Liverpool Institution* (Liverpool, 1828), Appendix.
[3] D. E. Williams, *The Life and Correspondence of Sir Thomas Lawrence, Kt.* (London,
1831), II, 515–16.
[4] *Address delivered in February, 1829, at the General meeting of the Members of the
Liverpool Institution* (Liverpool, 1829), p. 20.

the one side of it was the county of Chester, replete with nobility, gentry, and wealthy individuals; and on the other, the populous towns of Stockport, Rochdale, Bury, and Bolton, full of opulent and public spirited men, who found Manchester a point where they could, equally with their Cheshire neighbours, gratify their taste, and enroll their names in its public institutions for the fine arts. In most of these towns, there were collections, and in all of them numerous wealthy individuals, liberal supporters of the arts. In Bolton-le-Moor, which thirty years since, had but few claims to civilisation, and still fewer to taste and refinement, there were now some important collections, and what was much more important, a subscription was now on foot for the building of a gallery intended for the productions of modern art. He mentioned this as highly honorable to the spirited individuals who promoted it, and to the Manchester amateurs, who set so laudable an example.[1]

This dash of cold water only excited the leaders of Liverpool to undertake greater responsibilities for art in the community.

II. AN INDEPENDENT ACADEMY

The exhibition of 1830 was the last held by the Academy in the rooms of the Royal Liverpool Institution. Artists and public had complained that the situation of the building was inconvenient, the entrance to the galleries, unsuitable. Spurred by the financial success of the exhibitions, the Liverpool Academy severed its formal connections with the Institution, but it did not become completely independent at this time. It was allied with a Society of Amateurs 'of taste and opulence' that emerged at the end of 1830 to assist art. The Mayor, seven Aldermen, twelve members of the Corporation, and fifty-four other resident gentlemen made up the society. The executive committee included many serious collectors of art. Winstanley was the secretary. A sum of money was placed at the disposal of this committee by the Corporation, and they dispensed some £100 to £150 yearly in prizes to artists. The devotion that some merchants, lawyers, and ministers felt for the fine arts was now further institutionalised in Liverpool as it was in other cities.

At the banquet of 1831, Winstanley, who had canvassed London artists for contributions,[2] told the guests how the Academy had obtained a new home in Post Office Place through the aid of Aldermen Wright and T. C. Porter and Sir John Gladstone. Since the Academy was dependent on the Corporation and the wealthy for this home, it was inevitable that some of the influential members of the Society would assume a proprietary attitude and antagonise artists who wished to direct their own affairs. However, the relationship for the moment seemed friendly enough and in 1831 the Society awarded prizes. William Broxall received £50 for his picture in the

[1] *Kaleidoscope*, 14th September 1830, p. 86.
[2] Liverpool Academy, Council Minute Book, 13th April 1831. Liverpool Record Office.

exhibition and local artists received prizes for 'professional merit and improvement'.[1]

Organisational changes were rapid in the next few years. In 1832 prizes were again awarded by the Society, but in 1833 no exhibition was held, because of renewed financial difficulties. In 1834 the Society was not mentioned in the exhibition catalogue, though it was stated that the Mayor and Corporation had distributed £135 in prizes. The Society of Amateurs had disappeared. The problem in Liverpool, as in other communities, such as Birmingham and Edinburgh,[2] was the belief of the patrons, on the one hand, that an informal, lay-dominated academy met all the basic needs of art, and the hostility of artists, on the other, to any form of lay control. Patrons insisted on their 'wiser' leadership, while the artists felt they were looked down upon. In Liverpool, the artists now felt they were strong enough to stand alone and they did, helped substantially for the next decade by an art-union organized in 1834.[3] In 1835, the Mayor and the Corporation were again thanked for their patronage. In 1836, even municipal patronage ended, and only one prize, £50, was awarded, which came from the funds of the Academy.[4] The Liverpool artists placed their trust in the beneficial operation of the laws of the market place, and they were not disappointed. Those who loved English art gave as enthusiastic support to these exhibits in Post Office Place as they had to those at the Royal Liverpool Institution. Many members of the Royal Academy not only exhibited their outstanding works but also carried away the Liverpool prize. In 1839 J. R. Herbert received the £50 for 'The Bridge of Venice', while an altar piece, 'The Intercession of Christ', by C. W. Cope won favour in 1840 and the following year Thomas Webster took the prize with 'The Boy with Many Friends'.

Members of the Academy initiated auxiliary projects. From time to time engravings and books on art were purchased or presented to the society, and by the early forties there were monthly meetings for the discussion of art.[5] Plans were made to open the exhibition two evenings a week to the working classes at a reduced fee of 6d. In 1845 W. G. Herdman, an enthusiast for working-class education, proposed that the fee be reduced to 2d. on the last days of the exhibition, in order that the largest possible number of the working people might benefit from the many moral lessons depicted in the paintings.[6]

---

[1] *Kaleidoscope*, 23rd August 1831, p. 477.
[2] See Joseph Hill and William Midgley, *The History of the Royal Birmingham Society of Artists* (Birmingham, 1929), and *The Royal Scottish Academy*, ed. Charles Holme (London, 1907).   [3] See ch. V.
[4] Liverpool Academy, Council Minute Book, 10th April 1837. Liverpool Record Office.
[5] Liverpool Academy, Council Minute Book, 30th March 1842. Liverpool Record Office.
[6] Liverpool Academy, Council Minute Book, 29th November 1845. Liverpool Record Office.

Several artists were appreciated in Liverpool before they gained national fame. The most widely publicised example is the Pre-Raphaelite Brotherhood. In 1851 the Liverpool Academy's prize of £50 was given to a Pre-Raphaelite painter for the first time. On a motion of William Windus, who had recently seen and admired Millais' brilliantly painted and minutely detailed 'Christ in the House of His Parents' at the Royal Academy, it was awarded to William Holman Hunt for his 'Valentine rescuing Sylvia from Proteus'. The Pre-Raphaelites also carried away the prize in succeeding years.

The accomplishments of several Liverpool artists were praised at the Academy's exhibitions. Some of these artists gained national recognition, made London the centre of their activity, yet regularly sent pictures down to Liverpool. Here are examples. In the thirties Samuel Austin found here a steady market for his rustic figures and his coast scenes with boats and shipping. Mrs. Mary Harrison[1] sent her charming nature studies. She was accustomed to paint chiefly roots of wild flowers surrounded by grasses, moss, and dead leaves, though sometimes she would delineate cut sprays of garden flowers, or a branch of blackberry bush, lying near a bird's nest with violets, cowslips, crocuses, primrose, snowdrops, or roses. In France, during the reign of Louis Philippe, she was much sought after, and called the 'Rose and Primrose Painter'. Modest sums were asked for these studies, and they quickly moved from the walls of the exhibitions.

William Windus, the enthusiastic convert to the teachings of the Brotherhood, sent to the Royal Academy in 1856 'Burd Helen', and in 1858 'Too Late', two of the most distinctly characteristic Pre-Raphaelite studies, with their high degree of finish and the appeal of homely detail. Ruskin's criticism of the second work, followed by the death of his wife, caused Windus virtually to give up painting as a career. He destroyed most of his later canvases before moving to London in 1879 and was almost forgotten as an artist.[2]

Richard Ansdell moved vigorously in Liverpool and London art circles in early Victorian England. At the age of twenty-one, he set up as an artist in Liverpool, while attending the classes of the Liverpool Academy, of which he afterwards became a member, and eventually president. The turn of his mind was towards animal painting, about which he probably learned most from the observation of nature. His first appearance at the Royal Academy was in 1840, when 'Grouse-shooting, Lunch on the Moors' and 'A Galloway Farm, the property of the Marquis of Bute', were hung. In 1842 he gained favourable comment with the historical study, 'The

---

[1] Ellen C. Clayton lavishes praise on her in *English Female Artists* (London, 1876), Vol. I.

[2] Mary Bennett, 'William Windus and the Pre-Raphaelite Brotherhood in Liverpool', *The Liverpool Bulletin*, VII (1958–9), p. 26.

Death of William Lambton at the Battle of Marston Moor'. 'Here as in most of his pictures the subject was not the main thing and was selected for representation because the scene was on Marston Moor and the agonies of a wounded horse could be well portrayed there.'[1] The *Art Union*, admiring this work and 'Portraits of Red Deer in Knowsley Park', declared that the artist had established his claim to a distinguished place in his profession. Ansdell was honoured three times with the Heywood medal at the Manchester exhibitions, and in 1855, he received a gold medal at the Great Exhibition in Paris, which had a very important collection of pictures.[2] He was elected A.R.A. in 1861 and R.A. in 1870. Since there was a public that liked animal pictures seasoned with a dash of theatrical sentiment, Ansdell had no difficulty in finding purchasers for his works, and during the last twenty-five years of his life, his average price for a picture was £750. With profits from engravings, a large income came to this popular artist.

Another Liverpool artist who explored the animal world was William Huggins.[3] When he was a student at the Liverpool Academy, and only fifteen, he took a prize for a design, 'Adam's Vision of the Death of Abel'. In the same year, 1835, he contributed to the exhibitions of the Liverpool Academy. Ambitious to excel as a painter of history, the persistent preference shown for his studies of animals, in the Landseer manner, rather annoyed him. His skill in this line was the result of much sketching in boyhood at the Zoological Gardens in Liverpool. Among early works illustrating Scriptural and other subjects were: 'Daniel in the Lions' Den' (1841), 'The Disobedient Prophet Slain by the Lions' (1843), 'Christian About to Turn Back for Fear of the Lions' (1848), and the 'Aerial Combat, the fight between the Eagle and the Serpent', from Shelley's 'Revolt of Islam'. In 1842, he made his first appearance at the R.A. with 'Androcles and the Lion'. He was elected as associate of the Liverpool Academy in 1847 and a member in 1850, although he was never honoured by the R.A. Huggins also had a considerable practice as a portrait painter, using his talent as a painter of animals to good account by introducing them as accessories. A good example is 'Tired Friends', a portrait of Mr. Case, a Birkenhead magistrate, with his horse.

The works of several landscape artists were well-known in the North. In 1843 John Wright Oakes began modestly as a landscapist with a three-guinea 'Sketch on the Lancashire Coast'. He seems to have attended classes at the Liverpool Academy, but his training was

---

[1] 'Richard Ansdell', *Dictionary of National Biography*, Suppl. I, 52.

[2] Sir Edwin Landseer, a more popular animal painter, received a Grand Medal of Honour. For an interesting survey of this exhibition see John Canaday, *Mainstreams of Modern Art* (New York, 1962), pp. 141–55.

[3] His reputation has been revived. For a just appreciation of his work see Jeremy Maas, *Victorian Painters* (London, 1969), pp. 81–2.

probably very desultory. After he exhibited ten landscapes of local or Welsh subjects at the Liverpool Academy, in 1846, in the following year he was elected an associate and next began exhibiting in London. In 1848 his pictures at Liverpool included subjects in the Lake District, one of which, 'On the River Greta, Keswick', marked his first appearance at the Royal Academy. His prices were moderate, thus appealing to the middle-class patron of the provinces. In 1854 his highest price was 150 guineas for 'The Vale of Bersham'; in 1855, £100 was asked for 'Twil-du' and 'Loch Ranzar, Arran'. There were many other Liverpool artists too who painted familiar and unfamiliar landscapes for the same modest prices. Richard Bond specialised in scenes of the Scottish border; George Dodgson concentrated on the scenery of Yorkshire, Wales, and the Lake District; and William Linton found inspiration in the nearby countryside.

An artist might struggle against great odds. Henry Dawson, the landscape painter, had a varied career before he took a house and settled down with £30 clear in his pocket in Liverpool, at first having neither friends nor introductions. It was not long before he found a patron in Mr. Richardson, a picture-dealer, who paid him £12 for a small forest scene called 'The Major Oak'. After this, though his funds were often very low, he was able to maintain himself for a time. While at Liverpool, he studied briefly at the Academy, but on the whole his instruction was slight. Growing dissatisfied with inadequate patronage, he moved on to London. The entry in his diary for 1850 shows the scale of his income, his expenditures, and also the temper with which he and other artists engaged in the struggle of life: 'June 8—This day had more money in my possession than ever I had at one time of my own, namely £148. This will enable me, with God's blessing, to stand a twelve month's siege, if I should not sell another picture, and all this good fortune notwithstanding my apparent ill-luck at the Academy. Surely goodness and mercy hath followed me all my days. O God, make me more thankful of these great benefits.'[1] It was long before he gained any reputation in the south of England. Though well treated at the British Institution, his pictures were, with one exception, ill-hung at the Royal Academy, and almost to the end of his life it was the residents of Birmingham, Liverpool, Leeds, and Nottingham, and not those of London, who bought his later pictures, landscapes in the style of Turner.

The majority of Liverpool artists received modest sums for their works shown at the provincial exhibitions. Here is a good example. The landscapist John Pennington, a member of the Liverpool Academy in 1822, showed four pictures; the largest, a 'View on the

[1] 'Henry Dawson', in M. Bryan, *Dictionary of Painters and Engravers*, revised by G. C. Williamson (London, 1913) I, 674.

Banks of the Canal, near Bootle'. was priced at £21. He was a regular contributor to the exhibitions until 1840, his total contributions numbering nearly one hundred. His subjects were chiefly local, but sometimes he submitted scenes from North Wales, the Lake District, Derbyshire, and Cheshire. He did not advance greatly in reputation, and the exhibition prices of his pictures remained stable. In 1835, a 'View near Black Combe, Cumberland' was 22 guineas, in 1836 'View near Hale' was 25 guineas. A newspaper critic in 1828 observed that 'Mr. Pennington's prices are always moderate, which shows that he is modest and void of pretense to a high rank of his profession.'[1]

The portrait painters who had pioneered on the provincial art scene were the first to be battered by the camera. James Pelham II (1800–74)[2] is typical of the artists who were hurt. After he settled in Liverpool in 1846, he frequently exhibited portraits and miniatures. He was elected an associate of the Academy in 1847, a full member in 1851, and in 1854 secretary, in which capacity he took an important part in arranging the Academy's exhibitions. Although he exhibited portraits until 1854, the progress of photography so greatly interfered with the the practices of miniature and portrait painters that, like many others, Pelham had to turn to another branch of art. In his case, it was the painting of domestic genre subjects, usually on a small scale. In the case of other artists, it was a question of learning to use the camera.

While the Academy honoured those moving within the pale, all went well. Tribute to the outsider brought disaster. Between 1850 and 1858, John Millais, Holman Hunt, and Ford Madox Brown each received the Liverpool prize on two occasions. This partiality for the Pre-Raphaelites was too much for most of the public, and for many of the artists. Fierce controversy broke out in the local press and spread to London where the *Athenaeum* fought a sharp battle with the *Spectator*. Then a rival body sprang up calling itself the Liverpool Society of Fine Arts, as the Academy lost support on every side. The unfortunate Academy struggled on for a few years more, but the last prize was given in 1861 and the last open exhibition held in 1867.

In spite of this apparent failure, the idea of an annual exhibition of art attracted the public. The Corporation, therefore, as representative of the people, now came forward to sponsor exhibitions. In 1871 they opened, in the ten-year-old museum in William Brown Street, the first of a long series of Liverpool Autumn Exhibitions which still continue. The artists contributed, the crowds came to

[1] *Ibid.*, IV, 91.
[2] There were three James Pelhams: father, son, and grandson: I (d. 1850), II (1800–74), and III (1840–1906). The first two were miniaturists and portrait painters, while the third painted landscape and genre.

the first exhibition, but there was much criticism of the location. Through the generosity of Andrew Walker,[1] a new gallery was erected. It is quite clear that the primary purpose of the building was to afford facilities for the great annual show, which was now a feature of the life of Liverpool and which came to be known familiarly as 'the Academy of the North'. These exhibitions were immensely popular, and in the days when the wealthier shipowners and cotton brokers still lived within easy reach of the centre of town, its soirées were an important feature of the life of the middle classes of Liverpool. The charge for admission and commissions on sales of pictures provided handsome profits: in 1884, nearly £5,000 was taken in at the doors, and pictures to the value of more than £12,000 were sold. The profit, as a means of inducing artists of eminence to contribute to the annual exhibitions, was spent on the purchase of pictures directly from the exhibition and these pictures were added, with further gifts, to the rapidly growing permanent collection. In 1893, the Liverpool Institution lent the Roscoe Collection to the Gallery and what had been very contemporary was given historical depth.

III. THE ART EDUCATION PROGRAMME OF THE LIVERPOOL ROYAL INSTITUTION

The proprietors of the Liverpool Royal Institution believed that a sound education in art required not only a collection of casts from the antique but also paintings or copies of paintings of the Old Masters. There was nothing extraordinary in the Institution's collection of casts, but the collection of paintings was unique. Appreciation of the collection's true worth, however, came only in this century.

Roscoe and his friends believed that the artists and students of the Academy would improve their art and enlightened gentlemen would correct and improve their taste if there was a catholic selection of paintings in the community. In the detailed plan of the Institution of 1814, specific reference is made to the worth of 'Specimens of Art'. The possibility of starting an Institution collection came when Roscoe was forced to place his personal collections on the market after the Napoleonic Wars.

In the early nineteenth century, Roscoe collected the works of

---

[1] 'When Sir William Brown (Brown, Shipley & Company) gave the Brown Library, a journalist could remind his readers that the prospect of a baronetcy rather than any native generosity had inspired the gift. . . . Sir Andrew Barclay Walker, the brewer and distiller who provided Liverpool with its art gallery, was regarded with no more enthusiasm by this abrasive commentator. Walker's philanthropies, he intimated, were planned as instruments for his own social and political advancement, first to a knighthood and then to a baronetcy.' David Owen, *English Philanthropy: 1660–1960* (Cambridge, Mass., 1964), pp. 453–4.

the Old Masters, not merely for his own pleasure, but also, it would seem, for the eventual benefit of the community. The nature and purpose of Roscoe's collection of paintings is suggested by this extract taken from the advertisement of his sale catalogue.

The following works . . . have been collected during a series of years, chiefly for the purpose of illustrating, by reference to original and authentic sources, the rise and progress of the arts in modern times, as well in Germany and Flanders as in Italy. They are therefore not wholly to be judged of by their positive merits, but by reference to the age in which they were produced. Their value chiefly depends on their authenticity, and the light they throw on the history of the arts. Yet as they extend beyond the splendid era of 1500, there will be found several productions of a higher class, which may be ranked amongst the 'chef d'oeuvres' of modern skill.

Hopes had been indulged by the present possessor that the works of Literature and Art included in this and the two preceding Catalogues (i.e., books and prints), might have formed the basis of a more extensive collection, and have been subsurvient to some object of public utility; but the circumstances of the times are not favorable to his views, and they are now therefore offered to the public, in detail without reserve. The catalogue may serve, however, to give an idea of the entire collection, when the works that compose it are again dispersed.[1]

Roscoe's purpose, it is apparent, was didactic—to form an illustrated history of art for the instruction of artists and the general public. He believed his survey revealed the progress of the art of painting from the late middle ages to the age of Raphael. Roscoe, like other *philosophes* of the Age of Enlightenment, believed that man, through his own intelligent efforts, could transform the conditions of human life and that the beginnings of this transformation could already be seen in the sciences and the arts. His collection of paintings, therefore, had a very high purpose. His philosophy was one that called for the greatest efforts of man to improve his standards and to maintain them.

Roscoe and his friends lived through an age which saw the opening of many of the great national collections of Europe: Florence, Vienna, Paris, Berlin, Madrid, and London.[2] 'In contrast to the present day, the museum represented one of the most progressive

---

[1] Quoted in Michael Compton, 'William Roscoe and the Early Collections of Italian Primitives', *The Liverpool Bulletin*, IX (1960-1), 29.

[2] Maria Ludovica, Grand Duchess of Tuscany and the last of the Medici, willed to the state of Tuscany in 1737, the collections of the family in Florence and in other parts of Italy. The magnificent gesture of the last of the Medici was followed shortly afterwards in Dresden with the opening of that city's museum. The enlightened purpose of that collection, according to its first catalogue, prepared by its curator, Riedel, in 1765, was to honour the achievement of the best artists and to improve taste. The process by which the public obtained control over art and art collections was speeded up when, in 1793, France's revolutionary government nationalized the property of the crown, renamed the Louvre's museum 'Museum of the Republic' and opened it to the public. A sample of these treasures is shown in Hans Tietze, *Treasures of the Great National Galleries* (London, 1954).

institutions of the age. For that generation art really meant something holy.'[1] The idea of the historical collection was familiar to
Roscoe and other collectors of engravings. Earlier he had written
An Idea of a Chronological Collection of Engravings. His great example of
progression was collections not of paintings but of drawings and
prints, which were considered all important for the correct education
of the artist and gentleman. These historical or illustrative collections of drawings had a history going back to the Renaissance world
of Vasari and included many English collections of the eighteenth
century. Roscoe had a considerable collection himself. The ultimate
source of his ideas on the progress of the arts, however, came from
the histories of Vasari, Baldinucci, and Lanzi.

When the Liverpool bank, William Clarke and Sons, suspended
payment in 1816, Roscoe, in an attempt to save the situation, disposed of his collections of books, engravings, and paintings, as well
as his country estate. The loss of these treasures was a hard thing,
but Roscoe and his friends conceived of a plan to keep his collection of paintings in Liverpool. In spite of what the sale catalogue
says about 'without reserve', he bought in a large part of his historical collection through local dealers. After this was valued by Winstanley at 1,553 guineas, Roscoe generously offered it for 1,200
guineas to the Liverpool Royal Institution. 'I shall think myself
sufficiently gratified if the liberality of my townsmen shall so far
second my wishes as to prevent a collection form'd with a view to
public utility from being dispersed.'[2] In 1819, this collection was
bought by public subscription. A catalogue of the paintings, compiled by Roscoe for the Institution, was published in the same year,
with a brief introduction, which emphasised the educational purpose of the collection.[3] Roscoe's connoisseurship was not much
better than the standards of his time and the majority of the attributions in the catalogue are incorrect. However, he did gather together
and eventually sell to the Liverpool Institution a group of primitives,
which contains real masterpieces, and interesting pictures of later
periods.

In the 1820s, while the directors were concentrating on the development of the lecture programme and the Academy's exhibitions,
the permanent collection of art did not increase significantly. In
1829, J. A. Yates, Joseph B. Yates, Benjamin Arthur Heywood, John
Gladstone, Thomas Winstanley, and James T. Winstanley presented
four historical pictures by Labruzzi to the Institution that they
thought 'would be highly useful connected with the study of the
Fine Arts. As the object of the Institution is to assist and promote

---

[1] Hans Sedlmayr, *Art in Crisis: The Lost Center* (Chicago, 1958), p. 28.

[2] William Roscoe, Liverpool, June 16, 1818, Letter to Dr. Thomas Stewart
Traill, Roscoe Papers 486A, Liverpool Record Office.

[3] *Catalogue of a Series of Pictures, illustrating the Rise and Early Progress of the Art of
Painting in Italy, Germany, etc.* (Liverpool, 1819).

general science and the progress of the Fine Arts.'[1] With the abandonment of the lecture programme in 1840 because of declining interest in popular lectures, the general committee determined to increase the collection of paintings and to construct a permanent gallery to house both pictures and casts. A proposal brought before the annual meeting of 1840 to devote £1,200 of the institution's funds to this objective was approved, provided that a similar sum was subscribed by the general public. Thomas Winstanley prepared a prospectus with his usual zeal, and the matching sum came in. Next, a committee to oversee construction of the gallery and purchase additional works of art was appointed.

The new building contained two large galleries: the one on the lower floor designed for the display of the casts and sculptures, the upper one for pictures. The building had faults and Benjamin R. Haydon was quick to note them:

Poor old Winstanley, Dr. Freckleton, and others when building their gallery took me over to show it to me as a wonderful thing, and it certainly was, for they had so placed the light, at the sides instead of in the middle, that no picture could ever be seen. I pointed out this defect to them and to their architect, but he laughed at my objections, finished the roof, and brought the pictures. Not one could be seen. Ashamed of his blunders and of spending so much money, they applied to me for a plan and I sketched one for them and referred them further to *Borter House* at Rugby as the true method of lighting a picture gallery. Three hundred pounds more were collected, the roof altered, so as to place the light in the middle and now the pictures are to be seen to perfection.[2]

Haydon, who was none too kind to lesser men, ends his tale with a self-compliment. 'The other day when going through their gallery once more to see the effects of my suggestion, I was much amused to hear first one and then the other, boast to me that they had always said so. . . .'[3]

Thomas Winstanley acted as the general artistic advisor to the Liverpool Royal Institution during these years. On 7th April 1842 he brought to the notice of the gallery committee the availability of a collection of pictures owned by Mr. Bullock, and the committee authorised him to enter into negotiations. In May, the committee agreed, 'that a discretionary power be confided to Mr. Winstanley (now in London) to expend on paintings a sum of money not exceeding £300.'[4] In June he presented a list of the paintings that he had purchased and informed the Committee that, while he was in London, he had selected for his own firm fifteen pictures that he

[1] Dr. Thomas Steward Traill, *Address of February, 1829* (Liverpool, 1829), p. 23.
[2] B. R. Haydon, Liverpool, 1st April 1844, letter to his wife in Benjamin Robert Haydon, *Correspondence and Table Talk of Benjamin Haydon* (Boston, 1877), II, 445.
[3] *Ibid.*
[4] Entry of 5th May 1842, Gallery Committee Minutes, p. 23. Liverpool Royal Institution Archives, No. 41, University of Liverpool Library.

would sell to the Institution at cost. This offer was accepted. Later, in the same year, the committee purchased works supposedly by Vasari and Spagnoletto from Winstanley. Above all, it must be remembered that, largely on his advice, the Institution acquired further primitives of the fourteenth and fifteenth centuries. For twenty-five years he helped the Royal Institution form its collection and by the end of this period, to the thirty-seven pictures of the Roscoe collections were added another eighty or so works, including a Signorelli and a Bellini.

There was much in the collection of the new gallery for those who wished to study the art of the past and acquire a finer taste. Unfortunately, the gallery was never popular with the general public and after the activity of the early forties, the interest of the proprietors waned. The gallery did open doors for the art students of the Academy, for whom increased facilities were now available. From an early date, students had been granted access to the collections for study three evenings a week. With the opening of the new gallery, it was possible to admit students on four evenings, two of which were devoted to a life class, supervised by members of the Academy.[1]

The people of Liverpool passed the Institution's collection by when the Walker Art Gallery opened. Only when the bulk of the Institution's collection was given to the Walker Art Gallery in 1893 did scholars and the public begin to appreciate the full measure of the Roscoe and Winstanley endeavour.[2]

[1] Liverpool Academy, Council Minute Book, 31st January 1843. Liverpool Record Office.

[2] The gem of the Roscoe collection was and is 'Christ returning from the Doctors to his Parents' by Simone Martini. Other admired works are 'Portrait of a Young Man (with the Conversion of St. Hubert)' by Jan Mostaert; a 'Pieta' by Ercole De'Roberti and 'Portrait of a Man with a Helmet' by Il Rosso.

CHAPTER IV

LIVERPOOL'S RIVAL

I. THE ART PROGRAMME OF THE MANCHESTER ROYAL INSTITUTION

By the 1820s, Manchester had become the metropolis of a manu-facturing region that drew the bulk of its most important raw material, cotton, from the U.S.A., and by the 1830s, the new rail-ways had begun to increase the tempo of manufacturing and merchandising. Towns such as Bolton, Bury, Rochdale, Oldham, Ashton, Stalybridge, Hyde, and Stockport were the manufacturing sections of one great urban centre, Manchester, whose merchants and manufacturers concentrated their activities on wholesale mer-chandising, the finishing processes such as dyeing and bleaching, or the manufacture of textile machinery.

'Cotton made modern Manchester. It created a small class of wealthy men—they were perhaps the first men to think of themselves as a "class"—and a large class of "working men" who were often doomed to severe suffering.'[1] Many of these businessmen were very practical, energetic, and tough, devoting a large part of their lives to making money. Richard Cobden, early in his career, noted that in the town there was 'but one opinion or criterion of a man's ability—the making of money . . .,'[2] and de Tocqueville solemnly declared: 'Everything in the exterior appearance of the city attests the individual powers of man; nothing the directing powers of society. At every turn human liberty shows its capricious creative force. There is no trace of the slow continuous action of govern-ment.'[3] On closer examination, however, one finds merchants and manufacturers who were enlightened, cultured, and pious. In the late eighteenth century, men of this type had aided in the founding of the Manchester Literary and Philosophical Society, the Circu-lating Library opened in 1765, the New Circulating Library established in 1792, and the most elegant of these libraries, the Portico, which circulated books from 1806. Although these men had never learned to turn a Latin hexameter, they appreciated the works of Scott, Southey and Wordsworth, and *The Edinburgh Review* or the *Quarterly Review* was often found on the tables of their libraries. They could also appreciate the sights of the Rhine valley and Venice. These men were much conerned with the condition of the poor and

---

[1] Asa Briggs, *Victorian Cities* (London, 1964), p. 85.
[2] John Morley, *The Life of Richard Cobden* (London, 1881), I, p. 22.
[3] de Tocqueville, p. 105.

were active in municipal affairs. Culture and enlightenment, as they conceived of them, did not mean withdrawal to a remote estate, but civic improvement: schools, concert halls, public libraries orphanages, churches, and museums and art galleries. These traders and manufacturers were joined in their endeavours by an equally concerned group of professional men: doctors, lawyers, editors, and publishers.

In the 1820s Thomas and Richard Potter, George William Wood, John Edward Taylor, and Joseph Brotherton joined such older men as Robert Philips, Samuel Greg, Samuel Jackson, Thomas Preston, and Thomas Renshaw to organise what Richard Potter called 'a small but determined band of free traders and reformers.'[1] The average age of the younger men was thirty-three; most of them were dissenters and all were successful business or professional men connected with the cotton industry. Sir James Kay-Shuttleworth believed that Wood, the Potters, and their associates deserved great credit for advancing municipal reform.

I cannot look upon the great avenues of commerce which have opened through the centres of this city without reflecting how difficult it was (for these men) to obtain the revenue for these improvements by the establishment of your gas-works, . . . nor can I forget these improvements, for the origination of improved sanitary arrangements, for your representation in Parliament, for your municipal incorporation, for your increased security of property, health, and comforts among all classes of the community, you are indebted to pioneers. . . .[2]

These men lent their reforming zeal also to cultural projects, the most ambitious being, perhaps, the Royal Manchester Institution, whose beginnings were unpretentious. An auctioneer and print seller, Thomas Dodd, first suggested that a deeper appreciation of art would develop in well-to-do homes if there were an art society in the community. He already discerned varied interests in the arts among 'the more enlightened classes of the community and foresaw that if in a degree they were directed and diffused among the ingenious although uninitiated minds of the community, great and highly intellectual results would ensure, to the benefit of all classes engaged in operative employments of manufacture.'[3]

Envisaging a print club similar to the one Gregson had organised earlier in Liverpool, Dodd next addressed a circular to influential and affluent citizens, proposing that each subscribe £10 and in return Dodd would purchase books and prints at his discretion. Whatever the sum raised, Dodd would add as much on his own

---

[1] Leon S. Marshall, *The Development of Public Opinion in Manchester* (Syracuse, 1946), p. 223.

[2] *Manchester Examiner and Times*, 27th February 1866.

[3] Frederick Boyle, 'The Last of the Grand School of Connoisseurs', *Memoirs of Thomas Dodd, William Upcott, and George Stubbs, R.A.* (Liverpool, 1879), pp. 34–5.

account, and all the articles would be sold at a private auction to subscribers of the scheme. Every subscriber would have a right to his £10 worth and as much else as he chose to buy. The circular became a topic of conversation among the connoisseurs as well as the artists of the Manchester area. Charles Calvert, a leading painter, visited Dodd and suggested that a more appropriate undertaking would be an exhibition of art similar to those of other provincial communities, and that Dodd, familiar with the national art scene, might help organise such an undertaking. Dodd yielded and as a result, a general meeting of artists took place at Jackson's print warehouse in Market Street.

From 1760 to 1820 Manchester was a market for, rather than a vital centre of, art, the practice of art being largely confined to those who painted portraits. In 1767 Peter Romney described the Manchester art scene. 'There is one Pickering, who lives altogether in this town, a face painter, and a second Cranke, but who neither draws nor colours so well. He is, in short, a mere old woman in painting, and is quite adapted to the Manchester people, who are old women in every thing, except trade and manufactures. This you think is dictated by a spirit of disappointment, but I believe it will be found true, taking the people in general.'[1] After a short stay in Liverpool, Romney returned to Manchester, found greater success, and gained the friendship of such enlightened men as Dr. Thomas Percival.[2] Once in Manchester, an impoverished William Hazlitt lived on little more than coffee for two weeks while painting a half-length portrait of a manufacturer who paid him five guineas when the canvas was finished.[3] Among other artists who left a brief imprint on the city were Joshua Shaw, William Marshall Craig, Theodore Fielding and Daniel Stringer. Shaw specialised in flower pieces and clever copies of Old Masters, which the unscrupulous touted as genuine Berchems and Boths. Craig's staple was the flattering miniature; the last two artists concentrated on portraits. Perhaps, more lasting impressions were left in the North by John Rathbone, Daniel Orme, Mather Brown, and Henry Wyatt. Rathbone, known as the 'Manchester Wilson', created rather undistinguished landscapes in oil but handled watercolours with greater vivacity. Orme, the son of a Manchester merchant, studied at the Royal Academy and then practiced in London and later in Manchester as portrait painter, miniaturist and engraver. Mather Brown, an American pupil of West, roamed the provinces, searching for portrait commissions and giving lessons. Two of his Manchester pupils, William Bradley and Thomas Henry Illidge, emerged as leading portraitists of early Victorian England. Henry Wyatt,

---

[1] Romney, p. 298.
[2] *Ibid.*, p. 301.
[3] Herschel Baker, *William Hazlitt* (Cambridge, 1962), p. 1 2.

after studying with Lawrence, found much favour in the North with his portraits and such anecdotes as 'Fair Forester', 'Preferred Kiss', and 'Gentle Reader'.

By the 1820s the small group of artists residing permanently in Manchester sought the social status and economic rewards connected with an academy. Their spokesman was Charles Calvert, who had been apprenticed to the cotton trade and began business as a cotton merchant in Manchester, only to abandon commerce for art, becoming a landscape painter. Much of his time was devoted to teaching, but all of his spare moments were spent in the Lake District, the great inspiration for his mountain and lake scenery, his favourite subjects.

Dodd and the artists resolved to seek the sustained support of the community through the creation of a society of patrons. A circular, again written by Dodd, suggested the worth of such patronage, specifically pointing to the utilitarian and moral benefits that would result:

An alliance between commerce and the Liberal Arts is at once natural and salutary. The wishes of mankind increase with the means of gratifying them, and the superficial wealth, which is the fruit of extensive and flourishing trade, finds an object in those elegant productions of human genius and skill, which minister to the luxury of the imagination. Nor do the arts fail to reward the patronage, which is extended to them: they bestow an intellectual grace upon society; they refine the taste and soften the manners; they not only furnish employment for the riches, which must otherwise accumulate in useless abundance, but provide contrasting influence to the gross and sordid spirit, which is too often the result of an undivided attention to mercenary pursuits.[1]

These arguments were successful in bringing artists and businessmen together in the large room of the Exchange on 1st October 1823. During the meeting, the following resolution was passed unanimously: 'That the diffusion of a taste for the Fine Arts, in this populous and opulent district, by establishing a collection of the best models that can be obtained, in painting and sculpture, and by opening a channel through which the works of meritorious artists may be brought before the public, and the encouragement of literary and scientific pursuits, by the delivery of public lectures, are objects highly desirable and important.'[2] A hundred and forty persons subscribed £50 apiece to found an institution that was uncompromisingly cultural in character. The gentlemen of Manchester like those of Liverpool were pooling their energies in a group enterprise

---

[1] *The Manchester Institution for the Promotion of Literature, Science, and the Arts* (Manchester, 1823), p. 9.
[2] Royal Manchester Institution, Council Minute Book, 1823–35, p. 25. Central Reference Library, Manchester.

that was designed in part to create and diffuse a taste for the fine arts through the study and exhibition of works of art, in order to raise the cultural level of Manchester and to encourage the growth of English art.

A limited competition was announced for the design of a building suitable for study and exhibitions, and that of Charles Barry was chosen, his first major commission and his only Greek public building.[1] The editor of the *Builder* considered the work one of significance because the architect had reinvigorated neo-classical themes. Barry integrated the portico into the design, whereas in so many Greek works of that period the portico was merely tacked to a many-windowed façade.[2] Mounting costs during construction provoked criticism and brought suggestions that the design be modified, Benjamin Arthur Heywood, as enthusiastic a supporter of the Royal Manchester Institution as of the Liverpool Royal Institution. warned that distinction could not necessarily be purchased for a small sum: 'There is more to be considered than the calculation of pounds, shillings, and pence and there is some valuable feeling connected with the reflection that our little Forty Pound Freeholds will hereafter and forever be considered to give posthumous fame in the character of a family heirloom which makes me more willing to make the cost sixty pounds . . .'[3] His wise voice prevailed, and what is now the City Art Gallery emerged as the most distinguished building in Manchester of the period preceding the accession of Victoria.

Distinguished patrons of English art lent their names and influence to the endeavour. Sir John Fleming Leicester, 'the munificent patron and encourager of mature genius',[4] offered to seek the king's favour for the enterprise. He felt sure that George IV, 'whose love for the Fine Arts, I doubt not',[5] would honour the undertaking with his royal patronage. Leicester also encouraged artists of his circle to lend support. 'That distinguished artist, Mr. Ward, who is now with us at Tabley, requests me to assure you that he is greatly rejoiced at the formation of this Establishment for the promotion of the Arts, and that he will do everything in his power in aid of a yearly exhibition, if such is intended by sending some of his works, and also by endeavouring to produce the works of other Artists of established reputation.'[6]

Later, Sir John offered 'to apply to such gentlemen that appear

---

[1] Alfred Barry, *The Life and Works of Sir Charles Barry* (London, 1867).

[2] Cecil Stewart, *The Stones of Manchester* (London, 1956), p. 32.

[3] B. A. Heywood, 1827, letter to Dr. Davenport Hulme, Royal Manchester Institution Letters 1823–1832, p. 73. Central Reference Library, Manchester.

[4] The phrase is Raeburn's, quoted in Boase, p. 104.

[5] Sir John Fleming Leicester, 15th January 1824, letter to G. F. Bury, Royal Manchester Institution Letters 1823–1832, p. 5. Central Reference Library, Manchester.

[6] *Ibid.*

to me likely to give their assistance'.[1] He was successful, however, only in obtaining encouraging words. His greatest service was that of publicist. In 1825 he wrote to Dr. Davenport Hulme, requesting a copy of the elevation of the new building, 'which all the world of taste may have an opportunity of seeing in my Gallery in Hill Street; nor am I without hope that I may have an opportunity of submitting it to His Majesty, when it could I think be highly gratifying to the members of the Institution as well as of incalculable importance to the Architect, to have it in their power to report that the King, whose taste is excellent, admired and approved of it.'[2]

Sir Thomas Lawrence,[3] the President of the Royal Academy, also gave his support wholeheartedly to the plan for the exhibitions of contemporary English art, but warned the proprietors that frequent exhibitions of the works of Old Masters jeopardised the progress of English art, because the public too often fell down and worshipped before old varnish and dark colours, 'finding real advantages in the efforts of Time, as a true and perfect test to the apparently inadequate exertions of modern art—making the mere contrast of appearance and surface, proof of superiority, and thus connecting unavoidable result, into intentional refinement.'[4]

Before the programme of the R.M.I. began, Benjamin Arthur Heywood presented a gift of £500, the yearly interest of which would be used to purchase medals, awards for the outstanding works of art and science examined by the institution. He wished to offer the meritorious student more than 'the mere expressions of praise'[5] for his exertions.

On the eve of the opening of the first exhibition of contemporary art in 1827, the governors reaffirmed their devotion to the fine arts. 'The dignity and importance of the Fine Arts in adding lustre to a national character is abundantly proved in the history of mankind; a successful cultivation of them being almost necessarily connected with a high degree of civilisation. ...'[6] The proprietors of the R.M.I.,

[1] Sir John Fleming Leicester, 31st December 1824, letter to Dr. Davenport Hulme, Royal Manchester Institution Letters, 1823–1832, p. 35. Central Reference Library, Manchester.

[2] Sir John Fleming Leicester, 19th January 1825, letter to Dr. Davenport Hulme, Royal Manchester Institution Letters, 1823–1832, p. 35. Central Reference Library, Manchester. The taste and patronage of George IV are discussed in Roger Fulford, *George IV* (London, 1949).

[3] For his patrons, see Kenneth Garlick, *Sir Thomas Lawrence* (Boston, 1955). For his collection of art see Columbus Gallery of Fine Arts, *Sir Thomas Lawrence as Painter and Collector* (Columbus, 1955).

[4] Sir Thomas Lawrence, London, 15th January 1824, letter to the Secretary, Royal Manchester Institution Letters, 1823–1832, p. 3. Central Reference Library, Manchester.

[5] Benjamin A. Heywood, 26th January 1824, letter to the Governors of the Royal Manchester Institution, Royal Manchester Institution Letters, 1823–1832, p. 7. Central Reference Library, Manchester.

[6] Royal Manchester Institution, Council Minute Book, 1823–35, p. 215. Central Reference Library, Manchester.

guided by the experiences of men in London, Leeds, and Liverpool, first concentrated on establishing an institution that would stimulate an interest in art through exhibitions and lectures, while only second did they consider the need of young artists for professional instruction. In the home of the R.M.I. was a room for artists and students, but there was no organised school of design in which the principles of high art as modified by neo-classicism prevailed. A group of casts, placed in the basement of the Portico Library, gave the students a rather dim view of the achievement of the Greeks. Here a number of students studied and made drawings which were submitted for one of the Heywood prizes.

The proprietors of the R.M.I. believed that lectures on literature science, and the fine arts, presented by authorities in their field, were of the utmost importance for their programme. Lectures on art and architecture would deepen and broaden the taste of the members and of the art community. The great popularizer of Gothic, John Britton, delivered a course of eight lectures on 'the architectural antiquities of all nations',[1] in 1836, in which he guided his audience through 'the most distinguished buildings of different ages and countries' by 'the medium of graphic illustration and critical description'.[2] 'More historical than technical, more general than particular, the Lectures now announced are intended to excite and emulate curiosity'[3] and in the end impart a greater understanding of the 'manifold beauties and utilities of architecture'.[4] In 1837 Benjamin Robert Haydon presented a course of six lectures on painting, and in 1840 another six lectures on the history of art and design, in which he discussed, among other topics, the art of Greece, that of the Middle Ages and the Renaissance, and the state of art in contemporary England. Three years later H. Heyhams lectured on the history and progress of civilisation, using transparencies of the monuments of the ancients and the architectural remains of the Middle Ages, while in 1845, R. W. Buss analysed the technique of fresco painting, and in 1846, George Wallis outlined 'the history, principles, and practice of Ornamental and Decorative art'.[5] The Institution also sponsored *conversazioni* at which papers on the arts were read and discussed. In Manchester, as in Liverpool, the proprietors were introduced to a rather unsystematic survey of the arts.

The surveys of contemporary art were more rewarding. The governors fortunately met none of the problems that had confronted the members of the L.R.I. The first exhibition in 1827, a blend of

---

[1] *Syllabus of a Course of Eight Lectures on the Architectural Antiquities of All Nations, illustrated by above 250 drawings, by John Britton, Esq. F.S.A.* (1836).

[2] *Ibid.*

[3] *Ibid.*

[4] *Ibid.*

[5] *Syllabus of a course of four lectures on the History, Principles, and practice of Ornamental and Decorative Art* (1846).

London and local talents, was a financial success. It was followed in the autumn of 1827 by an exhibition of water colours and another successful exhibit of oils in 1828. Contributors to the first exhibition were S. Austin, A. W. Callcott, R.A., C. Calvert, A. Cooper, T. C. Hofland, W. Havell, T. H. Illidge, J. Northcote, W. Linton, Henry Liverseege, C. H. Schwanfelder, C. Towne, James Ward, R.A. and S. Williamson of Liverpool. Watercolourists who contributed to the second exhibition were S. Austin, C. Barker, C. Calvert, D. Cox, Peter De Wint, Copley Fielding, John Glover, Richard Hargreaves, Arthur Perigal, Samuel Prout, Sass, John Varley, and R. Westall. The exhibitions 'were visited by great numbers of persons and numerous sales of pictures took place—The admissions money on each occasion amounted to considerably more than the expenses incurred. . . .'[1] Further, a Manchester artist received a prize of 20 guineas, a sum drawn from the Heywood Prize Fund. The exhibitions of contemporary art in 1829 and 1830 were well attended, and a great number of pictures were sold. 'There appears to be increasing taste for works of modern art and the sales which took place in 1829 amounted to £1363. 15s. and those in 1830 to £986.'[2]

Then, in 1831, the committee organized the Institution's first exhibition of Old Masters, selected from collections of friends of the Institution, in order to further 'the promotion and encouragement of the Fine Arts, and the improvement of the public taste . . .'[3] The committee emphasised specifically the moral value of such an exhibition: 'When there is reason for presuming that the contemplation of the more noble works of art may contribute in no small degree, to elevate and purify the sentiments of a people, the subject at once assumes a sort of national importance. . . .'[4] The organisers particularly wished viewers to notice the works of Reynolds, Wright, and other members of the English school, which were hung in a separate gallery in order that 'the visitor may more easily compare them with their foreign rivals and distinctly observe their characteristic perculiarities: and . . . how far the diversity may be owing to climate, national character, or the manners and customs of the age and country in which the artists lived.'[5] Among those who lent paintings were William Townsend, James Beardoe, Edward Loyd, George Scholes, T. J. Trafford, Samuel Barton, and Mrs. James Hardman, members of the gentry or business community.

The 1832 exhibition included oils, water colours, architectural

---

[1] Royal Manchester Institution, Council Minute Book, 1823–35, 15th February 1829, p. 251. Central Reference Library, Manchester.

[2] *Ibid.*, 14th March 1831, p. 334.

[3] Royal Manchester Institution, *Catalogue of the Exhibition of Pictures by Italian, Spanish, Flemish, Dutch and English Masters, with which the Proprietors Have Favoured the Institution, for the Improvement of Taste in the Fine Arts, and the Gratification of the Governors and the Public* (Manchester, 1831), p. 3.

[4] *Ibid.*

[5] *Ibid.*

designs, drawings of machinery, and proof impressions of modern engravings. It was very well attended and sixty-five of the pictures were sold for the sum of £1,100. Artists were pleased with the sales, 'which . . . were far more numerous than any other provincial Exhibition of that year.'[1]

Provincial artists, particularly Manchester artists, also benefited from these exhibitions. In 1834, the members heard:

It affords the Council much pleasure to state that there is evidently considerable improvement in the productions of our native Artists which appeared at the last Exhibition compared with those Exhibited at the early period of the Institution and they consider they will not be claiming too much of this society when they say that the improvement may in a great degree be attributed to the Exhibitions—the honorable emulation—excited by the comparison of their works not only with those of their fellow townsmen but likewise with those artists residing at a distance has induced many of our artists to exert their best energies and the effect has been a considerable improvement in all . . .[2]

This exertion had its financial rewards. Nearly 100 pictures were sold during the exhibition for a sum surpassing that of any previous year.[3] The members of the Institution had placed Manchester in the first rank as a centre of patronage of English art.

In the 1840s, however, there was a feeling that the quality of the exhibitions was declining. Remedies were found. First, the annual exhibition was no longer held at the same time as that of the Royal Academy. Second, a prize of 100 guineas was offered to the exhibitor of the best oil painting. Third, a group of Manchester art lovers went to London and interviewed the president of the Royal Academy and a number of eminent artists, whose co-operation was solicited and in every case promised in return. The exhibitions soon regained their attractiveness. In 1850, 'forty-two pictures were sold, amounting in value to £1,339, being more than double the amount realised by the sales of the previous year.'[4]

The attempt of the R.M.I. to bring art to the working classes was successful when in 1844 the exhibition was open certain evenings at a reduced rate of 6d: 'It is but right to add that, during the whole time of the Evening Exhibitions, the most marked interest in the various works of art, was evinced by that class of society for whose convenience and gratification, more particularly, the plan of Evening Exhibitions was first suggested.'[5] When in 1847, during the last

---

[1] Royal Manchester Institution, Council Minute Book, 1823–35, 29th March 1833, p. 448. Central Reference Library, Manchester.
[2] Ibid., 31st March 1834, p. 498.
[3] Ibid.
[4] Report of the Council for the Year 1850–51 (as read and agreed upon at the Annual Meeting of the Governors, held March 31, 1851) (Manchester, 1851), p. 1.
[5] Royal Manchester Institution, Proceedings of the General Meetings, 10th March 1845, p. 61.

two weeks, the exhibition charge was two pence in the evening, nearly eleven thousand people paid admission at the door. Though there was orderliness and a respectful attitude,[1] whether a serious appreciation of art developed among the many may be questioned.

From the first, there was correspondence between artists and members of the Institution concerning the availability of works, prices, and other matters. In 1827 W. Linton, the landscape painter, gave a capsule report of the London scene and what Manchester could expect from London artists.

To your inquiry respecting contributions from the first artists, it is almost impossible to give a satisfactory reply—Sir Thomas Lawrence and the portrait painters will send as it may happen to suit their convenience— Having had letters they will as usual observe the appointed days without thinking answers necessary—so will the other artists—Wilkie is in Rome— Mulready is applied to, as also to several of the Academicians, who have little to send, the very eminent ones have usually commissions, and care little about exhibiting them when executed as Turner, Landseer, Callcott. . . . The great support will be derived from those who are on the ascending list, in as well as out of the Academy, indeed they form the great mass of the exhibitors of interest and are alone likely to have pictures to spare.[2]

The analysis was true to a certain extent, but, unexpectedly, the most prominent artist might provide a work at a price. For example, in 1833, F. R. Lee, the artist, wrote a Committee member, Fraser:

I have seen my friend Collins and communicated your wishes with regards to having a picture for the Manchester Gallery—He very much regrets your not calling on him. Mr. Wilkie having led him to hope that you would have done so—The Price of his 'Skittles Players' is 400 guineas, and as he never exhibits an unsold Picture at any Provincial Exhibition, I am fearful there is no chance of your having it upon those conditions, but I have seen a picture in his room which was painted for Watson Taylor at 300 guineas, just before his failure, which I esteem as one of Mr. Collins' best works and an orna- ment to the British school, and provided you think Manchester would pro- duce a purchaser at £250, he would be happy to send it down—of course, it never passed into the collection of Mr. Watson Taylor although it was ex- hibited at Somerset House as his property—The beautiful picture of 'Re- turning from the Haunts of the Seafowl' now exhibiting is not engaged; the price 300 guineas, but I cannot do better than inform you that he feels much gratified by your admiration of his works, and your desire to have one of them in your Exhibition.[3]

Benjamin Robert Haydon, less secure, was willing to try the Manchester market with an historical work, sending instructions for hanging and reasons for the price.

[1] Royal Manchester Institution, Proceedings of the General Meetings, 27th March 1848, p. 90.
[2] W. Linton, London, 29th March 1827, letter to (?), Royal Manchester In- stitution Letters, 1823–1832, p. 75. Central Reference Library, Manchester.
[3] F. R. Lee, 21st June 1833, letter to Fraser, Royal Manchester Institution Cor- respondence A. 3, No. 101, Central Reference Library, Manchester.

Newton has resolved to send the 'Achilles' and it will go tomorrow or next day—Pray take care of it, and do let it have a centre, because if the Picture is well hung and sells—Shall in future support the Exhibitions. The price is 400 gns., a very inadequate price, for 5 months incessant labour—

People have no idea of the research, time, trouble, thinking, knowledge and labour to paint an historical picture in this Country—an upholsterer is allowed to charge for his time, if a painter were allowed the same privilege, artists would be more respectable men—and keep up their character like the rest of their countrymen—

Pray do your best for the Picture.[1]

Haydon's words strike a sympathetic note, but in Manchester the laws of the market place prevailed, and the artist who made his way successfully placed a relatively low price on his work and was ready to barter. In November 1832, William Etty wrote:

Sir,

I only arrived yesterday from Yorkshire, or I would have answered your obliging communication immediately—I have recently refused 80 guineas for the 'Storm' offered me by a gentleman of Cambridge—it is a large picture, and one of those I have studied 'con amore' and at least I ought to have ninety guineas for it but if the gentleman you speak of likes to have it at eighty-five guineas—he may—and the 'Nymph Fishing' at forty-five—or the ultimate—forty guineas—[2]

In 1836, Charles Hancock wrote: 'I shall be happy to sell my picture to Mr. Stubbs for 40 guineas—As possession is nine points of the law, Mr. Stubbs thinks I suppose he may as well quietly enjoy the possession of my frame.'[3] A less happy artist was J. Tennant, who wrote bitterly:

The Blackburn gentleman must have the picture for this simple reason that cash is so needful to me—that I can't afford to refuse his offer albeit this is a bitter pill to swallow. In consideration of having the picture so low, you must be kind enough to endeavour to get cash, i.e., a note or bill payable on London. I am sorry tho' not surprised at hearing sales are going so indifferently in Manchester—for which by the way I suppose we are indebted to the confounded Railroads—I shall entirely leave you to act with the remainder of my pictures according to your discretion, as I have priced them rather high to meet the bartering system.[4]

---

[1] B. R. Haydon, London, 9th August 1836, letter to A. T. Myall, Royal Manchester Institution Correspondence A. 4, No. 225, Central Reference Library, Manchester.

[2] William Etty, London, 5th November 1832, letter to T. W. Winstanley, Royal Manchester Institution Correspondence A. 3, No. 214, Central Reference Library, Manchester.

[3] Charles Hancock, London, 30th August 1836, letter to A. T. Myall, Royal Manchester Institution Correspondence A. 4, No. 319, Central Reference Library, Manchester.

[4] J. Tennant, Bexley Heath, Kent, 3rd September 1836, letter to A. T. Myall, Royal Manchester Institution Correspondence A. 4, No. 325, Central Reference Library, Manchester.

All during this period, sales figures were tied to the economic conditions. In the catalogue of 1829 the committee remarked: 'That nothing except the combined depression under which the trading part of the community labours, can withhold from the artist of talent a degree of patronage commensurate with their deserts; and they venture to hope, severe and general as the pressure is, that means may still be found to prove that Manchester is neither unable or unwilling to afford the recompense due to the exertions of superior endowments.'[1] Of another dark year, 1837, Myall wrote:

The sales last year were few at most places except where great exertions were made to get up a Lottery as at Liverpool. The sales in London were not half compared with the year before and this year I fear they will be few. The British Gallery on the first day sold only one four guinea Picture and only about five since. I was rather more fortunate on our first having sold thirteen from £5 to £65 each. We have a fair exhibition this year—yet I fear it will be dull in sales as I have only sold between 30 and 40.[2]

Which artists of Manchester benefitted from the Exhibitions? Such portraitists as Bradley, Illidge, and Benjamin Faulkner used the exhibitions to display examples of their talents for depicting the successful businessman in sober garb and his wife adorned with symbols of wealth. Charles Calvert sought purchasers for his quiet landscapes, while Henry Liverseege presented scenes from Scott and Shakespeare. The patronage of Liverseege became the great endeavour of Manchester men. Cunningham wrote: 'The fine arts flourish most where wealth and knowledge abound; they are less needed in places where men have to produce subsistence before they sacrifice to elegance. That Manchester lately a village but now a town with two members of parliament, encouraged as well as produced Liverseege, must be taken as proof of increasing wealth and growing taste.'[3]

Of Liverseege's early studies, little is known. He first appears on the art scene as a painter of portraits, 'chiefly remarkable only for the sort of staring Saracen head style of likeness in which common spirits deal'.[4] These portraits brought a modest income and a limited reputation, while also allowing him to study problems of form and expression vital to the success of dramatic scenes. For him, however, it was difficult to break away from sustaining portrait work. In 1827, he painted three small pictures representing banditti and sent them to the Manchester exhibition. They were disposed of with difficulty and at a small price. He was not, however, dis-

---

[1] Royal Manchester Institution, *Catalogue of the Exhibition of the Pictures by Modern Artists, in the Gallery of the Institution* (Manchester, 1829), preface, p. 6.
[2] A. T. Myall, London, 9th April, 1838, letter to G. T. Maulley, Royal Manchester Institution Correspondence A. 4,unnumbered, Central Reference Library, Manchester.
[3] Allan Cunningham, *The Lives of the Most Eminent British Painters, Sculptors, and Architects* (London, 1880), III, 126.   [4] *Ibid.*, p. 127.

heartened; he had found out where his strength lay. Regrouping his energies, he completed 'Adam Woodcock' from Scott's *Abbot* which was admired and purchased by Lord Wilton. The patronage of nobility now encouraged manufacturers and bankers. He had no difficulty disposing of his next work, based on the interview between Isabella and the recluse in the *Black Dwarf*. The fame of this work brought many inquiries about the artist. The interested were told that 'he still lived with his generous uncle and aunt; was well-to-do in the world; that London booksellers were atracted by his reputation; and that he no longer painted signs for alehouses or portraits at five guineas a piece'.[1] From 1826 to the close of 1832, Liverseege painted those works that brought him his reputation and many were exhibited at the Institution. In August 1831 he showed three works: 'Don Quixote', the 'Fisherman', and 'Cobbett's Register'. Although he had intended to send the 'Don Quixote' to Liverpool to compete for the 50 guineas prize, he was prevailed upon to exhibit it in Manchester. About this time, he received 130 guineas for 'The Recruit', and his sketches brought large prices—Manchester did not fail to support her son.

From the first, the members of the exhibitions committee wished to inaugurate a regular purchasing plan to further stimulate artists. An entry in the minute book in 1827 discloses this.

The Committee conceiving that it will be an encouragement to artists to send their best works to future Exhibitions if one painting be bought by the Institution at each Exhibition, and as the proceeds of the Exhibition have much more than paid the expenses thereof they have—subject to the approval of the next general meeting—purchased with part of the surplus receipts of the Exhibition one of Mr. Northcote's pictures—'Othello, or the Moor of Venice' for 30 gns. That being in their opinion the best executed painting of those calculated for the institution, and they recommend it for the consideration of the next general meeting whether it would not be advisable for the benefit of the Institution at future Exhibitions that permission should be given to the Committee to purchase at each Exhibition one painting for the use of the Institution.[2]

The governors agreed that this was a wise plan.

In the following year, the committee made 'a few purchases out of the surplus proceeds of the Exhibition Fund'. When the Council voted to purchase William Etty's 'The Florentine' in 1832, criteria were listed. 'This purchase was made on account of the intrinsic value of the Picture which will always be an ornament to the Institution and afford an admirable study for the students . . . [and] encourage first rate artists to send down their best pictures for Exhibition. . . .'[3]

[1] *Ibid.*, p. 128.
[2] Royal Manchester Institution, Council Minute Book, 1823–35, 2nd August 1827, p. 235. Central Reference Library, Manchester.
[3] *Ibid.*, 29th March 1833, p. 448.

In the next decade, the members of the Institution revealed their pride in the achievements of the English school by organising a permanent gallery for their collection, with the hope that it would be the nucleus of a community collection. It was reported in 1845: 'During the past year, the Paintings belonging to this institution have been cleaned and repaired and have been placed, temporarily, in the Exhibition Room. The Council, however, are desirous to form a permanent Gallery, in which to place the works of art, and hope that the present collection will form a nucleus to which the inhabitants of the Town and Neighbourhood will not be disinclined to add their contributions.'[1] The gallery was opened in 1848, and at the same time a short catalogue was prepared by R. Winstanley. To put the finishing touch to the undertaking, the council purchased Ansdell's 'The Chase', 'a work of such high merit, and which is so creditable to the talents of this promising Artist'.[2]

For over half a century the governors of the Royal Manchester Institution arranged exhibitions and lectures to meet the intellectual needs of a considerable body of private subscribers. The classical building in Mosley Street became the City Art Gallery in 1882, when the Corporation accepted the offer of the governors to present the building and its contents to the city.[3]

The Royal Manchester Institution offered a setting and marketplace for the works of local artists, but no academy constructed on traditional lines had as yet emerged in Manchester. Only in 1845 did the artists of the region band together. Their objectives were stated in the 'Artists' Prospectus': 'First—to institute a class for the study of the antique and the living model—the want of which has long been felt by the students and artists of this town as an insuperable bar to professional advancement. Secondly—to collect a library for reference, comprising history, poetry, archeology, optics, anatomy, chemistry, as applied to colour, architecture, sculpture, painting, and engraving.'[4] The *Art Union* considered this step long overdue. 'It cannot be disputed that there is unquestionable incongruity and absurdity in an Exhibition existing without a school. Its tendency must be to produce imitation of imitation—to cause deterioration, not progress or improvement.'[5] The artists were forming a line that would connect the studio with the public exhibition room and the private gallery. They deserved only praise.

No princely manufacturer or banker came forward to underwrite the endeavour, but the artists were not without resources. Each of the twenty-two members of the Academy agreed to execute a picture,

[1] Royal Manchester Institution, Proceedings of the General Meetings, 10th March 1845, p. 61. Central Reference Library, Manchester.
[2] *Ibid.*, 27th March 1848, p. 90.
[3] S. D. Cleveland, *Guide to the Manchester Art Galleries* (Manchester, 1956), p. 11.
[4] *The Art Union: A Monthly Journal of the Fine Arts, etc.* 1st October 1845, p. 316.
[5] *Ibid.*

contribute it to an exhibition and sale, the proceeds of which would aid the fledgling Academy. The most outstanding members of the Manchester Academy in the forties were C. A. Duval, W. K. Keeling, and James Stephenson.

Duval exhibited regularly, in London and in the local exhibitions at Liverpool and Manchester from 1833 to 1872, portraits and narrative pictures, his chalk studies of children receiving particular praise. One of the earliest of his commissions came from Daniel Lee for a portrait of Daniel O'Connell. Establishing a reputation as an artist of the significant historical event, he painted a picture containing one hundred portraits of the leading Wesleyans in the United Kingdom, when they met in Manchester to celebrate the centenary of Methodism, now in the Salford Art Gallery, and another historical scene depicting the chief members of the Anti-Corn Law League. Among his other works, praised at the exhibitions, were 'The Ruined Gamester', 'Columbus in Chains', 'The Declaration of Samuel', and 'The Morning Walk'.

Nathaniel Hawthorne spent one of his pleasantest evenings in England at Duval's 'very pretty' house at Carlton Grove, while he was visiting the Arts Exhibition at Manchester in 1857. To the American author, Duval looked like an artist, 'and like a remarkable man, with his careless dress and broad, bold brow'.[1] The dinner was admired, 'because it was so comfortable, unpretending, and satisfactory for all the purposes of a friendly dinner . . .'[2] The predominance of the Irish element, Hawthorne thought, produced this happy state of affairs. There was much talk about the Exhibition and English art and artists. Hawthorne was particularly impressed by the fact that the Duvals were raising twelve children on an artist's income. 'Now DuVal is certainly not a foremost man among English artists; indeed I never remember to have heard his name before; and it speaks well for the profession that he should [be] able to live in such handsome comfort, and nourish so large a brood.'[3]

About 1835, W. K. Keeling returned to Manchester to practise as a painter in oil and water colour and to give lessons in drawings. He made some excellent studies from *Gil Blas*, a few of which were engraved in Heath's *Annual*. Many of his earlier works, especially his illustrations to Sir Walter Scott and other authors, were in the manner of his friend, Henry Liverseege. He was awarded the Heywood medal by the Institution in 1833 for an oil painting, 'The Bird's Nest', while other examples of his work are 'Gurth and Wamba', 'Touchstone, Audrey, and William', and the 'Intercepted Letter'.

---

[1] *The English Notebooks*, ed. Randall Stewart (New York, 1962), p. 563.
[2] *Ibid.*
[3] *Ibid.*

James Stephenson was apprenticed to an engraver on Market Street. While there, he made the acquaintance of Henry Liverseege; probably on his advice, he went to London at the end of his apprenticeship and entered the studio of William Finden. About 1838, he returned to Manchester and established himself as an historical and landscape engraver. Besides furnishing illustrations for *Manchester As It Is*, and for other books, he executed for Agnew & Sons, the dealers, portraits of prominent members of the Anti-Corn Law League, among others, Sir John Bowring, Edward Baines, and Lawrence Heyworth. During this period, he engraved Duval's portrait of Richard Cobden, George Patten's portrait of John Frederick Foster, and John Bostock's portrait of Daniel Grant, the patron of Etty and one of the original 'Cheeryble Brothers', and in 1842, for the British Association, which met that year in Manchester, he executed a portrait of John Dalton.

The Academy in Manchester was reorganised in 1857 and James A. Hammersley, the headmaster of the Manchester School of Design, became president. He made vital contribution to the fine arts as well as the applied arts while he resided in Manchester between 1849 and 1862. A landscape of large size, exhibited at the autumn exhibition of 1850, 'Mountain and Clouds, a scene from the top of Loughrigg Fell, Westmoreland', is a good example of his work in oil. Honoured with royal patronage, he painted for Prince Albert the castle of Rosenau, the prince's birthplace, and a companion landscape.

Hammersley and most other English artists of early Victorian England found the patronage of merchant princes more satisfying than that of royalty. Manufacturers and traders were buying works of art at an increasing rate as the nineteenth century unfolded. What were their preferences? In the age of Reynolds they had admired the canvases of George Morland and Francis Wheatley who painted domestic scenes in the manner of Greuze. In the early nineteenth century, influenced by the essays of Charles Lamb, the novels of Scott, and the sweet ballads of Thomas Moore and other Romantic poets, domestic subjects became sentimental, and such works as Wilkie's 'Blind Fiddler', Collins' 'Pet Lamb', and similar essays by Cooper, Mulready, and Westall unashamedly solicited tearful responses from the men of the North. History was a source of fascination, particularly scenes of British history that introduced authentic portraits of heroes such as Cromwell.[1] The religious or mythological painting stirred emotions. In 1816, the young John Martin had exhibited 'Joshua Commanding the Sun to Stand Still' at the British Institution, a work that ushered in the vogue for the

---

[1] The interest in contemporary battles dates from Penny's and West's painting of the death of General Wolfe. Edgar Wind, 'The Revolution of History Paintings', *Warburg Institute Journal*, II (1938–39).

apocalyptic. Pious businessmen often stood before canvases depicting patriarchal figures of the Old Testament and the Book of Revelations and found religious meaning in them. Hawthorne, in 1857, found Duval at work on one of these moral essays. 'He showed us, also, a picture on the easel,—Samuel's mother delivering him up to Ely [sic]—which seems to promise well; and the subject, I think, is a virgin one, though other parts of Samuel's career have been often painted.'[1] There was a ceaseless demand for oils and water-colours that mirrored the unspoiled landscape of Scotland, Wales, and the Lake District, and more distant places. Ruskin emphasised that the great support of the English school of watercolourists were middle-class families such as those who frequently made purchases at the exhibitions of the Royal Manchester Institution. Ruskin wrote:

It is especially to be remembered, that drawings of this simple character were made [sixty years since] for [the] middle classes, exclusively; and even for the second order of the middle classes, more accurately expressed by the term bourgeoisie. The great people always bought Canaletto, not Prout, and Van Huysum, not Hunt. There was indeed no quality in the bright little water-colours which could look other than pert in ghostly corridors, and petty in halls of state; but they gave an unquestionable tone of liberal-mindedness to a suburban villa, and were the cheerfulest possible decorations for a moderate-sized breakfast-parlour opening on a nicely mown lawn.[2]

Both established artists and novices responded to the opportunities of the provincial exhibitions and benefited financially. Although artists ordinarily sent their works, from time to time, they made personal appearances in the hope of improving their finances. When Etty visited the North and Midlands to evaluate the exhibitions and to negotiate sales and commissions, he was rewarded with the friendship and patronage of the Grant brothers of Manchester and Joseph Gillott of Birmingham. Seeking a commission or two, Ford Madox Brown visited the Liverpool exhibition on his return from the Lake District in 1848.[3] Such a visit helped to lay the foundation for the close relationship between Liverpool and the Pre-Raphaelite Brotherhood.

[1] Hawthorne, p. 563.
[2] Notes by Mr. Ruskin on Samuel Prout and William Hunt, Vol. XIV of The Works of Ruskin, ed. E. T. Cook and Alexander Wedderburn (London, 1904), p. 373.
[3] W. M. Rossetti, Pre-Raphaelite Diaries and Letters (London, 1900), p. 96.

CHAPTER V

ART UNIONS IN LANCASHIRE

I. THE LIVERPOOL EXPERIENCE

The art unions of Lancashire, more than mere lotteries for the distribution of the works of art, developed into organisations concerned with educating the taste of hundreds of subscribers, disseminating information about art and artists, and providing new opportunities for patronage to English artists. The appearance of the art unions in early Victorian England marked a recognition of the changing status of the artist in the rapidly developing industrial society where the older patterns of patronage no longer sufficed and where cultural leaders emphasised the desirability of creating a national culture based on contemporary achievements rather than upon the culture of past ages. Designed to spread support for the arts among a larger segment of the population, the concept of the art union was part of 'the great art movement' of the thirties to open galleries and other institutions to the public, with which Joseph Hume and others were associated. The majority of English artists welcomed such a new enterprise as the art unions, expecially in 1837, a year of serious recession, in 1841 when recession moved into depression, and in 1842, than which there was 'no gloomier year in the whole nineteenth century'.[1]

In 1835, the House of Commons appointed a committee 'To inquire into the best means of extending a knowledge of the Arts and of the Principles of Design among the People (especially the manufacturing population) of the country, and also inquire into the constitution, management and effects of Institutions connected with the Arts.'[2] William Ewart, a leading proponent of such an inquiry, was made chairman, and was assisted by a committee which included Ridley Colbourne, Sir Robert Peel, and other national leaders devoted to the arts, Joseph Brotherton, Benjamin Hawes, Henry Thomas Hope, Joseph Hume, and Thomas Wyse.

The questions examined by the committee were many, but they coalesced under three headings: the establishment on the Continent of government-sponsored schools of design, the opening of art galleries to the public, and the various means of furthering an appreciation of the arts. Dr. Gustave Waagen, Director of the Royal Gallery at Berlin, and Baron von Klenze, Architect to the King of

[1] Briggs, *The Age of Improvement*, p. 295.
[2] Anthony King, 'George Godwin and the Art Union of London 1837–1911', *Victorian Studies*, VIII (December 1964), p. 101.

Bavaria, were important witnesses and in their report, drawn up after two sessions, the committee focused on an item of evidence presented by these two men,

> the institutions established in Germany, under the name of 'Kunst-Vereine', and now becoming prevalent in this country. These associations for the purchase of pictures to be distributed by lot form one of the many instances in the present age of the advantage of combination. The smallness of the contribution required brings together a large mass of subscribers, many of whom without such a system of association would never have become patrons of the arts. Messrs. Waagen and Von Klenze highly estimate the advantages conferred on the arts by such associations, which appear to have been introduced into Prussia by M. von Humboldt.[1]

Dr. Waagen stated in his evidence that the first *Verein*, established in Berlin in 1825, had an annual income of £1,200 ten years later, and that by its democratisation of patronage, several gifted artists found employment, and national works of art were distributed throughout the country. Many other unions were flourishing, not only in Prussia, but also in Bavaria, Saxony, Wurtemberg, and Hanover, 'by which an interest in the arts had been spread in an extraordinary degree in Germany'.[2] From these suggestive remarks was born the Art Union of London, the most successful of the art unions in England in the nineteenth century.

The pioneers of the movement in Britain were already extending patronage in Scotland and in the English provinces. Henry Glassford Bell, the last of the Scottish literary sheriffs and one of the founders of the Royal Scottish Academy, believed that Scottish art was dying in the early thirties because of limited patronage. In the Academy report of 1833, as in all preceding reports, the artists strongly deplored the indifference with which the public regarded their exhibitions. After Bell and his friend, David Octavius Hill, impressed with the success of the German unions, organised in Scotland the Edinburgh art union, in 1834, the artists' outburst of high spirits reminded one of 'the jubilations at a farmers' club dinner at the commencement of a war'.[3] In the same year, the Liverpool Academy organised a union with the hope of extending patronage.

In Edinburgh, Liverpool and later in Manchester, where an art union was sponsored by the Royal Manchester Institution, the organisers of the unions believed that their chief mission was to advance the cause of English art by offering additional encouragement to painter, sculptor, and engraver. They recognised the existence of a potential market for works of art among those who possessed

---

[1] Review of the annual reports of the Art Union of London, the Royal Irish Art Union, and the American Art Union, *The Westminster Review*, XII (June, 1844), p. 515.
[2] *Ibid.*
[3] 'Art Unions', *The North British Review*, XXVI (February 1857), p. 509.

a cultivated taste but did not have the financial resources to buy works of art. All recognised the depressing effect insufficient support had upon artists and the future development of a vigorous school of national art, and they proposed to achieve by a scheme of mutual co-operation what was beyond the grasp of individual resources. Specifically, the executive committee of the Association for the Promotion of the Fine Arts in Scotland purchased works exhibited at the Royal Scottish Academy by means of a fund gathered together through a subscription of one pound from each subscriber; at the close of the exhibition, the purchased works were distributed by lot among the subscribers. Supposedly all would benefit from this simple plan. The exhibition would be enriched by additional works, and the annual selection and drawing would stimulate further interest in art and improve taste. In the late thirties and early forties, artists were thankful that these unions were flourishing in many parts of the kingdom, because artists were battered by recession and depression. During this period of economic depression, individuals did not stop purchasing works of art completely, but the number of individuals who could spare funds for such luxuries was often severely limited.

The phenomenal success of the London Art Union was due in part to certain innovations. Subscribers were allowed to choose for themselves the works of art to the amount of their prize or even add sums out of their own pockets in order to take home higher priced works that appealed to their taste. Liverpool was to adopt this selection process in the late thirties, while Manchester favoured the more autocratic method of selection. The London Art Union also offered annually an engraving to its members. Thus, no one was a loser and a subscriber who had never won a painting could turn to his portfolio of engravings and feel somewhat soothed. The larger provincial art unions soon introduced the annual distribution of engravings.

The impact of the patronage of the art union in Liverpool was considerable in the thirties. *The Art Union*, the first monthly magazine devoted to the fine arts, which took advantage of the art unions' activities and their object of rousing the artistic interests of the people, in 1839, reported that the recent exhibition had been more successful than any previous one. The ordinary sales amounted to £1,843; and the sum raised by 'The Society for the encouragement of Fine Arts', now modelled after the Art Union of London, was no less than £1,480; thus £3,323 was spent in the purchase of pictures.

This intelligence is very cheering, and as the Society is increasing its funds, and the taste for pictures is gradually progressing in the wealthy port of Liverpool, we may hope that the next year's report will be even more satisfactory. The metropolitan artists will, no doubt be stimulated by this news to contribute some of their best works. It should be borne in mind that a vast number of strangers from the adjoining counties visit the Liverpool exhibition, more especially from North Wales; and that, consequently, sources of reputation and profit, of no ordinary kind, are thus opened to our painters.[1]

In the following year, 1840, Samuel Eglington, the Secretary of the Liverpool Academy, emphasised that times were not good in Liverpool, yet the art union helped considerably to assist English art. 'We have raised far more than we could possibly have anticipated by "The Society for the Encouragement of Modern Art" on the admirable plan of the Art Union of London, and by private sales; our receipts at the door have also been greater than hitherto; and what is of still greater importance, we have supplied proof of increasing good taste, and the gradual improvement diffused by the various means which have been resorted to for the purpose. . . .'[2] The private sales amounted to £1,380, a drop of almost £500 from the previous year, while the amount of the art union fund and sums added by prize holders for pictures of a higher value was £1,023, a drop of only about £200 from the previous year.

In the same year, 1840, readers of *The Art Union* were also informed that prior to 1834 and the establishment of the art union, 'comparatively nothing was done for art by the wealthiest port of Great Britain'.[3] This is an exaggeration, of course. The efforts of Gladstone, Winstanley, the Mayor, and the Council, and other lovers of art must not be forgotten. Many of these men now served faithfully on the committee of the art union. Figures supplied by this contributor show that the amount of sales at the exhibitions increased each year, except one, in the thirties, and the yearly sales greatly exceed those of the twenties. In 1834, sales amounted to £1,174; in 1835, £2,500; 1836, £2,700; 1837, £2,500; and 1838, £3,300. No figure was given for 1839, but, as noted, there was an increase over 1838.[4]

From its inception, the merchants, bankers,[5] and artists, who directed the art union in Liverpool considered this foundation a supplement to private patronage, not a substitute. They hoped that the scheme would stimulate further sales of English art. And in Liverpool, in the thirties and forties, there was a healthy balance between private and art union patronage. *The Art Union* emphasised this point in 1841:

It is gratifying to be able to state that the season has been a successful one; there is one feature which is highly satisfactory; it is that the amount of sales by private parties is considerably larger than the former year. This is

---

[1] *The Art Union*, 15th March 1839, p. 33.
[2] *Ibid.*, 15th January 1840, p. 6.
[3] *Ibid.*, 15th September 1840, p. 147.
[4] *Ibid.*
[5] George Holt, J. P. Heywood, Josiah Booker, and William Rathbone were but four of the businessmen on the committee for 1845–46. *Prospectus of the Liverpool Art-Union* (Liverpool, 1845), p. 1.

pleasing as it tends to prove the great and wholesome influence the exhibition of the finest works of art has on the public taste; for whilst societies for the encouragement of art, on the plan of the Art Union, are most praiseworthy in their operations, valuable in their results, and worthy of our most active exertions, it is gratifying to know that individual patronage is on the increase, and taking a lead. . . .[1]

In any one year, the prize sums distributed at Liverpool were not particularly large. In a fairly successful year, 1844, there were one for £60, one for £50, one for £40, two of £30, two of £25, five of £20, six of £15, ten of £10, and four of £5; in all thirty-two prizes. Yet it was not impossible to find at this period paintings by well-known artists going for moderate prices. At the Hick sale in 1843, 'The Cobbler' by Rhodes brought £10 15s., Barker's 'Children playing with an Ass', 18 guineas, Beverly's 'Shipwreck' fetched 15 guineas; Linton's 'Carisbrook Castle', £14 1s.; Poole's 'Bo-Peep', £32 11s.; Bradley's 'Rosebud', £26 15s. 6d., and Herbert's 'Pardon', £27 6s.[2] There were many pictures of modest price by novice and established artists in the provincial exhibitions. For example, Frith sent his first attempt at genre painting, a small composition of two lovers, to Liverpool in 1840, and it was sold for £15: 'It was long before I could reconcile myself to the idea of being paid for a portrait; that anyone could be found who would give me fifteen golden sovereigns for a child of my imagination, astounded and delighted me, and at the same time urged me to further effort.'[3]

The first decade of the patronage of the art union in Liverpool was the most important for art. In 1845, the secretary, James Palmer, announced in a paid advertisement that, since the establishment of the art union in 1834, the sum of £8,734 had been subscribed, to which the additional sum of £2,415 was added by the prize holders, making a total of £11,149 beyond the amount of regular sales during the exhibitions.[4] Less, however, was going to the artists in the forties, once the issuance of engravings became customary. For example, in 1844, the art union subscription amounted to £881, but only £570 was distributed in prizes, because of the cost of the engraving and advertising, so important for the London and the provincial art unions, and other costs took the rest.

Bad times in 1847 and 1848 brought a sharp slump in membership. Although the 630 subscribers of 1849 represented a doubling of the membership over the two previous years, only £315 was distributed in prizes, the remainder going for the engraving and expenses.[5] There seemed to be no end now to the inducements! In 1851, each subscriber at Liverpool received, first, three engravings,

[1] *The Art Union*, 15th January 1841, p. 13.
[2] *Ibid.*, 1st April 1843, p. 90.
[3] W. P. Frith, *My Autobiography and Reminiscences* (London, 1887), I, 57.
[4] *The Art Union*, 1st January 1845, p. 28.
[5] *Ibid.*, 1st February 1850, p. 63.

two of which, 'Katherine' and 'Bianca' were from pictures by Frith; second, free admission to the exhibition of the Liverpool Academy; and third, most dazzling of all, a chance of obtaining one of the grand prizes, consisting not only of paintings from the exhibition at 'the Academy but also of statuettes of 'The Italian Boy' by Claggett, executed in parian by Copeland, and of artist's proofs of 'Christ and the Woman of Samaria', engraved by Bellini after a picture by Herbert, and 'Origin of the Stocking Loom', engraved by Holl after a painting by Elmore.[1]

Serious lovers of English art in Liverpool, who disliked the merchandising aspects of the art union, in 1852 successfully eliminated the distribution of engravings. In 1853 the executive committee proudly announced that during the past year a larger sum was spent on the purchase of paintings than had been spent for several years, because the sole object of the art union now was 'the distribution of good and genuine Pictures. Some of the engravings which were given to the Subscribers and Prize-holders in years past, were of the most inferior description, and in one instance an engraving was issued, which had been presented to the subscribers of a Weekly Newspaper.'[2]

In the hard times of the early forties, the art union in Liverpool was a boon to artists, but it did not stand by them in the next period of depression. Though there was 'unparalleled distress'[3] in Liverpool in the winter of 1846–7, private patronage was generous, the artists receiving £2,500 from this source. With the improvement of economic conditions in the fifties, the art union counted for much less in the history of patronage and the individual much more. Throughout these years, leading business and professional men continued to support the endeavour. In 1854 George Holt, Benjamin Heywood Jones, and Josiah Booker continued to serve on the committee of the art union.

II. THE MANCHESTER ART UNION

In October 1840, the *Manchester Guardian* announced a general meeting of the Royal Manchester Association for the Patronage of the Fine Arts for the purpose of appointing a managing committee and other officers.[4] Highly successful merchants, bank directors, founders of manufacturing establishments, and professional men, the same element that controlled the parent foundation, the Royal Manchester Institution, became the strength of this managing committee, which was assisted by a network of agents who sold subscriptions to this art union in various towns and distributed prizes

[1] *Ibid.*, 1st August 1851, p. 231.
[2] *Prospectus of the Liverpool Art-Union Season, 1853 and 1854* (Liverpool, 1853), p. 2.
[3] *The Art Union*, 1st March 1847, p. 100.
[4] *Manchester Guardian*, 14th October 1840, p. 1.

and engravings. Between six and seven hundred shares were quickly taken and more than twenty pictures and ten proof engravings were purchased by the Committee for distribution among the shareholders in its first weeks of operation.[1]

This association, like others, described itself as something more than an agent for a lottery: 'The objects of the Association are to encourage artists to send choice and valuable pictures to the exhibition; to disseminate a love and taste for the arts in every department, to enable all classes to become acquainted with, and likewise possessed of, works of art, which will greatly assist in forming a chaster and more correct taste in all ranks of life, but especially among the artisans and others employed in our various manufactures.'[2] It is somewhat difficult to ascertain how the last hope was to be realised because of the subscription fee. The annual membership was one guinea, a sum that most workers could little afford for art. After the payment of expenses, the remainder of the money was to be divided into various sums, none lower than £5, and drawn for by the members, a middle-class group of business and professional men.

Manchester, one of the most dynamic centres of patronage in the late twenties and early thirties, had fallen behind other provincial cities and needed the stimulus of an art union. *The Art Union* was very critical of the exhibition of 1839. Not a single picture of the first class and very few of the second were hung. The saving grace was the loans from Manchester collections and those of the neighbouring gentry. Supposedly only one small picture was disposed of during the first fortnight, but this may have been due to the fact that 'the worthy cotton-spinners were deep in the game of a contested election'.[3] It would seem that less expensive pictures moved off the walls and leading artists were making no great effort to show their works in Cottonopolis. *The Art Union* saw the possibility of more extensive sales with an art union on the landscape, but the journal criticised the committee for issuing an engraving. Too often the print was poor, too much was spent on the endeavour and too little on the purchase of paintings. The Manchester men, however, were dazzled by London's success with engravings. 'A very important branch of art will be encouraged, and the subscribers will receive, almost, if not entirely, the value of their subscriptions.'[4]

How successful was the art union of Manchester? The first art union distribution placed £823 in the hands of the artists, while private purchases and art union purchases totalled £2,256, an increase of £714 over the previous year. Among the artists who benefited from the drawing were Creswick ('Market Day', £63), Cotman ('A Sea View', £26 5s.), Linnell ('The Young Student', £21), and

---

[1] *Manchester Guardian*, 31st October 1840, p. 1.
[2] *The Art Union*, 15th August 1840, p. 125.
[3] *Ibid.*, 15th September 1839, p. 137.   [4] *Ibid.*, 15th August 1840, p. 126.

Watts ('Heath Scene', £10 10s., and 'Fishing Boats off Broadstairs', £7 7s.).[1] *The Art Union* did admit the committee's choice of an engraving of Constable's 'Vale of Dedham in Essex' was an excellent one. No one could deny that the art union represented salvation the following year, 1841, that year of depression, when the art union subscriptions amounted to £876, but the total sales at the exhibition were a mere £1,200.

Had the art union enriched the quality of the Manchester exhibits? 'No,' thundered *The Art Union* in 1843. Too many of the pictures in Manchester were 'the remainders' of the exhibits of the Society of British Artists in London. The artists showing there were 'lucky in persuading prize-holders that the surest and safest way to encourage British art is to remove pictures from their walls. This may be very just and fair, but it is neither just nor fair to transplant the refuse to Manchester. . . .'[2] In 1842, at the Manchester exhibition, pictures were purchased from twenty-five artists, twelve of whom were members of the Suffolk Street group. The organisers of the exhibitions in Manchester were not seeking the works of leading English artists in order to assist in the development of a higher taste among townspeople and artists of the Manchester region. They had grown careless, letting the annual exhibition become a mart for showy and inexpensive works. Too many paintings with very low price tags were chosen in order to make the subscribers of the art union happy. Of the twenty pictures purchased by the committee, no fewer than fifteen were at or under the value of fifteen guineas each: 'such arrangements do deteriorate art. Who can deny it?'[3] No doubt there was too much trafficking in pictures at four and five guineas by an organisation that should have been seeking works of a higher calibre.

The Art Union not only criticised this backsliding, but they were most caustic when it came time to review the engraving issued by the art union in the same year. With great earnestness, the committee told how they had made their selection. In May, they had advertised for specimens, and by the end of September several prints were receiving their consideration. They had chosen one by Posselwhite, entitled the 'Hop Garland', from a painting by Witherington. They had attempted 'to choose a Print which should be acceptable to the subscribers as a work of Art, and, on the other hand, not to make the choice so expensive as improperly to curtail the amount expended on pictures.'[4] Yet, said *The Art Union*, contemptuously, more than half of some £700 was spent on this engraving done by one Posselwhite, who was unknown in London art circles.

The council of the Royal Manchester Institution reacted strongly

---

[1] *Ibid.*, 1st June 1841, p. 105.   [2] *Ibid.*, 1st January 1843, p. 17.   [3] *Ibid.*
[4] *Annual Report of the Committee of the Manchester Association for the Promotion of the Fine Arts* (Manchester, 1843), p. 3.

to the criticisms of the exhibitions. *The Art Union* was able to report in 1844 that the exhibition was of finer character than many previous ones. In 1845, several members of the Royal Academy contributed works, and Samuel Jones Loyd, Joseph Fielden, and Joseph Gillott, lent works from their collections, which added further interest to the exhibition and offered local artists the opportunity of studying highly praised works. The council had thrown off its lethargic air: 'They gave timely and repeated notices of the opening and their call was responded to not only by the resident artists, but by those of the metropolis. The result is that, although, of course many unworthy pictures are "placed". the majority are good works, and among them are many of the highest merit.'[1]

The managing committee of the art union showed less willingness to undertake reforms. The criticism concerning the high cost for the production and distribution of prints was ignored, except in the bad years, when there was no print. In a good year, 1844, the total amount received in shares was £988, and the engraving of Stone's 'The Heart's Misgivings', advertising and other expenses absorbed £443. The pool for prizes of £545 was divided into thirty-six sums. There were the respectable: one of £100, one of £50, and two of £30, and the less respectable: ten of £10 and twelve of £5 each.[2]

Although the business and professional men who controlled the affairs of this art union were often men of great wealth, they recognised that the basis of their power lay in their capacity to gauge the extent and limits of the taste and aesthetic experiences of the subscribers, many of whom were from the lower middle class and for the first time were introduced to the possibility of possessing a 'real hand-painted picture' taken from the walls of the exhibition. Before the heyday of the art unions, they would never have dreamt of asking the price of such pictures. The members of the managing committee were acting in a dual capacity, conforming to public taste to a certain degree, while at the same time attempting to attain goals which they felt were worthwhile. The purchases that the managing committee made from the large numbers of pictures that passed before them each year and the subjects they selected for engravings involved the exercise of judgment and taste.

The art union at Manchester, which had been of great importance to the artists in 1841, was of little help in the late forties. In 1848, there were only 300 subscribers, but all of the subscription was spent on the purchase of paintings. With the coming of better times, the art union in Manchester resumed the practice of distributing something to everyone.

[1] *Annual Report of the Committee of the Manchester Association for the Promotion of the Fine Arts*, 1st August 1845, p. 265.
[2] *Ibid.*, 1st November 1844, p. 330.

III. STRENGTHS AND WEAKNESSES OF ART PATRONAGE

The financial success of the art unions did not go unnoticed by other interested bodies, particularly the print sellers and art dealers of Liverpool and Manchester. No sooner was 'the art union in operation in Manchester, than Mr. Grundy, at the Repository of Arts, announced in the *Guardian*, that he had a splendid collection of watercolours that he would dispose of on the principle of the art union. There were 120 prizes and 1,200 shares were issued at one guinea each. Every subscriber would be a winner because he would receive the full value of his subscription in prints, in case he did not obtain a major prize.[1] A group of London print sellers and art dealers tried the same tactic in 1842, when they organized the 'National Art Union', which was supposedly supported by many established artists. In reality the artists were cool to the project and the genuine art unions denounced the scheme as a shabby one, calculated to move dead stock from the print seller's shelves. The print sellers were bested in this round, but they were not beaten. In February 1843 a letter appeared in the *Morning Herald* warning that 'the public may not be aware that every subscriber to . . . Art Unions is liable by Act of Parliament to a penalty of £20 which can be enforced by any common informer.'[2] The Acts referred to were the various Lottery Acts of George III; and it must be admitted that more than one subscriber in London and the provinces was looking for something for nothing and felt no deep obligation to the needs of English art and artists.

The opponents did not stop here. A deputation of the print sellers themselves, condemning the London Art Union and 'certain schemes assuming similar objects',[3] for the mass distribution of prints each year that undercut their enterprises, were successful in procuring a legal opinion from Mr. Serjeant Talfourd pronouncing all such societies illegal.

The art community was filled with gloom, fearing that this vigorous source of patronage was to disappear. Friends, however, rallied from many quarters. Leading periodical protested against the ban. For example, *The Westminster Review* emphasised that there was more good than evil in the system:

In the provinces, in Scotland (even earlier than in London), and in Ireland, the same principle of association has been acted upon with similar success; and at this moment there is in the hands of the committees throughout the United Kingdom a comparatively enormous sum of money, intended to and spreading widely the love of the arts of design, and to give encouragement to

---

1 *The Manchester Guardian*, 2nd September 1840, p. 1.
2 Quoted by King, p. 113.
3 *Ibid.*, p. 114.

artists, objects so important as fairly to overrule the otherwise valid objections to any approach, however distant, to a lottery system.[1]

The Review emphasised strongly how depressed provincial art circles would be without the patronage of the art unions.

In the provinces, great excitement has been caused among the artists as it is admitted on all hands that the provincial schools of art, as at Birmingham, Liverpool, and elsewhere, cannot be supported without the aid of funds raised by the local art unions. Previously to the establishment of the Irish art union the fine arts were entirely neglected in Ireland. In the first twelve months of its existence, £1,200 were subscribed for their advancement, and a larger sum each year afterwards, by means of which the arts have been revived in a degree that could not have been anticipated.[2]

Fraser's Magazine was somewhat more dramatic: 'The Art Union is a hospital where the poor patient has been fostered, healed, and sent on her way rejoicing, with bread to eat.'[3]

Members of parliament were helpful. Lord Monteagle (Thomas Spring-Rice), until 1839 Chancellor of the Exchequer in Melbourne's government, introduced the problem to the members of the House of Lords, and by July a temporary bill emerged legalising art unions and permitting the distribution of paintings and engravings for that year. At the same hour, Thomas Wyse, M.P., worked vigorously to establish a Select Committee on Art Unions. Appointed in May 1844, and re-appointed in February of the following year, the committee was headed by Wyse himself, who was assisted by Viscount Palmerston, the Solicitor General, Viscount Adare, Messrs. Ewart, Ridley Colbourne, Baring Wall, and others. The evidence taken in 1844 and 1845 is important for an evaluation of the aims and accomplishments of the London and provincial art unions as patrons of English art.

From the first, the committee showed that it was the friend of such co-operative undertakings. The task of the group was 'to consider the objects, results, and present position of the Art Unions, how far they were affected by existing laws and what were the most expedient means to place them on a safe and permanent basis to render them subservient to the Improvement and Diffusion of Art through different classes of the community.'[4] The secretaries of the London, Glasgow, Birmingham, and Dublin societies were questioned. Despite the unfriendly criticisms of Etty and one of the print sellers, the final report was most positive in its endorsement of the societies as vigorous promoters of the arts of Britain.

Much good had come to young and established artists, for the influence of the unions had been 'direct, immediate, and extensive,

---

[1] *The Westminster Review*, p. 517.
[2] *Ibid.*, p. 519.
[3] *Fraser's Magazine for Town and Country*, XXX (October 1844), p. 472.
[4] *Sel. Cttee. Art Unions*, title page, quoted by King, p. 116.

and in a pecuniary point of view, beneficial',[1] the outstanding example being Ireland. From 1835 to 1839, purchases from the Royal Hibernian Academy had amounted to a paltry £1. 1s. After the Dublin Art Union was established, the amount spent had been well over £6,700. It was stated also that the Royal Scottish Academy would have to shut its doors if the Edinburgh Art Union were disbanded. No such dramatic figures or statements were presented concerning the influence of the unions on Liverpool and Manchester art circles, but, as we have seen, the patronage of the unions was a very powerful influence in the early forties.

The positive or negative effect on the engraver and publisher was explored. While some of the witnesses were sharp in their condemnation, it was not necessarily the unions that deserved their bitter reproaches, but the invention, electroplating, which had flooded the markets with inexpensive prints. One of the most famous and influential publishers, Colnaghi, testified that the unions were not a depressant because they had brought an increased interest in print collecting and much added business to glaziers and framers.

The major question, and the one that divided educated circles most, was that of the influence of the art unions on the quality of English art. There were five charges: 'The art unions produced in art an injurious stimulus, they tended towards the production of inferior painting and encouraged inferior artists, they diminished ordinary patronage with a consequent loss of "High Art", they neglected other branches of art, and connected art with gambling and jobbing, and none of these disadvantages was balanced by compensating advantages.'[2] Just what was an injurious stimulus? Etty equated it with over-production of inconsequential works, while Lady Eastlake, who was *not* called upon to testify, was very explicit:

These Art Unions have been most pernicious things—in other words a cabal for encouraging trumpery painters. There might as well be a club for encouraging bad singers. The world has been too long accustomed to spend its money on those who could give best work for it, whether in book making, picture making, or shoe making, that we may depend upon it there is some good reason for this arrangement. It sounds all very good and charitable to talk of giving encouragement to modest merit, but where is the real charity of misleading people as to the amount of talent they possess, or the pursuit of that which they can't attain?[3]

Somewhat later, the brothers Redgrave were equally caustic. For them, the art unions encouraged the production of showy pictures of a low class to be sold at a low price, pictures that were

---

[1] *Ibid.*
[2] *Ibid.*, p. 117.
[3] Lady Elizabeth Eastlake, *Journals and Correspondence* (London, 1895), I, 50, entry for 13th February 1843.

painted with no desire of improving the mind of the beholder, pictures which were manufactured by formula:

> To show the quantities in which such works are produced, we were assured by one who counted them, that a single family of landscape painters, who exhibit under various names, had in the several metropolitan exhibitions of a single season, more than 140 pictures, all painted up to an average showy standard, yet good enough to prove that, if guided by better aims, the painters had sufficient talent to produce works of true art, rather than remain mere manufacturers of pictures. This effect of art unions is attributable to their very nature. The best interests of such societies consist in pleasing the largest number of their members, in distributing many small prizes rather than one or two good pictures; in fact, fostering mediocrity rather than excellence . . .[1]

The Redgraves had their day when the art unions were again examined in the sixties.

In the forties the weight was on the side of the unions. Sir Charles Eastlake, 'than whom there can be no more competent judge',[2] according to the committee, gave them his endorsement. Established artists and the less known had benefited. As to encouraging a lower style of art, 'it is to be imagined that but few painters in this mercantile country paint for any other object than to sell and in the hope to sell, consult the reigning taste, whatever it be, of the public'.[3] The committee did admit that the governing bodies sought engravings that would be popular with the subscribers, but, otherwise, it would not admit that the unions were the breeding places of inferior works.

A good summary of the debate was presented some years later by Frith. For him the art unions had been:

> The means of assisting many young painters, who without such aid would have been compelled to abandon their profession. Good and evil are mixed together in all human institutions, and the Art Union of London is an example of the truth of the rule. Subscribers to the lottery are allowed to select their picture prizes, and the consequence is that works of indifferent merit are often chosen, and men are encouraged in the pursuit of art who ought not to have studied at all. So much for the mischief of the Art Unions. For the other side, instances could be shown of pictures of undoubted merit having escaped from being returned unsold to their producers, by enlightened selectors of Art Union prizes.[4]

The committee believed that the respectable art unions, such as those of Liverpool and Manchester, had contributed 'to interest, at

---

[1] Richard and Samuel Redgrave, *A Century of Painters of the English School* (London, 1866), II, 626.

[2] King, p. 117. 'He has done so much for art and given so much pleasure to society . . .' Harriet Martineau, *Autobiography* (London, 1877), I, 367. Elizabeth Aslin discusses the influence of Eastlake's *Hints on Household Taste* (1868) on the history of design in *The Aesthetic Movement* (New York, 1969).

[3] *Ibid.*   [4] Frith, I, 90.

home and in the colonies, a great portion of the educated classes in the nature and advancement of the Fine Arts'.[1] The committee, discussing next how the worthwhile art unions could operate within the framework of the existing laws, after deliberation concluded that the unions could be given special licenses to operate.

Your Committee at first felt disposed, from the financial nature of the question, to entrust that duty to the Board of Trade, but seeing that the Board of Trade in consequence of new duties laid upon it can scarcely pay attention to such objects and wishing they could place it under a department specifically charged with the interest of art (such as exists in almost every country in Europe), are constrained to recommend that . . . such powers and duties be confined to a Committee of the Privy Council.[2]

In its conclusion, the committee made a number of recommendations. The members believed that the democratic system of the London and Liverpool art unions, which allowed prize winners to make their selections, weakened rather than strengthened art. It was preferable for the committees of the art unions to select the prizes. This was the practice in Manchester and most of the other provincial cities. What criteria should the governing committees use in their selection of paintings and engravings? The aims of art, according to the committee, were twofold: 'The development of the highest moral and intellectual elements, and their development with national modifications. . . . We would not even exclude the more homely scenes of common life, sensible that, provided they be combined with moral influences, they must always be useful, as they are oftentimes the only intelligible mode in which Art can speak to a large portion of the community.'[3] These ideas were not strange to the members of the governing committees in Manchester and Liverpool.

The report closed by recommending that the governors of the art unions in Liverpool, Manchester, and other cities should submit their regulations to the Privy Council, and when these were approved a charter of incorporation would be presented. The friend of the art unions, Wyse, soon put a bill, embodying these proposals, before the House and it received the Royal Assent in August 1846. The art unions of Liverpool and Manchester were declared legal as they worked for the advancement of the fine arts.

Although the cultivated denounced the art unions from their inception for encouraging the production of, and taste for, small showy pictures at low prices, they were in the thirties and forties 'a real boon to the artists themselves during the period when sales were few'.[4] They also extended the patronage of art by introducing

[1] King, p. 118.
[2] Ibid.
[3] Ibid.
[4] Oppé, p. 119.

many members of the middle class to the possibility of possessing original works of art, which had always seemed beyond their reach. The maintenance of the prizes at the same low levels in the fifties when the more extensive private patronage developed made the art unions of Liverpool, Manchester, and other cities much less important than in the previous decades.

CHAPTER VI

OTHER MANIFESTATIONS

I. LITERARY AND PHILOSOPHICAL SOCIETIES

The foundation of the great provincial literary and philosophical societies is clearly associated with the interest in applied science stimulated by the Industrial Revolution. Certain members of the business and professional classes, who founded and supported these institutions, were also interested in 'literary' problems, and lectures and discussions on the fine and applied arts found a secondary place in programmes. These societies, which were the intellectual centres of the towns in which they were established, were, therefore, important in moulding taste.

The Manchester Literary and Philosophical Society, founded in 1781, became the model for many societies of this type. It had its origin in private, informal gatherings at the house of Dr. Thomas Percival, who had been one of the first students enrolled in War- rington Academy. After studying at Edinburgh and Leyden, he arrived in Manchester in 1767 and quickly won a reputation with his writings on social and economic subjects. In his *Autobiographical Sketches*, Thomas de Quincey described him as 'a literary man of elegant tastes and philosophic habits, who had been a favoured cor- respondent of the most eminent Frenchmen who cultivated litera- ture jointly with philosophy. Voltaire, Diderot, Maupertuis, Condorcet, D'Alembert had all treated him with distinction.'[1]

The Society developed into a public institution, with regularly appointed officers and fixed agenda and many of the papers read before it were published in its official *Memoirs*. Also prominent among the founders was Dr. Thomas Barnes, minister of Cross Street Presbyterian (afterwards Unitarian) Chapel, and it was here that the majority of the early meetings took place. The rules provided that the subjects of conversation should include natural philosophy, chemistry, literature, civil law, general politics, commerce, and the arts, but religion, 'the practical branches of physic', and British politics were excluded. The intellectual centres for many of the founders were Paris, Edinburgh, or Glasgow, and they were quite proud of their independence from London. This attitude emerges in the preface to the first volume of the *Memoirs*.

The *Memoirs* of the Society give no indication of how the first and subsequent meetings were conducted, but it appears from the

---

[1] *The Collected Writings of Thomas De Quincey*, ed. David Mason (Edinburgh, 1889), I, 130.

minutes that the members were more willing to listen to papers than to do the research necessary to present them. As encouragement, a gold medal worth 7 guineas was offered to the author (whether a member or not) 'of the best experimental paper on any subject relating to the Arts and Manufactures which should be read before 1785, and a silver medal, of the value of one guinea, to any member under the age of twenty-one, who should do the like in Literature and Philosophy.'[1]

An early contributor was Thomas Henry, doctor, successful manufacturing chemist, and one of the first secretaries of the society, who took a particular interest in problems connected with the applied arts and the textile industry.[2] In an early paper, he emphasised how important it was for textile manufacturers to develop a taste for art:

A taste for the Polite Arts, especially of drawing and design, should appear as a desirable acquisition to the manufacturers of the finer and more elegant wares. If not possessed of this, he is always dependent on others for the patterns of his fabrics. Whereas, were he capable of inventing them for himself, he would possess considerable advantages over his less accomplished neighbors. His imagination would continually supply him with something new; and of what importance novelty is, in these times of fashion and fancy, everyday's experience furnishes continuing proofs. It is this supereminent taste that has distinguished the productions of a Wedgwood and a Bentley above all their competitors in the same line of business. Such taste would doubtless be equally beneficial to the manufacturers of the fine cotton and silk goods of Manchester, and he would be enabled to equal in elegance of pattern, as he excels in strength of fabric, the manufactures of neighbouring and inimical rivals.[3]

At the meetings of the Literary and Philosophical Society and in the lecture hall of the College of Arts and Science (1783–7), Dr. Henry had a fine opportunity to discuss the problems of design as related to textile manufacturing, and his lucid observations found a place in the *Memoirs*.

One of the intentions of the founders of the Manchester College of Arts and Sciences was to encourage the further development of science and particularly its application to industry. Thomas Barnes, in his first proposal for this institution, declared that the sciences most relevant to local industry were chemistry and mechanics. He wished also to see an experimental museum established, displaying all the machines related to the manufacture of textiles and the

---

[1] *Memoirs of the Literary and Philosophical Society of Manchester*, I (Manchester, 1785), xv.
[2] A. E. Musson and E. Robinson, 'Science and Industry in the Late Eighteenth Century', *Ec.H.R.*, 2nd ser., XIII (1960), p. 229.
[3] Thomas Henry, 'On the Advantages of Literature and Philosophy in General, and especially on the Consistency of Literary and Philosophical with Commercial Pursuits', *Memoirs*, I (Manchester, 1785), 9.

materials required for experimental work in dyeing, printing,[1] and other processes. Machines and materials would be constantly in use, and progress in research would be communicated to the community at large. In some ways, Barnes envisioned an experimental centre for the applied arts.

A note in the second volume of the *Memoirs* of the Manchester Literary and Philosophical Society, published in 1785, declares that the evening college had met 'with considerable success'.[2] During the two previous winters, numerous gentlemen had heard lectures on different scientific subjects, the Literary and Philosophical Society providing many of the lecturers. Here are some of the courses from the prospectus: 'Chemistry with Reference to Arts and Manufactures' by Thomas Henry, 'On the Theory and History of the Fine Arts' by George Bew, 'On the Principal Branches of Natural and Experimental Philosophy' and 'On Geography' by Henry Clarke, and 'On the Origin, History, and Progress of Arts, Manufactures and Commerce' and 'On Commercial Law' by Thomas Barnes. The most successful courses were those given by Thomas Henry on chemistry, bleaching, dyeing, and calico printing. Much of this material was incorporated into essays placed in the *Memoirs*. Guided by Henry, the members of the community were discovering much about the techniques of applied art as well as textile manufacture. Some better educated skilled workers, as well as gentlemen, attended these lectures. Though the college itself remained in existence for only a few years, it established a precedent and helped to prepare the way for other institutions in Manchester and other industrial towns. Specifically, the college was the forerunner of Owens College, founded seventy years later, which eventually evolved into Manchester University.

The papers presented at the meetings of the Literary and Philosophical Society on the fine arts and literature during the first decade of its history were not numerous. The first volume of papers published in 1785, includes 'An Attempt to Show that a Taste for the Beauties of Nature and the Fine Arts, has no influence favourable to Morals' by the Rev. Samuel Hall; and 'On the Comparative Merit of the Ancients and the Moderns with Respect to the Imitative

---

[1] 'In the early eighteenth century British textiles were often poorly finished. Superior linens had to be bleached in Holland, becoming "Scotch Hollands", and the Dutch were considered better dyers. West Indian cotton yarn might be sent for red dyeing in Turkey or East Indian yarn bought already dyed.... Export markets could be won or lost by good or bad dyes. Wrote Macpherson, "the superiority of a colour is sufficient to secure an extensive sale to the goods dyed or printed with it". Manchester merchants could only sell coloured cottons in Africa when more attractive Indian cloths were unobtainable. Conversely the British held markets in Spain and Portugal with good quality woollens to whose dyeing special attention was paid.' Susan Fairlie, 'Dyestuffs in the Eighteenth Century', *Ec.H.R.*, 2nd ser., XVII (1965), p. 489.

[2] *Memoirs of the Literary and Philosophical Society of Manchester*, II (Manchester, 1785), 42.

Arts' by Thomas Kershaw. The second volume of contributions, also published in 1785, contains 'Remarks on the Knowledge of the Ancients respecting Glass' by Dr. Falconer of Bath. The third, appearing in 1790, included 'Essay on the Supposed Druidical Remains near Halifax in Yorkshire' by Thomas Barritt, 'Account of an Ancient Monument in Hulme Abbey, Northumberland' by John Ferrier, and 'Observations on the Art of Painting Among the Ancients' by Thomas Cooper.

The contribution on druidical remains and that on Hulme Abbey emphasise the popularity of archaeology in the eighteenth century. This was a key element of the Gothic Revival, whose origins have been traced by Sir Kenneth Clark to the taste for ruins that formed part of the Romantic Movement in literature; to the school of architecture of Batty Langley that introduced carpenters to the mysteries of Gothic; and to the writings of Horace Walpole, and especially to his Gothic villa, Strawberry Hill. Sir Kenneth gives greatest weight to the archaeological element. The 'scholarly interest in archaeology, followed by a sentimental delight in decay, is the true source of the Revival; and it just overlaps with the use of Gothic as a traditional style. Renaissance forms reached England so late, and were acclimatised so slowly, that Gothic was still being employed when it became the subject of antiquarian inquiry.'[1]

In the early nineteenth century when the presence of Dalton dominated the meetings of the Manchester Literary and Philosophical Society, papers on science ousted all others. However, a Literary and Philosophical Society like that of Newcastle continued to encourage the communication of papers on the arts as well as the sciences. The founders had specifically suggested that:

the romantic scenery, especially the banks of the Tyne, and other rivers would furnish a variety of subjects for the pencil and for the lovers of picturesque description, and these might occasionally entertain the society . . . the profusion of antiquities, not only in Newcastle but along the Roman Wall, which though they have furnished abundance of employment for many pens, are not by any means exhausted, will engage the attention of the patient enquirers after these venerable monuments of extinct customs and religion.[2]

When the Literary and Philosophical Society was re-established in Liverpool in 1812, papers on art were read, and these were an element in moulding middle-class taste. The members of the Liverpool society were interested in becoming better informed about the sources of architectural inspiration, specifically the characteristic features of the Greek and Gothic styles. The roots of the Greek revival as well as the Gothic revival go well back into the eighteenth

[1] Sir Kenneth Clark, *The Gothic Revival* (London, 1950), p. 14.
[2] Robert Spence Watson, *The History of the Literary and Philosophical Society of Newcastle-Upon-Tyne* (London, 1897), p. 37.

century. The importance of Robert Wood,[1] Stuart and Revett[2] and the aristocratic Society of Dilettanti[3] in forming a specific critical taste for Grecian architecture was considerable. Beautifully lithographed plates were calculated to give subscribers to such a publication as the *Unedited Antiquities of Attica* 'very definite ideas on the subject of correct Greek design'.[4] In the late eighteenth century there also appeared specimens and examples of Gothic architecture, so sumptuous that only the wealthy could afford them. The entrepreneur who popularised engravings of Gothic by publishing them cheaply and in great numbers was John Britton, when he began the publication in 1805 of his *Architectural Antiquities of Great Britain* in which he combined the picturesque approach with careful scholarship. The illustrations, particularly those of Frederick Mackenzie, are distinguished works and these volumes 'gave the average cultivated man a far truer idea of Gothic forms than he had hitherto had, so that after their publication the old fantastic parodies of Gothic were no longer possible'.[5]

The 'average cultivated man' of Liverpool became more familiar with the 'scientific principles' of Gothic when Thomas Rickman lectured at the Literary and Philosophical Society in Liverpool. An architect and writer, he, like many others, was at work on the actual facts and principles of the Gothic style.[6] Much time and energy went into the problems of terminology; there was an attempt to substitute 'English' for the opprobrious term 'Gothic', and there was also debate on the origins of the pointed arch. Rickman examined both of these problems and presented his findings to the members of the Literary and Philosophical Society.[7]

His first contribution to the Literary and Philosophical Society in 1812 was entitled 'Distinctive Principles of Grecian and Gothic Architecture'. In this and succeeding lectures, Rickman classified Gothic as previous architectural writers had classified the neo-classical, and he also favoured an English origin of the Gothic style. He distinguished the Norman style, and Early, Decorated, and Curvilinear English styles. Within each area, he discussed the typical forms, beginning with doors and then passing on to windows, arches, piers, capitals, buttresses, cornices, niches, towers, parapets, vaults, façades, porches, fonts, and finally the appearance as a whole. The architectural information that Rickman initially transmitted

---

[1] *The Ruins of Palmyra* (1753) and *The Ruins of Balbec* (1757).
[2] *The Antiquities of Athens* (1762).
[3] *Ionian Antiquities* (1769).
[4] D. Pilcher, *The Regency Style* (London, 1947), p. 65.
[5] Clark, p. 106.
[6] Henry-Russell Hitchcock, *Early Victorian Architecture in Britain* (New Haven, 1954), I, 12.
[7] For a full survey of what has been thought and written about Gothic style see Paul Frankl, *The Gothic: Literary Sources and Interpretations through Eight Centuries* (Princeton, 1960).

to the gentlemen of Liverpool, he spread abroad when in 1819 he published *An Attempt to Discriminate the Styles of English Architecture from the Conquest to the Reformation*, and his designations 'Early English', 'Decorated', and 'Perpendicular', quickly passed into common currency. The book proved immensely popular, a seventh edition being printed in 1881.

The men who listened to Rickman, often members of building committees for new hospitals, town halls and, churches, did not repudiate neo-classic forms. John Foster designed for them in 1828 the Liverpool Custom House, a vast structure with domical roof, Ionic porticoes, and antae. Earlier he had built two large churches, one classical on the St. Martin's model, the other Gothic, both situated in middle-class suburbs. As the works of Rickman, John Britton, and Sir Walter Scott circulated, however, men of the North were more and more attracted to Gothic, 'particularly as a style for new churches. Interest in this style was moving from the merely Picturesque to a serious sentiment for Gothic as a national style . . . it remained only for liturgical enthusiasms to be added to the patriotic and the Victorian Gothic Revival had been born.'[1] Rickman taught the men of the North by example as well as by words, for in the churches he designed, he always attempted to introduce correct detail, an effort that won him the respect of many Victorians.[2]

Members and guests of the Liverpool Literary and Philosophical Society presented papers on other aspects of the arts. Henry Hole discussed the origin and progress of engraving, while Dr. Traill traced the origin of painting and sculpture in the ancient world and described the process of lithography. Edmund Aikin analysed the styles of architecture of the Elizabethan age, and John Lightfoot gave a description of the past and present state of Kenilworth Castle. In 1821, Roscoe lectured on the principal manuscripts in the library at Holkham.[3] In 1829, Thomas Winstanley, a frequent speaker on art topics in this period, read a paper on the 'Progress of Painting in England', while in the thirties, Solomon Gibson, the brother of the famous sculptor, read papers on architectural subjects. In 1841, *The Art Union* was very happy to hear that Thomas H. Illidge had read a paper 'On Composition, and Light and Shade in Painting' which he had illustrated with references to numerous engravings and diagrams.[4] Science came first in Liverpool, but the arts were not neglected.

[1] John Summerson, *Architecture in Britain 1530 to 1830* (Baltimore, 1958), p. 299.
[2] The leaders of the Camden Society had reservations. Eliot Rose, 'The Stone Table in the Round Church and the Crisis of the Cambridge Camden Society', *Victorian Studies*, X (Dec. 1966), p. 123.
[3] *List of Communications Laid Before the Literary and Philosophical Society of Liverpool, since its Institution in 1812, to the End of Session Tenth*, 1821 (Liverpool, 1821).
[4] *The Art Union*, 15th March 1841, p. 47.

II. ARCHITECTURAL SOCIETIES

On 3rd December 1835, a group of junior architects and engineers founded the Liverpool Society for Promoting the Study of Architecture and Engineering. Their objectives were 'to promote the diffusion of taste for the Fine Arts and Sciences',[1] and 'to endeavour to raise their Professions to their proper rank in the estimation of society'.[2] The society also proposed the establishment of a library and museum, and the exchange of designs between members. The society had only a brief life, however, and its influence on the development of taste in Lancashire was ephemeral. It is interesting that it included among its aims that of founding a school of architecture, an achievement not realised for another sixty years.

Manchester architects were more successful in organising a society, which made its appearance in 1837. *The Architectural Magazine* blessed it and optimistically predicted that the example would be followed in all of the provincial cities of size in Great Britain. Although the officers and members of the council were practising architects, the rules allowed the introduction of amateurs and they were there in goodly numbers. 'In our opinion, on their introduction into architectural societies much of the architectural improvement of the country will depend, for what corporation of professional men ever yet improved their own profession?'[3] No doubt the editor believed that Manchester was teeming with men of independent taste and judgment.

In order to encourage a greater interest in problems of art and architecture, the Manchester Architectural Society sponsored a series of *conversazioni*. *The Architectural Magazine* lavished praise upon the society for organising these, because of their 'delightful and instructive nature'.[4] At the fifth, works of art were exhibited. Members lent drawings, many of them architectural subjects, by Prout, Stanfield, Cattermole, Crouch, Richard Lane, J. W. Hance, and Duval and paintings by Bradley, Liverseege, and Duval. George Peel contributed three bronzes, while Agnew and Zanetti, the dealers, furnished numerous other works of art. At these *conversazioni*, painters and architects had an opportunity to discuss with civic leaders problems of art and architecture and to review designs of proposed buildings for the community. In 1838 they examined designs submitted in competition for the Catholic Church, confident that 'public examination is the most effectual mode of insuring just decisions in competitions'.[5] Two years later, when the Society

---

[1] *Report of Part of the Resolutions adopted at a Meeting of Junior Architects and Engineers, held December 3, 1835, for the purpose of taking into consideration the propriety of establishing a Society of Young Architects and Engineers* (Liverpool, 1835), p. 1.
[2] *Ibid.*
[3] *The Architectural Magazine*, IV (London, 1837), p. 351.
[4] *Ibid.*, V, 280.   [5] *Ibid.*, p. 281.

examined some twenty-five designs that were submitted for the new Independent College, 'The general opinion was, so far at least as the first premium was concerned, the decision had been judicious.'[1]

The Society continued to be an influential body until it disappeared in 1845. During its brief life, it had given architect, artist, and middle-class patron an opportunity of enjoying each other's works or possessions and, in the end, had helped to deepen the understanding of members for works of art and architecture.

Spurred by a greater understanding of architectural principles and a vigorous civic pride, Lancashire men called upon architects and builders to create imposing edifices in their communities in the early Victorian period. A magnificent example of princely patronage is St. George's Hall in Liverpool. When a committee of gentlemen advertised in 1837 for designs for St. George's Hall, the advertisement was cut out of *The Times* and sent to Harvey Lonsdale Elmes. The young architect went to Haydon, asking whether he should submit a design. 'By all means, they are noble fellows at Liverpool. Send in a design, and mind, let it combine grandeur with simplicity. None of your broken-up and frittered abortions, but something grand.'[2] Elmes set to work with burning enthusiasm and in the end triumphed. The hall, a vast building based on a study of the Thermae of Caracalla,

in matter and form was academic, but the composition was new, the power of expression more profound. The youthful architect had succeeded at one great stroke of plan and mass, not by trifling with details, eking out ornament or regrouping columns and porticoes. There was no other disguise in his methods but great force united to extreme simplicity. Elmes' success was that he got rid of the trammels of indecision and sentimentality. He had the gift of vision and the perception to benefit by the purpose and example of other great architects.[3]

After the death of Elmes in 1847, Charles Robert Cockerell designed an interior with cast iron balconies supported by caryatids, plaster wall decorations, Corinthian columns, and great chandeliers, all of which brought genuine splendour to Liverpool's most impressive building.

In Liverpool, Manchester, and other bustling cities there were appearing imaginatively designed business blocks. In 1843 the *Companion to the British Almanack* featured Brunswick Buildings, an office block in Liverpool, one of the earliest public buildings in England designed specifically for this purpose. Soon leading architects, such as Charles Robert Cockerell, were seeking commissions for this type of building. The analogy with Renaissance Italy was

---

[1] *The Art Union*, 15th March 1840, p. 42.
[2] *The Art Union*, 1st February 1848, p. 52.
[3] A. E. Richardson, 'Architecture', *Early Victorian England 1830–1865*, II, 192.

complete—here were the city merchants and manufacturers, bestowing their munificence upon large and intricately decorated palaces of commerce and fine civic buildings. One might suggest that the analogy was conscious—Brunswick Buildings imitate the *palazzi* of the Medici, the Strozzi, and the Pazzi, with a heavy rusticated base supporting three storeys of classical windows and a monumental cornice.

Between 1840 and 1860 the architecture of Manchester was generally accepted as more advanced and more progressive than that of any other city in the country.

Art in Manchester, [wrote the editor of *The Builder*] has sprung into vigorous existence, and the town is now a striking example of good taste. A new school of architects has sprung up, many of them young men, and it is greatly to the credit of the merchants of the town that they have had the judgment to use the services of architects, in which they are seldom applied to, and it is greatly to the credit of the architects that these appeals have been replied to by them almost universally in the best manner.[1]

What so impressed the editor were, of course, the great warehouses, that, during this period, were giving Manchester a new look.

Here, [wrote Bradshaw in his first *Guide to Manchester*] are structures fit for kings, and which many a monarch might well envy. There are eight or ten sovereign princes in Germany whose entire revenue would not pay the cost of one of these warehouses. The industrial and scientific energy which has reared them is an honour to our country and speaks well for the future of Manchester. The artistic display is all but equal to the noble enterprise which gave them being. They are, indeed, the most splendid adornment of this city and really monumental whether we regard their splendours, their properties or their durability.[2]

What distinguished these Manchester warehouses was the adoption of the *palazzo* style and the imaginative use of iron and terracotta. The *palazzo* style eliminated the application of orders, dear to the neo-classicists, with basement storey below and attic storey above. Now, there were not even pilasters. Only the cornice remained. The internal structure consisted of a cast-iron framework that was largely independent of the walls, making numbers of large windows possible. The first of these commercial palaces was built by Edward Walters in 1839 at 15 Mosley Street, for Richard Cobden. That successful manufacturer of calicoes first met Walters in Constantinople and persuaded him to return to Manchester to set up a practice. Walters planned for Cobden a façade of red brick, trimmed with stone quoins and capped by a cornice below the attic storey, in this adaption of the Renaissance style to Victorian needs. The windows in the second and third storeys were grouped

[1] Quoted in Stewart, *The Stones of Manchester*, p. 36.
[2] *Ibid.*

together under stone segmented arches with carved keystones. The rest of the windows had segmented arches of brick. This building would have been identical to dozens of warehouses that succeeded it, if it had incorporated a monumental entrance and a rather more lavish application of stone trim. Edward Walters developed this theme over and over again, sometimes, if the budget were liberal, in stone, or in stucco. By the 1850s, the warehouses of Manchester were more impressive than the mills: massive, simple, austere, they were later to be praised for their 'real beauty'. They were held to represent 'the essentials of Manchester's trade, the very reason for her existence'.[1]

III. THE MECHANICS' INSTITUTES

The mechanics' institutes may be regarded as a democratic expansion of the literary and philosophical societies and as an extension of the movement for elementary education for the children of the working classes. Behind this dynamic movement were intelligent artisans and enlightened members of the middle class to whom the further education of the people meant national progress and strength, and not revolution.[2] The mechanics' institute movement, which had its origins in early nineteenth-century Scotland, spread to London in 1823, and with the enthusiastic support of Lord Brougham soon took root in the provinces. The mechanics' institute had forerunners here in the various workingmen's libraries, book clubs, and mutual improvement societies. An early example in the North is recorded in 1810 in a manuscript in the Chester City Library, that bears the title 'Mechanic Institution established in Chester MDCCCX', and includes proposals issued by John Broster, a local bookseller and antiquarian, for the creation of a library and reading room for masters, workmen, and apprentices.[3] In Liverpool, Egerton Smith, editor of the *Liverpool Mercury*, was the chief sponsor of a Mechanics' and Apprentices' Library and Reading Room that opened in 1823.

Although in London and in the provinces the influential kept a firm hand on the affairs of the institutes, not necessarily was this foreordained. In London, there was a bitter dispute over the question of whether an appeal should be launched for subscriptions from the well-to-do. Francis Place, who was an important voice in the councils of the institute, answered affirmatively, but more radical voices, such as those of J. C. Robertson and Thomas Hodgskin, wanted the working class in full control of these institutions. After long debate, the Place forces won out, and although the working

---

[1] Briggs, *Victorian Cities*, p. 103.
[2] Lawrence Stone, 'Literacy and Education in England 1640–1900', *Past and Present*, No. 42 (February 1969), p. 137.
[3] Kelly, p. 117.

men had a majority voice in the managing committees of the London and provincial institutes, the well-to-do were most influential in decision-making. A large part of the success of the institutes was due to the help given by business and professional men.

From Edinburgh, Glasgow, and London as centres the movement spread with great rapidity, in London's suburbs, the industrial areas of the North, and in the seaports. Among institutions founded during this early period were those of Manchester (1824), and Liverpool, Warrington, and Bolton (1825). A great boost was given to the movement when Henry Brougham in a pamphlet entitled *Practical Observations Upon the Education of the People*, published in 1825, appealed successfully to manufacturer and trader to come forward and support the movement with their monies and time. In Manchester, Benjamin Heywood, a banker, worked diligently year in and year out to make the institute a success, and many other professional men were helpful. In Liverpool, John Gladstone, B. A. Heywood, members of the Rathbone and Yates families and Dr. Traill were enthusiastic supporters of the institute. The motives of these men were varied. Enlightened employers sought better educated and more industrious workmen; political leaders such as Brougham hoped that the institutes would provide an introduction to problems of self-government; philanthropists such as William Wilberforce saw them providing spiritual comfort for the ill-fed and ill-housed; clergymen believed that the workmen would learn to be responsible members of the community. 'Only a minority of people regarded the institutes . . . primarily as agents of cultural education, as a means of liberating the mind and enriching the understanding.'[1] While many artisans among those who filled the halls of the institutes only desired to improve their economic condition, there were others who were not merely interested in getting ahead in the factory, but were also genuinely interested in intellectual fare.

The enthusiasm of employer and artisan was dampened in 1826. There were two chief reasons. In that year, there was economic depression and throughout their history the institutes showed themselves very sensitive to economic upheavals. A second reason was that the average English working man, without a good basic education and tired at the end of a long day's work, was incapable of absorbing the materials of the lectures in chemistry, mechanics, and the other subjects that were the staples of the programme in these first years. It must also be remembered that a great many people were not interested in science; they were interested in politics and economics, which were excluded from the halls because of their controversial aspects. Some working men merely wished to find a place to relax and a bit of social life. But there was no place for such idleness. There were no newspapers or novels in the reading rooms. Is it

[1] *Ibid.*, p. 123.

any wonder that many of the working men returned to their public houses, clubs, or mutual improvement societies? For many years, the movement progressed at a sluggish pace, but in the early thirties, the movement resumed its forward march. The economic depression of the early forties brought retrenchment, but by 1850 the institutes were more buoyant than ever before.

There were large urban institutes, such as those of Liverpool and Manchester, with imposing buildings and hundreds of members; and at the opposite extreme were tiny village institutes, with a few members who met in hired quarters. There were three main departments in a mechanics' institute, the lecture department, the class department and the library and in the larger institutions, such as those of Liverpool and Manchester, all three functioned on quite a considerable scale. The mechanics' institutes movement also had its impact on middle-class education, for the literary and scientific institutions that appeared in London in the twenties were designed for commercial and professional workers and the athenaeums of the provinces served a similar function. In Manchester and other cities, employers and professional men, however, came to monopolise these institutions, that combined club facilities with a form of adult education more popular in character than that offered by the older literary and philosophical societies.

Though science was the great focus in the programmes of the mechanics' institutes, literature and art also had their place in the programmes. Art was given particular definition because of its importance in industrial design, and there was also a great deal of interest in art for art's sake. After the setback of 1826, art and literature found a more prominent place in lecture programmes, most institutions abandoning the attempt to provide serious courses in the sciences and substituting single lectures and occasional short courses on a variety of topics—science, history, literature, antiquities, and art.

In both Liverpool and Manchester, the directors obtained the talents of well-known and popular lecturers on art and architecture. At Manchester, R. N. Wornum (later appointed keeper of the National Gallery), Charles Calvert, George Wallis (later keeper of the South Kensington Museum), Benjamin Robert Haydon, and R. W. Buss, all painters, lectured on art; and George Godwin, the architect, who worked hard to educate public taste in art as guide of the London Art Union and, in his professional capacity, to improve the housing conditions of the working class, was outstanding.[1]

At times lecture and discussion touched upon problems of applied art. At the Athenaeum in 1845, George Jackson read a paper 'on the means of improving public taste in reference to art, with a view of exciting the authorities to this important object, in the general

---

[1] Mabel Tylecote, *The Mechanics' Institutes of Lancashire and Yorkshire Before 1851* (Manchester, 1957), pp. 150-1.

movement that is making for improvement'.[1] The formal presenta-
tion was followed by a lively discussion led by Richard Cobden and
Louis Schwabe, important manufacturers. They both emphasised
that Britain lagged in patronage of schools of design. Cobden declared: 'It is highly important that we should improve our designs,
to meet the improved taste of our customers in every quarter of the
globe',[2] while Schwabe was confident that in the near future there
would be a demand for better designed textiles. 'It is important that
this country should educate clever artisans, because if we do not,
other countries would do so (Hear! Hear!)'.[3] If England could not
supply superior design, her customers would go elsewhere, he declared.

The libraries and reading rooms of the institutes were important
instruments of education. These libraries were not very large, but
their collections were of great value before public libraries came into
existence. In the Liverpool Mechanics' and Apprentices' Library
were found books on mechanics and design, works that would be
particularly helpful to those who were employed in the carpentry
trade and other handicrafts.[4]

After the initial setback to the mechanics' institute movement,
much of the genuine educational work was transferred from the lecture rooms to the classrooms, where instruction could be given in
smaller groups, and, if necessary, at a more elementary level. In
1839, Manchester, for example, had 1,051 pupils in institute classes.
Over six hundred were learning writing, grammar, or arithmetic,
and the remainder were involved with problems of mathematics,
music, French, and drawing.[5] Some institutes attempted to buttress
their adult education programme by establishing day schools for the
children of members. The outstanding example is Liverpool, where
the boys' and girls' high schools, founded by the institute, still
survive.

Dr. Traill and many other patrons of the institutes were in favour
of courses related to design. At the inaugural meeting in Liverpool,
Dr. Traill declared in his address that there should be courses in
architectural drawing and perspective: 'The very essence of the arts
of the architect, the joiner, the carpenter, and of every worker in
metals, depends on general principles, a knowledge of which is necessary to those who hope to improve the arts which they practice.'[6]
Following his advice, quite early in the history of the institution,

[1] *The Art Union*, 1st January 1845, p. 17.   [2] *Ibid.*   [3] *Ibid.*
[4] *An Account of the Liverpool Mechanics' and Apprentices Library: being a succinct view of
the rise, progress, and objects of the institution; its constitution and laws. . . .* (Liverpool,
1824), p. 8.
[5] Kelly, p. 128.
[6] *Liverpool Mechanics' School of Arts. Address delivered by Thos. Stewart Traill,
M.D. . . . And Resolutions adopted at a General Meeting of the Inhabitants held on the 8th of
June, 1825; with an exposition of the Objects and General Regulations of the Institution*
(Liverpool, 1825), p. vi.

permanent teachers and lecturers in the area of the arts were appointed on a salaried basis. First, there were classes in landscape and perspective drawing; later, there were also classes for figure drawing, ornamental design, and modelling.

In 1843 *The Art Union* reported that to accommodate the pupils of the evening as well as the day classes, a sculpture gallery had been erected in which drawing would be taught, Benjamin Robert Haydon acting as general overseer of construction.[1] It was the proud boast of the Directors that this gallery contained the most numerous public collection of specimens of ancient and contemporary art to be found anywhere in the country except in the galleries of London and Edinburgh. In a period when the cast was considered to be as thought-inspiring as the original marble, there was some justification for this boast.

In 1850, on the recommendation of the Government School of Design, a more rational plan of art education was introduced at the Liverpool Mechanics' Institute. Hitherto, art classes were independent, and a student could join whichever he pleased. Henceforward, there were four classes of drawing and modelling: (1) Elementary, (2) Mechanical, (3) Architectural, and (4) Figure and ornamental, a student completing each of these classes in sequence. In 1853, classes (2) and (3) were united and the department became the School of Design. A year later, under the guidance of the Science and Art Department at South Kensington, the school on the Mersey became the South Liverpool School of Art.

In the first years of the Manchester Mechanics' Institution, the only subjects taught were mathematics and mechanical and architectural drawing. After 1830, there were changes in the educational programming of the Institution, the older insistence on studies relating to the occupations of members was breaking down and wider aims were outlined. Benjamin Heywood, perhaps the most influential patron, had strongly urged that the original plan be modified 'to adapt our instruction more to the taste and capacity of the working classes; to make it more elementary and more entertaining; to extend it to a greater variety of subjects and to connect it with moral improvement.'[2] In response to Heywood's appeal, the Institute introduced more classes of a cultural nature. One of the earliest of these was 'a new school . . . for Landscape, Figure, Flower and general Ornamental Drawing intended both to gratify the subscribers and to increase the interest of the establishment, as well as to serve as an introduction to the Mechanical and Architectural schools'.[3]

A proposal to establish a fully-fledged school of design at the

---

[1] *The Art Union*, 1st January 1843, p. 20.
[2] Quoted in Tylecote, p. 157.
[3] *Ibid.*, pp. 158–9.

Institute was discussed in 1828, came to nothing at the time, but Heywood reintroduced the subject in 1832. A member of the committee of the House of Commons examining the silk trade, he had learned much about the courses in design at the school of applied arts in Lyons: 'I think it of great importance that a similar school should be established in Manchester, where the silk manufacture is advancing so rapidly, and where calico printing is so large a part of the trade. There is one of the classes, namely, that of teaching the application of machinery to the transfer of patterns, which I should like to see at once established in this institution.'[1] After much discussion and debate in Manchester, a School of Design, independent of the Institution, was established. Reference to this institution was always polite, and Heywood believed that such a rival institution would apply the screw to the Institution's drawing classes, and put instructor and student on their mettle. Most likely, it was this incentive that brought changes in the drawing classes in 1841. The mechanical and architectural classes, instead of meeting separately once a week, were combined, and met together three times a week. And the directors, hoping to make the figure, flower, and landscape drawing class more immediately useful to artisans, arranged that this class should be used to introduce the application of general drawing to pattern designing.

The patrons of the institutes were interested in introducing the working classes to works of fine art that would teach moral lessons. When, in 1837, Heywood suggested that 'a collection, embracing objects of natural history, works of art, and mechanical contrivance'[2] be established at the Institute, the suggestion was taken up and a series of exhibitions was sponsored that were very successful. After the first of these, one of the vice-presidents of the Institution, John Davies, noted that he had suggested to Cobden that a gallery of art should be associated with or incorporated in the Manchester Athenaeum, when the designs for the building were being considered, but his idea had excited little interest. The success of the first exhibition at the Institute gave him great confidence. 'As to the utility of such institutions, everyone knew that the human mind at first received the principal part of its information from external objects; and there was no possibility of information of that kind being communicated more easily, nor permanently and every respect better, than through the medium of such institutions.'[3]

The first of these exhibitions was held from December to February 1837–8, and the last from December to March 1844–5. After

[1] *Addresses delivered at the Manchester Mechanics' Institution by Sir Benjamin Heywood, Bart. F.R.S. the late President—collected and published by the Directors* (London, 1843), p. 51. [2] *Ibid.*, p. 92.
[3] *Report of the Directors of the Manchester Mechanics' Institution; and Proceedings at the Annual Meeting of the Members, held in the Theatre of the Institution, on the 28th of February 1838* (Manchester, 1838), pp. 54–5.

each, the directors congratulated themselves, firmly believing that they had brought amusement and information to thousands of working men and thus had diffused 'a taste for the correct and the beautiful in the productions of art and manufactures which cannot but form important agents for increasing the improvement and happiness of the mass of society'.[1] At each of the exhibits there were displays of machines, architectural and engineering models, and scientific apparatus; a large section was devoted to natural history. The fine arts section was always one of size and importance, consisting of drawings, engravings, paintings, and examples of sculpture. There were many of those not so old Old Masters and interesting works of the English school, lent by some of the leading collectors of the area. *The Exhibition Gazettes* presented interesting commentaries on the collectors and their loans. Here is a typical survey. In 1840, the chief contributor was Henry M'Connel, a textile magnate, who sent fourteen pictures, including Landseer's 'chaste and earnest' work, 'Life in the Old Dog Yet', which had excited great admiration at a recent exhibition at the Royal Institution. McConnell also lent Eastlake's 'Slave Market', several landscapes by Turner and Leslie's study of 'Merrie England', 'May Day'. The Rev. J. Clowes of Broughton had contributed three works of the Old Masters. A solicitor, Edward Bent, had sent a varied selection: a picture by West describing the rescue of an officer from the tomahawk of an Indian, a 'striking' view of the Lake of Killarney by Charles Calvert, and an Italian landscape by Aglio, while the well-known patron, Daniel Grant, had generously offered 'The Sketch Book' by Lonsdale, 'The Harebell' by Watson, and the 'Love Letter' by Graham, thought-provoking anecdotes. From Thomas Agnew came 'Grace Darling', a study of the heroic lighthouse girl by Parker of Newcastle, which represented a room in the lighthouse 'with the rescued sufferers in highly characteristic situations, and portraits of Grace and her parents who are all there in the act of kindly administering to the necessities of their exhausted guests.'[2] There were also works by Callcott, Knight, and other English and continental artists, while John Knowles, M'Connel, and one of the Strutts of Derby were the chief contributors to the sculpture gallery. For the fourth exhibition, there was a 'Chinese Room' filled with treasures of the Orient and for the fifth exhibition there was an 'Ancient Hall', furnished with the art and furniture of the sixteenth and seventeenth centuries. In 1844 there was a special exhibition of cartoons, examples of design that would enlighten the artisan.

Fifty thousand people visited the first exhibition, and double that

---

[1] *Report of the Directors of the Manchester Mechanics' Institution; and Proceedings at the Annual Meeting of the Members, held in the Lecture Room of the Royal Institution, on the 28th of February 1839* (Manchester, 1839), p. 33.

[2] *The Exhibition Gazette (Late Bazaar Gazette): In Connection with the Easter Exhibition, 1840, at the Manchester Mechanics' Institution*, No. 1, 20th April 1840, p. 2.

number were admitted to succeeding ones. Heywood and his colleagues were surprised and delighted by the success of the first
exhibition and repeatedly emphasised the contribution the Institute was making to the intellectual development of the working class.
In Heywood's address of 1839, he praised 'the gratification afforded
by it to thousands, and tens of thousands who had never seen anything of the kind before . . . the new and nobler taste which it has
awakened in the mind of many of them . . . its value as an example
to other institutions, possessing rich and beautiful collections from
which the public have been hitherto excluded. . . .'[1] He added, 'It
was delightful to see the countenances, beaming with pleasure, of
the working men, their wives and their children, as they thronged
through the rooms, and gazed upon the different objects. . . .'[2]

The example of Manchester was followed elsewhere in England.
In 1839, the directors reported that deputations had come from
several towns in order to learn how they might organize their own
exhibitions. At Bradford Joseph Farrar, indefatigable in his efforts
to raise money, immediately made a profit of from £700 to £800 in
1840 by holding an exhibition modelled on that of Manchester.
Machinery and apparatus, manufactured goods of all kinds; geological specimens, birds and eggs; pictures and statues; antiques and
curios and a baronial hall were here. In Halifax, an exhibition
organised by the Infirmary, the Literary and Philosophical Society
and the Mechanics' Institution in 1840 balanced areas of science and
art. In 1840 the date of the Manchester exhibition was moved from
Christmas to Easter in order that it might not coincide with the
exhibition being held at the Salford Mechanics' Institution.[3] When
the first exhibition in Liverpool at the Mechanics' was held in 1840,
one of the highlights was a collection of engravings that were filled
with earnestness, passion, and feeling. A 'companion' to the exhibition emphasised that with decreasing costs it was not impossible
for members of the working class to have similar works in their own
modest dwellings. 'There is the advantage in print collecting, that a
small sum of money may go a long way in the purchase of facsimiles
in miniature of some of these splendid paintings which are utterly
beyond the hope of people of moderate fortunes even to possess or
even to see.'[4]

As in all these exhibitions, there were examples of the sublime and
the ridiculous. In 1840 there were portraits of Liverpool worthies,

[1] *Report of the Directors, etc.*, 1839, p. 102.
[2] *Ibid.*
[3] *Catalogue of the Exhibition of Works of Art, Manufactures, Models of Machinery,
Curiosities, Antiquities, etc. at York Buildings, Victoria Bridge, in aid of the funds of the
Salford Mechanics' Institution* (Salford, 1840). T. J. Trafford, William Garnett and
others lent works of the Old Masters. There were also contemporary works of art
for sale.
[4] *Catalogue of the Exhibition of Objects Illustrative of the Fine Arts, Natural History,
Philosophy, Machinery, Manufactures, Antiquities, etc.* (Liverpool, 1840), p. 30.

such as William Roscoe and Dr. Currie; curiosities such as 'The Last Supper' cast in iron and Lord Byron's camp bed, while in the architectural room there was a model of Stonehenge and a plan of the new assize courts. J. B. Yates, R. V. Yates, Edward Hardman, Richard Rathbone, and Thomas Winstanley had lent paintings from their collections of Old Masters and contemporary art. The names of such artists as Raphael, Veronese, Poussin, and Bronzino weighed rather heavily beside those of such Lancashire artists as Samuel Williamson, Charles Towne, Samuel Austin and W. G. Herdman. Similar surveys of art were organized in succeeding years, with thought always given to the educational nature of the project. In 1842 the compiler of the catalogue particularly pointed out the high purpose of 'The Anti-Slavery Conference' by Haydon. Here was Thomas Clarkson, lifting his arms and pointing to heaven, while he solemnly urged the members of the Anti-Slavery Association to persevere, until slavery was extinct.[1] The directors of the Mechanics' Institute in Liverpool were as convinced as those of Manchester that a new and nobler taste was developing in the minds of thousands of members of the working class through such endeavours.

IV. THE MANCHESTER SCHOOL OF DESIGN

Those who believed that the design classes of the mechanics' institutes did not compare with those of Lyons and that the taste of textile designers in the Manchester region was limited and unimaginative were given support when Haydon arrived on the scene in 1837: 'I found Manchester in a dreadful condition of Art. No School of Design. The young men drawing without instruction. A fine anatomical Figure shut up in a box; the housekeeper obliged to hunt for the key! I'll give it to them before I go.'[2] Nothing concrete was done, however, until January 1838, when Haydon returned to Cottonopolis.

A meeting took place in the Committee Room of the Mechanics, to consider the propriety of founding a school of design. I read my proposal which was received with cheers. Mr. James Fraser in the chair, Mr. Heywood was present. Some one wished an elementary school to be added before beginning the figure, but I urged the necessity of uniting the Artist and the mechanic, as in Greece and Italy and I think I impressed the audience. Finally, an active committee was formed to take the proposition into serious consideration, preparatory to calling a public meeting.[3]

---

[1] *Catalogue of the Second Exhibition of Objects Illustrative of the Fine Arts, Natural History, Philosophy, Machinery, Manufactures, Antiquities, etc.* (Liverpool, 1842), p. 53.
[2] B. R. Haydon, *The Diary of Benjamin Robert Haydon* (Cambridge, 1963), IV, 416.
[3] *Ibid.*, p. 454.

At a dinner during his visit, Haydon remarked upon the outlook of and recorded conversations with these businessmen-patrons:

Dined with a very fine fellow, Darbyshire, and met [Benjamin] Heywood (banker), [William] Fairbairn (Engineer), and others, with some nice women, one with a fine head—sat opposite me at table, at the end. We talked of the School of Design. Heywood said, 'It was astonishing how it would get on if men had shares bearing interest;—not but [that],' said he, 'I prefer donations.' This was a regular hint for starting a 'School of Design Company', and after all, perhaps, this must be the way in England. We'll see. Bankers are shrewd ones, Heywood's intellect is underrated here, but he has a great deal of natural humour. . . .[1]

The next day Haydon pressed his campaign in public: 'Lectured at Royal Institution and Mechanics. Audiences stuffed. Laid the subject of a School of Design before them. Enthusiastically received. Committee met today. Monied men must not be bullied. . . .'[2] On 30th January Haydon continued:

Dined with Fraser, a very fine fellow and the best Amateur Sketcher except Sir George I ever knew, Fairbairn, Engineer was there and Roby from Rochdale. I went to lecture which spoiled the Party and returned but we met to talk of Art and not a word was spoken—till Fairbairn and I talked on the School—and they were evidently sincere. . . .[3]

Haydon seemed to be succeeding with these wealthy and ambitious men until the last hour:

February 1 and 2. Closed last night with an enormous audience. Dined at Fairbairn's, engineer, after passing the morning at his vast Engine works. . . . We had a pleasant party, but the conversation in all Country cities is on domestic politics. On any broad question they get spitish and you see the drift is to rival another establishment, or mortify a political opponent. Turner, the surgeon, Fraser the Connoisseur, and Darbyshire the attorney see things broadly. The pain of the night was the sudden instability of Mr. Heywood, a banker, very brainless, very vain, very rich, and very kind-hearted. He likes to lead and must be guided, and he never leads till danger is past.
Fairbairn, I and Fraser had planned the School, formed the resolutions, but had never consulted him, nor did intend to till they were finished. He felt nettled and spoiled the Evening. After I told Fairbairn and Fraser he must apparently be consulted in everything.[4]

Haydon was positively enraged when he heard of what further steps were taken after his departure:

After I was gone, the Council of the Royal Institution appointed a sub-committee to inquire and report on the School of Design, and what did these

---

[1] *Ibid.*, p. 455.
[2] *Ibid.*, p. 456.
[3] *Ibid.*
[4] *Ibid.*

men do in their innocent ignorance? Why they wrote up to Poulett Thomson, who replied that the plan of founding a school of design in Manchester was of no use, for their school in London was doing nothing, and so the whole project fell to the ground. This is like the Poulett Thomsons of the World.[1]

A school of design did open, however, in basement rooms of the R.M.I. under the patronage of such men of wealth as Benjamin Heywood, Edmund Potter, and William Fairbairn, if not under the official patronage of the R.M.I.

From a materialistic point of view, it seemed very possible that a school of design might save Manchester some £20,000 a year, for that is what Manchester men were spending in France for designs for calico printing. The difficulty was to persuade the merchants and manufacturers to subscribe substantially to such a project and to decide how design in the school should be taught. There was only one precedent in England, the Central School at Somerset House, London, established in 1837. Here, and later in Manchester, there was considerable discussion and correspondence in the press on the best methods of teaching design. On one side were those who like Haydon favoured the study of the living model and on the other, those who preferred concentration on flowers and ornamental forms. The first master of the Manchester school was a firm believer in the importance of the study of the human figure.

The first report in 1839 stated that there were thirty-six pupils of whom twelve were qualified to draw from the round, either statues or busts, thirteen were good copyists, and eleven were elementary students. Classes were held from seven to nine in the evening. The declared object of the school was to impart systematically a knowledge of the principles and practices of art with a view of its application to manufactures. The director, John Zephaniah Bell, was an excellent teacher, but because of his devotion to the human form, it must be admitted he presided over an academy of painting rather than a school of industrial design.

Like other provincial schools of design, that of Manchester in the beginning faced financial difficulties. Heywood and James Thomson of Clitheroe, the calico printer, as well as other bankers and manufacturers who had shown interest in the project, failed to give generously. To gather more fees, morning classes from eight to ten were introduced. Apart from fees, the school depended entirely upon public subscriptions and donations, which in February, 1839, totalled only £365. Out of this the master's salary (£150) had to be paid, and plaster casts, books, flowers, and other equipment bought.[2] To alleviate the financial strain, steps were taken in 1840 to obtain a government grant, but not until 1843 was the school awarded an

---

[1] B. R. Haydon, *Correspondence and Table-Talk* (Boston, 1877), II, 398.
[2] Cecil Stewart, *A Short History of the Manchester College of Art* (Manchester, 1953), p. 20.

annual allowance of £250 on the understanding that the local committee would raise an equal amount by private subscription and comply with a system of instruction outlined by the Central School.[1] London wanted a school in Manchester which would instruct the student in the technique, as well as the principles, of ornament as applied to the manufacture of cottons. However, many of the manufacturers of the community who supported the school, disciples of Haydon, did not necessarily want this sort of programme. Masters came and went; accusations were hurled abroad; and the School of Design's effectiveness fluctuated drastically. The crucial point was the drawing of the figure, for which Haydon had originally been the protagonist: 'In the inevitable desire of the State to steer clear of artistic instruction, he divined the portrait-painting clique at the Academy. Equally inevitably art teaching and the figure won.'[2]

When the school in Manchester had reached the nadir of its fortunes in 1849, the Board of Trade turned to J. A. Hammersley, the landscape painter, who by his energy and intelligence rather than by the principles laid down by London, saved the school. Under his direction, the school recovered and grew. The syllabus underwent radical changes; the training of calico printers was no longer considered the primary object of the school. 'Design applied to textile fabrics', he said, 'cannot be counted its only or its highest aim.' [The teaching of decoration] 'must be absolutely free of the trammels of trade necessities, and no attempt should be made to teach the special adaption to machinery required. To teach that would not be to teach art but something that rather interfered with and subverts it.'[3]

In 1854 the school became a sectional department of the Royal Manchester Institution. Although it paid a fairly large rent to the parent body, the Institution was generous in many ways, making its lecture rooms available to the students of design and providing medals and prizes for the students. In fact the number of prizes offered was staggering, with large sums spent on medals. For example, the die of one medal cost £250, and in 1852, no fewer than ten silver medals were awarded, while a prize of £100 was offered by a gentleman as reward 'for the greatest amount of proficiency, assiduity and talent exhibited'.[4] This type of incentive system was very common in the history of academies.

The exhibition of works of industrial design organised by George Wallis, master of the school in 1845 and 1846, was an innovation. In the second half of the eighteenth century, the growth of industrialisation gave rise to the industrial exhibition, an endeavour that,

[1] *Ibid.*

[2] Oppé, p. 110.

[3] Quoted in Quentin Bell, *The Schools of Design* (London, 1963), p. 120. This is the standard work on the subject.

[4] Stewart, *A Short History of the Manchester College of Art*, p. 22.

from the first, was quite different from the fairs of earlier periods, for it had a wider and more definite purpose, didactic and moral, as well as commercial. The exclusively commercial purpose of the fair was now subordinated to the exaltation of progress in technology, science, industry, and agriculture. One of the first such exhibitions in England was that involving agricultural and other machinery opened in London at the Society of Arts in 1756. In 1845, Wallis organised at the Manchester Royal Institution the first exhibition of manufactured art works ever held in England, which contained articles created in textile fabrics, porcelain and precious metals, electroplated metal, carved wood, stamped leather, and papier mâché. The largest number of textiles came from the Thomson Brothers' firm, another sign that James Thomson was very interested in encouraging good design. Here, too, were the prize designs of the pupils of the school, and though the printed patterns on mousselines, chintzes, and furniture cottons did not realise *The Art Union*'s notion of perfection, they were indisputedly far in advance of the patterns which were prevalent in Lancashire a few years before this. *The Art Union* considered the exhibition of such significance that it devoted a whole issue to it.[1]

The editor believed that the leading manufacturers did not thoroughly understand that such an exposition was a great and important educational project. Not only could employers and employees compare various examples of manufactures, but

a large display of the best products of industry, independent of its training in taste and the power of appreciation, has a great moral value in inspiring the operatives with self-respect. The greater the triumph of national industry in the excellence and magnificence of the objects displayed, the higher will be his sense of the importance of having taken a share in the production of such a result, and the more keenly will his ambition be stimulated to extend the bases and strengthen the structure of national industry, and what is, in fact, the same thing, of national prosperity.[2]

The Art Union noted, after the exhibition had closed, that the organisers were somewhat disappointed by the support they had received:

The ends the Council had in view seemed to be less fully understood by the manufacturers of this town and neighbourhood than they had allowed themselves to expect. The Contributions from our own district were few, and, with some exceptions, unimportant, whereas those from a distance contributed by far the most valuable and interesting part of the Exposition: and, although there can be no doubt that much good was effected in creating and diffusing a better taste amongst our working population, between forty and fifty thousand of whom visited the rooms, yet the Council have to state that the result of the Exposition was a pecuniary loss to the school. . . .[3]

---

[1] *The Art Union*, January 1846. Special issue.
[2] *Ibid.*, 1 January 1846, p. 54.   [3] *Ibid.*, 1st April 1846, p. 139.

The Council of the School of Design continued on after Wallis had gone, and in 1849 another exhibition of art manufactures was held at the Royal Institution. Articles of silver, glass, bronze, parian and other materials were displayed and admired. *The Art Union* firmly believed that everywhere were signs of improved taste.[1]

Because of his pioneering work, the Royal Commissioners for the Great Exhibition of 1851 appointed Wallis a deputy commissioner, and he visited in 1850 several manufacturing districts and the whole of Ireland, making selections. The great Exhibition of 1851 contributed to the development of industrial art in Europe, helping to bring about the linking of museums and schools of applied art which was, perhaps, the most significant development in this area in the nineteenth century. The German architect, G. Semper, is often given credit for projecting this idea. Claiming that the machine was responsible for the decline of industrial art and wishing to improve and refine the sensibility of the working class, he suggested that most of the exhibits of the Great Exhibitions should be set aside in a permanent museum that would be a place of practical study, where a variety of works of art would provide materials for study and copying. The museum at South Kensington was the result. The patrons of the School of Design at one point had discussed the possibility of a similar institution. In 1839 *The Art Union* reported that Sir Benjamin Heywood and James Nasmyth were interested in establishing a museum of significant forms in which an endeavour would be made to contrast forms in general use with those of the best periods of ancient art—a modern flower pot, for example, with a series of Pompeian vases, in order that the taste of artisans would be improved.[2] Nothing came of this projection, but the Wallis endeavour was a link between this and the Great Exhibition of 1851.

V. THE BEGINNING OF PUBLIC MUSEUMS[3]

It is appropriate to conclude this survey with a brief reference to the gradual development of public museums and libraries in Lancashire.

In Western Europe, the encyclopaedic curiosity of the Middle Ages continued to be displayed in the collections of the Renaissance and Baroque periods. These collections often were attempts at a systematic synthesis of two worlds: the macrocosm of the animal, vegetable, and mineral world and the microcosm of the human world. The 'virtuoso' was interested in coins and flowers, insects and paintings alike, as types of curiosities. In the eighteenth century, the *Wunderkammer* often assumed a more scientific air, but Sir Hans

---

[1] *Ibid.*, 1st July 1849, p. 204.   [2] *Ibid.*, 15th September 1839, p. 137.
[3] A full-scale survey is David Murray, *Museums, Their History and Their Use* (Glasgow, 1904), 3 vols. Also see Sir Frederick George Kenyon, *Museums and National Life* (Oxford, 1927).

Sloane, whose collections form the foundation of the British Museum, was interested in science, antiquities and art. He gathered together Roman urns, lamps, gems, and inscriptions; Etruscan bronzes; Egyptian and Assyrian antiquities; and drawings by Durer and Holbein.[1] Lancashire was not without its collectors. In the eight eenth century, Sir Ashton Lever was known far and wide for his passion for collecting. At first he concentrated on birds, and his aviary at Alkrington Hall near Manchester was considered the best in Britain. After he purchased at Dunkirk several hogsheads of foreign shells about 1760, his attention was taken up with shells and fossils. Then in succession came collections of stuffed birds, costumes of savages, weapons and ultimately all kinds of natural objects. Visitors came from far places to view these wonders, but in 1774 Sir Ashton packed up his collections and went off to London.[2] For many years his museum provided amusement and instruction, though its influence had not touched the majority of townsmen in Lancashire.

During the first years of the nineteenth century, Lancashire patrons of art, such as Nicholas Ashton, Henry Blundell, Sir John Leicester, John Leigh Philips, and John Trafford supported and studied in an interesting museum in Liverpool owned by William Bullock and described in this puffing hand-bill: 'William Bullock, Silver Smith, Jeweller, Toy-man and Statue Figure Manufacturer, Museum of Natural and Artificial Curiosities; at his house, 24 Lord Street, Collection comprising upwards of eight hundred articles. Admission 1 shilling. Annual Tickets 10 shillings and 6 pence.'[3] What did the visitor find in the museum? The catalogue, which passed through seven editions, listed mammals, birds, reptiles, fishes shells, crustaceans, insects, and corals; a case of minerals, and works of art. Bullock's purpose was eminently serious, for he appealed to the patronage of 'those then, who look thro' Nature, up to Nature's God; or to speak less metaphysically, who can derive knowledge and entertainment from the contemplation of the works of the Supreme Power; or can examine with surprise and delight, the production of the untutored Indian, as well as those ingenious pieces of art of the more enlightened part of mankind . . .'[4]

For the lover of art, the armoury was the high point of a visit, whether or not one was caught up in the craze for Gothic:

On entering this room (which is painted in the Gothic manner, and lighted by an elegant arched window of stained glass) the contemplative visitor can-

---

[1] G. R. de Beer, *Sir Hans Sloane and the British Museum* (Oxford, 1953), p. 113.

[2] 'Sir Ashton Lever', *Dictionary of National Biography*, XXXIII, p. 137; W. J. Smith, 'Sir Ashton Lever . . ., 1729–1788', *Trans. Lancs. and Ches. Antiquarian Soc.*, vol. 72, for 1962, 1965, pp. 61–92.

[3] Quoted in G. H. Morton, *Museums of the Past, the Present, and the Future* (Liverpool, 1894), p. 20.

[4] *Guide to the Liverpool Museum*, sixth edition (Liverpool, 1808), p. 5.

not but feel a degree of respect and veneration for the memory of his fore-
fathers. Surrounded by such a multiplicity of armour and war-weapons, he
will, if not solely engrossed in other pursuits, be capable of reflection and
form to himself a variety of conjectures of times long past; his active mind
will contrast the manners, customs, and military exploits of those days, with
the present ones, draw a line of comparison for the different centuries; and
mark the progression of art and science, from a state little better than bar-
barous, to an age when refinement and ingenuity are nearly arrived at the
acme of perfection.[1]

When Bullock started on his peregrinations again about 1810, he
left Liverpool without a museum. Soon there was to be a museum in
the Royal Liverpool Institution, which attracted not only the members but hundreds of the working class when it was opened to the
public for a slight admission fee. In the forties the directors of the
Liverpool Mechanics' Institute were very proud of their museum
with its glass cases filled with collections of objects of natural history,
minerals and geological specimens, and 'an interesting and most
valuable Series of Models in Wax, illustrating the Growth of Plants
and Fruits . . .'[2] Around the gallery were other glass cases, displaying antiquities and curiosities. At Manchester, the Mechanics'
Institute in the late thirties possessed a modest museum containing
a heterogeneous collection, chiefly of fossils and birds, and animals'
skins and snake skins. More important was the Natural History
Museum, Peter Street, opened in 1835 through private effort. In
neither community were there public museums.

In the thirties a movement began to found art galleries and
museums for the people. One of the chief arguments was that
museums would be effective in curbing crime in the streets. This
argument was repeated at the annual meeting of the School of
Design in Manchester in 1845 by Joseph Brotherton, in a speech
that contained all the other favourable arguments. A museum,
filled with works of nature, as well as examples of ancient and modern art, with examples of manufactures, would aid in improving the
taste of the masses, 'who could not be expected to submit themselves
to a systematic course of instruction'.[3] The audience was reminded
that Manchester and Salford paid a £40,000 police bill every year
and that the expense of thirty-five policemen would pay the interest
on £50,000, the sum needed for a decent museum building. This
would be a penny a pound on the rates. Further, there was nothing
sectarian about a museum, and 'it would have the effect of weaning
the working classes from the public houses, elevating their minds
and promoting their happiness to a degree which could scarcely
be contemplated'.[4] The popularity of the exhibits at the Royal

[1] *Ibid.*, p. 85.
[2] *Catalogue of the Second Exhibition of Objects Illustrative of the Fine Arts, Natural
History, Philosophy, Machinery, Manufactures, Antiquities, etc.* (Liverpool, 1842), p. 57.
[3] *The Art Union,* 1 February 1845, p. 49.   [4] *Ibid.*

Institutions and the mechanics' institutes had clearly demonstrated the need and the desire for museums and galleries.

In this same year, 1845, William Ewart proposed in the House of Commons that municipal councils should be allowed to impose a rate for the establishment of museums and 'pointed out that with railway transport it would be easy to send casts from town to town'.[1] Ewart's bill was strongly opposed, but it was finally allowed to pass, on condition that its operation be limited to towns with no fewer than 10,000 inhabitants; the special museum rate was not to exceed a halfpenny in the pound; the charge for admission was not to be more than a penny; and the museums were not to be open on Sundays. Public libraries as well as museums could be established under the protection of this act, and Ewart was consequently encouraged to introduce in 1850 a further bill by which councils were explicitly empowered to establish both libraries and museums, the restriction to towns of 10,000 inhabitants was removed, and admission to libraries and museums was to be free. When these proposals were denounced by some as extravagance, Ewart agreed that the act should not be adopted in any town unless a poll of the rate-payers showed a two-thirds majority in favour of adoption.

The Acts of 1845 and 1850 made possible the establishment of rate-aided museums, but the local authorities were slow to avail themselves of this power. In Lancashire, Salford and Warrington were the first two communities to establish municipal museums. A committee of the Liverpool City Council investigated the possibility of establishing a city museum in 1850. A year later, the Duke Street News Room, which was to serve as a museum and library for eight years, was bought and in the same year, the thirteenth Earl of Derby presented his zoological collection to the city. The museum immediately attracted some five thousand visitors a week, but the News Room was not adequate. Happily, Mr. (subsequently Sir William) Brown came forward with the money for a new museum and library.

Manchester was the first town to establish a public library under the Act of 1850, and Edward Edwards was the outstanding first chief administrator.[2] From the beginning, Edwards aimed at making the Public Free Library more than an institution for the housing and circulation of books. Even in its first year, the library exhibited a small collection of framed engravings, 'to the gratification of many thousands of persons', many of whom already knew the pleasures of the exhibitions of the Royal Manchester Institution and the Mechanics' Institute.

In the first half of the nineteenth century men of taste in Liver-

---

[1] W. A. Munford, *William Ewart*, M.P. (London, 1960), pp. 127 ff.
[2] There is no better guide in this area than Edward Edwards, *Free Town Libraries* (London, 1869).

pool and Manchester did not limit their support of art to the programme of the Institutions. The discussions on art at the Liverpool Literary and Philosophical Society and the Manchester Architectural Society, the exhibitions at the mechanics' institutes and the debates and exhibitions at the Manchester School of Design are significant examples of cultural enlightenment.

CHAPTER VII

LANCASHIRE COLLECTIONS

I. THE VARIETY OF MOTIVES

The leading patrons of Lancashire at the end of the eighteenth century believed that a knowledge of art and the development of taste began with the Old Masters. Both modern artists and patrons were thought to be dependent upon the artists of the past because they had achieved a perfection of technique, as well as an insight into nature, that was worthy of admiration. 'Whoever has so far formed his taste, so as to be able to relish and feel the beauties of the great masters has gone a great way in his study,'[1] wrote Reynolds, and the educated of Lancashire who had learned about art from reading the *Discourses* agreed.

The students of Sir Joshua adopted a literary approach to art, believing that a poet might describe or a painter might paint a land-scape and the effect would not so much depend upon the different character of the representing medium as on the different abilities of the respective artists. Many of the educated, in true eighteenth-century fashion, thought that poetry was the superior medium as it allowed the creative personality to admire the subject from all sides and to penetrate it more deeply. Moreover, they believed that the superior painter represented neither more nor less in his picture than nature to the eye; a highly individual style and extraordinary ideas were the signs of the less skilled. Their ideal was an atmospheric naturalism. Like fashionable London collectors, the connoisseurs of Lancashire admired the masters of the sixteenth and seventeenth centuries, such as Raphael, Reni, Albani, Claude, Poussin, and the Carracci. When a change in the tide of taste brought a re-evaluation of the Italian primitives, the prices of the works of the Carracci and their followers began to go down about the middle of the nineteenth century while those of Botticelli, Filippo Lippi, Antonello, Fra Angelico, and their contemporaries increased.

New tastes and ideas also began to permeate English thinking about modern art in the Romantic Age. Reynolds had always in-sisted upon the necessity of artists learning from nature as well as from Old Masters, but with the influence of the writings of the Associationists, the works of Repton and Price on landscape and the picturesque, and the emphasis of the English Romantic poets on the intimate relationship linking man and nature, the English school

[1] Reynolds, p. 98.

122

of art began to stress nature and instinct more and formal training and experience less. In the first volume of *Modern Painters* (1843), Ruskin emphasised that painting, with all its technicalities and difficulties, was nothing but a noble and expressive language, essential as the vehicle of thought, but of no deep significance by itself. For him, thought was shown in the artist's interpretation of nature. He commanded the artist to explore the mysteries of wood and field. Often he emphasised that the sketch of the perceptive watercolourist might reveal greater truth and beauty than the most highly finished work.[1]

As sentiments of nationalism grew in this period, certain provincial collectors began to question the meaningfulness of collections of Old Masters and to turn their attention, instead, to collecting works of the English school. They saw no reason why English painters in harmonious relationship with the English environment should not create pictures equal to those of the age of Raphael and Leonardo. The native artist was encouraged to roam the countryside, to delve into the country's history and literature, and to depict the commonplace. Although the early patrons of English art in Lancashire were rather few in number, their influence was significant, and by the middle of the nineteenth century, it became fashionable as well as patriotic to form English collections. Lady Eastlake noted the new orientation in early Victorian England:

The patronage which had been almost exclusively the privilege of the nobility and the higher gentry was now shared (to be subsequently almost engrossed) by a wealthy and intelligent class, chiefly enriched by commerce and trade. The notebook of the painter, while it exhibited lower names, showed henceforth higher prices. To the gradual transfer of patronage another advantage, very important to the painter, was owing, namely, that collections, entirely modern and sometimes only of living artists, began to be formed. For one sign of the good sense of the 'nouveau riche' consisted in his consciousness of his ignorance upon matters of connoisseurship. This led him to seek an article fresh from the painter's loom, in preference to any hazardous attempts at the discrimination of older fabrics. Thus, such gentlemen as Mr. Sheepshanks and Mr. Vernon, who were the first founders of this class of collectors, contended and often with success for the possession of fine modern pictures, with patrons of rank and distinction.[2]

Like historians who saw the Great Reform Bill destroying the influence of the nobility and gentry in English politics, she failed to recognise that noble patrons still made their mark, though surrounded by middle-class troops. The Duke of Bedford, the Marquess

---

[1] Vol. III of *The Works of John Ruskin* (London, 1903).

[2] Sir Charles L. Eastlake, *Contributions to the Literature of the Fine Arts* (1848); 2nd ser. with memoir by Lady Eastlake (London, 1870), p. 147. For an interesting description of the Sheepshanks collections, see Frank Davis, *Victorian Patrons of the Arts* (London, 1963), Chapter X. S. C. Hall surveyed the Vernon collection in *The Vernon Gallery*.

of Stafford, and Lords Northwick, Lansdowne, Egremont, Yarborough, and Monson, extending liberal patronage to living artists, were formative influences. David Roberts, a beneficiary of noble and bourgeois largesse, noted:

In the spring of 1829 I painted for my kind patron Lord Northwick 'Chapel of the Virgin at Caen', for which he paid me eighty guineas, a small picture of St. Remy at Amiens for Mr. Samuels and the 'Town Hall at Louvain' all of which were exhibited in the Suffolk Street Gallery. I also fulfilled my promise and sent two pictures to the exhibitions in my native city—a duplicate of the 'Chapel of St. Jacques at Dieppe' to the Scottish Academy, and a repeat of 'Antwerp Cathedral' to the Royal Institution. The first of these was purchased by Mr. Trotter, Lord Provost of the City, the other by Mr. Gritton.[1]

The painter Roberts and the sculptor Gibson, internationally known, had the best of two worlds of patronage; artists of provincial reputation often depended wholly upon middle-class support.

II. COLLECTORS OF THE OLD MASTERS

Men of wealth in Lancashire purchased Old Masters and when their means were limited, they bought copies or commissioned artists to paint copies for them. Genuine works of artists of the sixteenth and seventeenth centuries, however, were few in most London and provincial collections in the late eighteenth century. The typical London sale of the years 1760–92 featured a collection of overpainted, dishonestly attributed daubs, among which a masterpiece might pass unnoticed. Often connoisseurs sought the opinion of leading artists, but their professional eyes could not penetrate layers of sooty varnish. If a work came direct from one of the great Italian collections, it might fetch a high price. Great names were bandied about with greater abandon. The foremost art authority of London and a keen judge of old drawings, Reynolds—or his executors—announced that he possessed seventy van Dycks, fifty-four Correggios, forty-four Michelangelos, twenty-four Raphaels, and even twelve Leonardos. Although no fewer than four hundred and eleven pictures were sold after his death, the price that was realised represented less than £25 a canvas.[2] Such names and such prices were found well into the nineteenth century in the auction rooms of Liverpool and Manchester. More genuine articles appeared on the markets of Europe at the turn of the century, when the political and economic upheavals in Italy, the Low Countries, and

---

[1] James Ballantine, *The Life of David Roberts* (Edinburgh, 1866), p. 31.
[2] William T. Whitley, *Artists and Their Friends in England* (London, 1928), II, 194–6. There were some good pictures in the collection: two Rembrandts, a Rubens self-portrait, and two versions of 'The Agony in the Garden', both by Giovanni Bellini and Mantegna.

Spain touched palace and convent. Dr. Waagen, about 1850, noted that two superlative Claudes, then at Leigh Court, had come to England at the time of the French Revolution. These ornaments of the Altieri Palace in Rome were bought by the English dealer Fagan for £9,000.[1] In 1823, the catalogue of the exhibition of Old Masters at the Liverpool Royal Institution stated that two works by Viviani 'were purchased in Paris in 1803, from the collection of a French emigrant nobleman'.[2]

The provincial collectors of Old Masters gathered together their treasures in various ways. There were visits to dealers in London, in other English cities, and on the continent. There were auctions in many communities. In London, Roscoe bought pictures for himself and for his friends, and sometimes he attempted a bit of speculation. In a letter to his wife, dated 24th February 1793, he writes: 'Should this same D[aniel] D[aulby] [his sister's husband] tell you I have bought a large and magnificent collection of pictures, don't believe him—it's no such thing—a few trifles—by which I shall gain cent per cent (Mr. R's for that) and Dan shall be the first man I take in.'[3]

Thomas Taylor, the art lover and amateur dealer, purchased works in Norwich for his friend, John Leigh Philips, the Manchester connoisseur, in 1781 buying 'five beautiful things of Bartolozzi's, four small Rembrandts, two large etchings, a beautiful French landscape in aquafortes, and three small things by Albert Durer'.[4] Norwich was recommended to Northern connoisseurs as a cheaper market than London for works of this kind. In 1782, Taylor scouted the London market for collectors of the North. He became a convert to the English achievements, no longer admiring those 'old prints and etchings so much sought after by your Virtuosos! They are infinitely eclipsed by the productions of the present day, have you seen the etchings of Bright from Mortimer's designs?' he asked Philips, 'answer me candidly can you produce from among your antique heads such a work as his? Or from the works of Rembrandt can you equal Worledge's etchings of the raising of Lazarus?'[5]

In 1814, John Ashton Yates, a Liverpool broker and friend of Roscoe, was buying in occupied Paris.

Among the dealers, I have met with fewer good things than I expected, of the old Italian Etchings and Engravings scarcely anything the German amateurs having lately been picking up everything they could in this way.

---

[1] G. F. Waagen, *Treasures of Art in Great Britain* (London, 1854–7), III, 181.
[2] *Catalogue of the Paintings, the Works of the Old Masters of the Various Schools, and of Deceased British Artists, Contributed by the Proprietors of Most of the Principal Collections in Liverpool and the Neighbourhood* (Liverpool, 1823), p. 2.
[3] Roscoe Papers, 3522, Liverpool Record Office.
[4] 'Selections from the Correspondence of Lieutenant Colonel John Leigh Philips, Part II', *Memoirs and Proceedings of the Manchester Literary and Philosophical Society*, fourth edition, III (1890), 12.
[5] *Ibid.*, p. 16.

I have just purchased 60 or 70 drawings and a few small Italian pictures. The prices demanded generally for paintings appear to me to exceed those of London dealers, more especially in the Flemish and Dutch schools; I learn that several considerable purchases of these have been made by gentlemen who have been here since the Peace—and if a really fine Italian picture makes its appearance, it is held for a great price.[1]

Collectors in Lancashire had the assistance of London and local dealers. Most of William Roscoe's collection was brought together in the first fifteen years of the nineteenth century with the help of dealers, and his relationship with them was typical. Certain works of art were sent up from London on approval. For example, in 1795, the London dealer, Thomas Philipe, notified Roscoe of a shipment and enclosed a list of prices for the prints and drawings.[2] 'The case containing the items has been dispatched by post coach to Birchfield. . . . The above articles are sent to you for your amusement, and if they in any degree answer the purpose, you may have frequent parcels in the same way.'[3] A letter of 1796 notes that Philipe had received returned items and was sending his account for articles retained. 'I shall be happy to have the Honour of serving you here and if in the meantime you wish for any amusement in any way I am always ready to serve you, and with more pleasure, as there is congeniality in our Taste.'[4] A letter of the same year reveals that Philipe, on occasion, acted as agent for Roscoe in London, purchasing prints at auctions on commission. Philipe also sent works to Liverpool auctioneers. In 1811 he wrote:

I suppose Mr. Dodd [of the R.M.I.] is at present levying contributions in your city—as soon as it may be proper after he has moved to some other quarter I shall think of trying my fortune at Liverpool with modern artists— but have been hitherto discouraged by Mr. Winstanley's tardiness, owing to my custom not being worth his while—I understand, there is another Auctioneer, less employed, who may be induced by a succession of small parcels, to undertake my little concerns.[5]

William Carey, that most enthusiastic publicist of the English

[1] John Ashton Yates, Paris; 23rd July 1814, letter to William Roscoe, Roscoe Papers 5376, Liverpool Record Office.
[2] The writings of De Piles, Comte de Caylus and D'Argenville helped the connoisseur with problems of aesthetic distinctions. Julius S. Held, 'The Early Appreciation of Drawings', *Studies in Western Art: Acts of the Twentieth International Congress of the History of Art* (Princeton, 1963), III, 91. Drawings began to command increasingly high prices during the nineteenth century. Collectors flocked to important sales such as those of the collections of the Marquis of Lagoy in Paris in 1834, and William II of the Netherlands in Amsterdam, in 1850. Roseline Bacou, 'Introduction', *Great Drawings of the Louvre Museum: The Italian Drawings* (New York, 1968), p. 11.
[3] Thomas Philipe, London, 14th January 1795, letter to William Roscoe, Roscoe Papers, 2961, Liverpool Record Office.
[4] Thomas Philipe, London, 4th February 1796, letter to William Roscoe, Roscoe Papers, 2962, Liverpool Record Office.
[5] Thomas Philipe, London, 24th September 1811, letter to William Roscoe, Roscoe Papers, 2966, Liverpool Record Office.

school of art, from time to time made sorties into the provinces from his London headquarters. In 1814, he wrote to Roscoe acknowledging the receipt of £8. 9s. 6d. for various drawings and announcing new acquisitions. 'I desired last summer to have visited Liverpool with a few paintings but other engagements prevented me.'[1] He concluded by tempting Roscoe with the description of a work. 'The picture which I mentioned . . . by Ghirlandaio is a most uncommon specimen of vigorous colour and even of joyous expression although the early Florentine Gothic style is visible in the design.'[2]

The two most prominent dealers of Liverpool were Thomas Vernon and Thomas Winstanley, who both handled Old Masters and contemporary works, though the latter was the more active in handling the earlier schools of art. A reviewer of Winstanley's *Observations on the Arts* wrote:

For more than thirty years he has been actively engaged in the buying and selling of pictures, during which period some of the finest works in this part of the kingdom have passed through his hands. Two instances, illustrative of this assertion, deserve to be placed on record. During the short peace in 1802. led by his favourite pursuit, the author visited Paris, where he purchased the head of our Saviour, painted by Leonardo da Vinci, which was so long a distinguished ornament of the collection at Allerton. The head was sold by Mr. Winstanley to Mr. Roscoe for forty guineas; and at the sale of the splendid collection at Allerton, it was sold to Mr. Coke of Norfolk for 300 guineas. The picture of Leo and his Cardinals, after Raffaelle, and del Sarto was also bought by Mr. Winstanley for Mr. Roscoe for less than half the price Mr. Coke gave for it at the same sale.[3]

Indeed, Winstanley was the principal agent of Roscoe for the procurement of his historical collection. Many of Winstanley's bills survive, and it is clear from them that he took a major part in helping Roscoe build up his collection. Roscoe bought fifty or sixty pictures from him. It is impossible to tell whether Winstanley had any influence on the taste of his patron, but the date of his establishment in Liverpool coincides loosely with the date at which Roscoe seems to have begun collecting most actively.

Winstanley wished to deal with patrons who were educated in the arts and in his little work, *Observations on the Arts,* he outlined a system for the would-be collector who possessed taste but only moderate income. 'My humble intentions are to show how that taste may be extended without danger and how the pursuit of collecting . . . may be made interesting and desirable.'[4] Basically, his system was an introduction to the great schools, past and present, with nothing original about the work. Winstanley emphasised that

---

[1] William Carey, London, 11th July 1814, letter to William Roscoe, Roscoe Papers, 735, Liverpool Record Office.
[2] *Ibid.*
[3] *The Liverpool Chronicle*, 24th January 1829, p. 26.
[4] (Liverpool, 1828), p. 11.

the hour was very propitious for merchant or manufacturer to collect Old Masters, for, after twenty-five years of prices 'at once ruinous to purchasers and hurtful to the progress of the arts among us'[1] prices had fallen. He admitted that the artful had taken advantage of the unwary, but he did not specifically state that the men of the North and the rest of England, as well, were becoming more and more suspicious of their 'genuine Leonardos' and were not ashamed now to display an English collection.

Auctions became more frequent in the early nineteenth century and announcements such as the following appeared in the Liverpool and Manchester papers to tempt the connoisseurs.

On Sale, by Private Contract, at apartments in Mrs. Mooney's No. 48 Bridge Street, Manchester, from Friday the 17th of March, to April the 7th, 1809, a small collection of Italian, French, Dutch, Flemish, German, and English CABINET PAINTINGS.

Also an ample selection of Drawings, comprising Sketches, Studies, and Designs, by esteemed Masters in the several schools from Massaccio, the star that preceded the day of Raphael, to Cipriani and Girtin, Westall, and Ker Porter.

And a collection of Rare Etchings and ENGRAVINGS on Wood and Copper, including a mass of specimens in history, landscape, and fancy subjects, commencing with the earliest era of the Art, and forms a continuation of nearly 350 years. Hours of Sale from Ten each morning to five in the afternoon.[2]

William Ford and Thomas Dodd were nationally known booksellers and print dealers in Manchester. William Ford, a native of Manchester, displayed his erudition and wares in Cromford Court. Dr. Dibdin, the eminent bibliographer, praised his catalogues 'for the pains which he exhibited in describing his books . . .'[3] He brought together books, manuscripts, tracts, engraved portraits, and illustrations of Lancashire history and biography, works much in demand in the period of romantic nationalism, while his interest in painting was lively. On a visit in 1809 to his shop William Carey admired a landscape by 'young Williamson'.[4]

Thomas Dodd had a long career as a London-based dealer serving the provinces before he settled in Manchester in 1819. He had acquired a remarkable knowledge of engravings while selling old books and prints in Tavistock Street, Covent Garden. His dealings in prints grew gradually, and his stock assumed immense proportions. In 1816, Dodd opened an auction room in St. Martin's Lane, and there he sold some famous collections, including that of General Dowdeswell. He also extended his business in prints and books to Liverpool, Portsmouth, Manchester, and other provincial cities.

[1] *Ibid.*
[2] Newspaper announcement, Mayer Papers, Liverpool Record Office.
[3] Quoted in *Manchester School Register*, p. 79.
[4] *Letter to I . . . A . . . Esq. A Connoisseur, in London* (Manchester, 1809), p. 4.

Suffering financial difficulties after the war and hoping to improve his fortunes, he moved to Manchester. In 1820, he informed William Roscoe that his new catalogue had just been published, but he complained that times were bad for book and print sellers.

Robert Hindley and Thomas Agnew were two other dealers of the period in Manchester. Of the former, Ford wrote:

> This gentleman no doubt will call himself a collector, but others will more appropriately designate him a dealer, for he is a dabbler in all sorts of Virtue, as Books, Prints, Pictures, Cameos, and Intaglios but of his Knowledge in these matters, many do call it in question, or at most allow it to be superficial.

> This gentleman had the honour of introducing to the Collectors of Pictures on his first appearance here a most notorious well-known character and Dealer, of the name of John Robinson Blakey later known under the appropriate application of

> 'Varnishhando'

> for which the Fine Arts and Collectors have been greatly indebted to him.[1]

The Agnew firm[2] became the most influential in Victorian Manchester. The *Manchester Directory* of 1810 lists two brothers by the name of Zanetti, both in business as carvers and gilders. That year Thomas Agnew arrived from Liverpool and began his apprenticeship, eventually becoming a partner. In 1826, when Vittore Zanetti retired, Agnew became the sole proprietor of the firm, which then bore the title Thomas Agnew and Sons. Originally, the firm had been known for its carving, gilding, glass, and picture framing, and the making of barometers, thermometers, and hydrometers. Only later did the firm concentrate on the sale of Old Masters and contemporary works and on the publication of engravings. Capital accumulation in Lancashire made it possible for Thomas Agnew to pass from the role of general dealer in art supplies to that of picture dealer, while the large fortunes accumulated in mid-century by Manchester merchants gave a tremendous impetus to collecting, and Thomas Agnew with his two sons, William and Thomas, took full advantage of the opportunity.[3]

Nathaniel Hawthorne, visiting Manchester in 1856, found Agnews stuffed with treasures. 'There are many handsome shops in Manchester;' he wrote, 'and we went into one establishment, devoted to pictures, engravings, and decorative art generally, which is much the most extensive and perfect that I have ever seen. . . . I saw some interesting objects purchased by them at the recent sale of the

---

[1] William Ford, 'Character of the Different Picture Collectors, in and about Manchester, faithfully and impartially Delineated' (Manchester, circa 1827), p. 5. MS. 827.79. F.1, Central Reference Library, Manchester.

[2] For a fascinating history of the firm see Geoffrey Agnew, *Agnew's, 1817–1967* (London, 1967).

[3] G. S. Willet, 'A Gallery of Art Dealers, I, Agnews', *The Studio*, CXLI (1951).

[Samuel] Rogers collection; among other things, a slight pencil and water-coloured sketch by Raphael. An unfinished affair, done in a moment, as this must have been, seems to bring us closer to the hand that did it than the most elaborately painted picture can.'[1] He also saw a copy of a handsomely illustrated edition of Byron's *Childe Harold*, presented by John Murray to Rogers. 'There was a new picture by Millais the distinguished Pre-Raphaelite artist,' he continued, 'representing a melancholy parting between two lovers or a husband and wife. The lady's face had a great deal of sad and ominous expression; but an old brick wall, overrun with foliage, was so exquisitely and elaborately wrought, that it was hardly possible to look at the personages of the picture.'[2] Mrs. Gaskell, from time to time, liked to show her girls the pictures at Agnews.[3]

In the North at the end of the eighteenth century a few merchants. and manufacturers had succumbed to the pleasures of collecting Old Masters. The collection of Edward Rogers, one of Liverpool's opulent merchants, was distinguished. 'Fond of music and painting, he devoted much of his leisure to those pleasing pursuits, and a well-chosen collection of pictures evinces the goodness of his taste.[4] The announcement of its sale emphasized that the collection contained 'undoubted Pictures' by Dutch, French, and English masters.[5] Daniel Daulby, the banker and Roscoe's brother-in-law, concentrated on works of the Dutch school,[6] and was particularly proud of his collection of Rembrandt etchings and compiled a descriptive catalogue of that artist's works.[7] Daulby, like Roscoe, believed in the ethical value of art study and justified his labour because he believed society afforded 'opportunities for enjoyment, as well as for contention, and that the hours of leisure are not improperly past in the gratification of innocent taste. . . .'[8] Roscoe's collection, described earlier, adorned Allerton until bankruptcy forced its sale. Two brothers, disciples of Roscoe, were outstanding scholar-connoisseurs in Liverpool in the early nineteenth century. Joseph Brooks Yates

---

[1] Hawthorne, p. 352.

[2] *Ibid.* The picture discussed is 'The Huguenot'.

[3] *The Letters of Mrs. Gaskell*, ed. J. A. V. Chapple and Arthur Pollard (Manchester, 1967), p. 202.

[4] *Gentleman's Magazine*, LXV (1795), 1958.

[5] *A Catalogue of a capital and extensive collection of valuable pictures, . . . Of the late Mr. Edward Rogers, of Liverpool* . . . (Liverpool, 1797), p. 1. Perhaps to be doubted as genuine were works by Claude Lorrain, Guido, Panini, Paul Potter, and Wouvermans. Works by Fuseli, Morland, Barrett, Mortimer, Stubbs, and other artists of the English school were, no doubt, genuine.

[6] *A Catalogue of a Superlatively fine Collection of Capital Pictures, by the most celebrated masters of the English, Flemish, and Italian Schools; . . . The whole being the Property of the Late Daniel Daulby, Esq.* . . . (Liverpool, 1798). The names of such Dutch painters as Rembrandt, P. Brill, DeHeem, and Steinwick are found here. Like Rogers, Daulby had a collection of English pictures.

[7] Daniel Daulby, *A Descriptive Catalogue of the Works of Rembrandt, of his Scholars, Bol, Livens, and Van Vliet* . . . (Liverpool, 1796).

[8] *Ibid.*, p. xviii.

filled his mansion at West Dingle with canvases of Old Masters, manuscripts, early block-letter editions, and a rich collection of emblems, while John Ashton Yates, the broker, formed a valuable collection of engravings and Old Masters.

The catalogue of the exhibition of Old Masters at the Liverpool Royal Institution in 1823 reveals that John Gladstone, Jacob Fletcher, Sir John Tobin, William Duff, and Francis Jordan, leading merchants of Liverpool, were the proud possessors of works of the masters of the sixteenth and seventeenth centuries. There were no attributions and only a copy or two. For example, Sir John Tobin had lent works by Giorgione, Domenichino, Titian, Berchem, D'Arpino, Brakenburg, and Canaletto. The compiler of the catalogue emphasised how important the study of such works were to the artists of the community. After Veronese's 'An Allegory of Wisdom and Strength', he wrote, 'The pictures of Paul Veronese are anxiously sought for by the admirers of the Venetian School: the proprietors of the British Institution made a purchase of one of a very high quality, for the purpose of its being studied by the artists of the metropolis.'[1]

How substantial were the reputations of these collections? On his first tour of England in 1835 Dr. Waagen visited Sir John Tobin in Liverpool and concentrated his attention on the illuminated manuscripts in his collection. A distinguished merchant 'who did as much to promote the commerce of Liverpool as any man of his time',[2] as slaver, privateer, trader in African palm oil, and promoter of the steam engine for transoceanic voyages, Sir John, in 1819, had bought Oakhill House, Old Swan, Liverpool. Here, assisted by the merchant's daughter, Sarah, a woman 'with much love of art, and a cultivated understanding', Dr. Waagen examined a Prayer Book of Mary of Burgundy and a Roman Breviary, the works of Flemish artists, and the Bedford Missal, a Book of Hours, written and illuminated in Paris[3] for John, Duke of Bedford, brother of King Henry V and Regent of France 1422–35. Though Dr. Waagen wrongly attributed the work to the Flemish school, he was correct in judging the work with its many large and small miniatures 'one of the most important monuments of this kind, which that age so fertile, in works of art, produced'.[4] Sir John had paid £1,000 for the Missal, 'perhaps the largest sum that ever was paid for a monument of this kind.'[5]

---

[1] *Catalogue of 1823*, p. 3.
[2] Baines, II, 538.
[3] The artist of the principal illuminations is known as 'the Master of the Duke of Bedford', and his atelier seems to have been the most flourishing and important in Paris in the early fifteenth century. D. H. Turner, *Illuminated Manuscripts Exhibited in the Grenville Library* (London, 1967), p. 46.
[4] G. F. Waagen, *Works of Art and Artists in England* (London, 1838), I, 173.
[5] *Ibid.*, p. 176.

Sir John Gladstone was a considerable collector of pictures. When he lived on Rodney Street in Liverpool, an inventory of his effects for 1813 disclosed in an entry that he had pictures, drawings and prints valued at £2,000. Later, at his home outside Liverpool, Seaforth House, he built a picture gallery, adjacent to the ceremonial bedroom that was occupied by Canning on the famous occasion when he was waiting for news about his succession to Castlereagh as Foreign Secretary. The works lent to the exhibition of 1823 reflect a somewhat cautious taste with the landscapes of Salvator Rosa and Jacob Ruisdael the most notable works. John Gladstone acted as executor of his friend and neighbour at Seaforth, Charles Robert Blundell of Ince, and as a reward he was left two paintings by Wilson that enhanced his collection.[1]

On a later visit to England, Dr. Waagen rode out to Obelisk House, Allerton, to view the collection of the merchant, Jacob Fletcher. 'These pictures are few but choice.' He made notes on a Murillo, a Titian, two works by Veronese, a Both, a Rachel Ruysch flower piece, and a Panini, satisfied with the authenticity of the works. Of the Titian, he wrote:

The Virgin as Mater Dolorosa, with folded hands. The ground dark. Half-length. Signed. Formerly in the Borghese Gallery, Rome. Of the frequently occurring examples of this composition, this is one of the best. The expression is intense and noble, of a full but subdued and warm colour. The hands expressive in action, and excellently coloured.[2]

Perhaps the most important collector to emerge from the trading and manufacturing community of Manchester in the late eighteenth century was John Leigh Philips, the successful textile manufacturer. After his death in 1814, the dealer Winstanley conducted a sale which brought in £5,474. 15s. and 3d. His collection of books combined so many facets of eighteenth-century taste, aristocratic connoisseurship, and intellectual curiosity that it may be considered atypical of Manchester at this period. Most of the volumes were in elegant bindings and many of them, especially those on natural history, were selected copies, enriched with valuable manuscript notes and additional plates and drawings.[3] His art collection, filled with paintings and prints of the European and English schools, was particularly known for its comprehensive survey of the works of Wright of Derby.[4]

[1] Letter from S. G. Checkland, Department of Economic History, University of Glasgow, 18th June 1969.

[2] Waagen, *Treasures of Art*, III, 420.

[3] *A Catalogue of the Valuable Extensive, and Well Chosen Library of John Leigh Philips. Esq. deceased, selected by him during a series of many years, with acknowledged judgement and at a liberal Expense, which will be Sold by Auction, by Messrs. Winstanley & Taylor, of Liverpool, at the Large Room in the Exchange, Manchester, on Monday the 17th of October, 1814—and 8 following days* (Manchester, 1814).

[4] *A Catalogue of the Valuable Collection of Paintings and Drawings, Prints and Etchings, Cabinet of Insects, &c. (The property of the late John Leigh Philips, Esq.) Which will be*

At Dukinfield Lodge above the Tame, near Ashton-under-Lyne, a large art collection enhanced the beauty of the octagon room and the other small but elegant rooms.[1] Many pictures were painted or purchased in the eighteenth century by the builder of the new seat, the adventurous artist, John Astley, friend of Reynolds and husband of the rich widow, Lady Dukinfield Daniell. Other works were purchased by their son and heir, Francis Dukinfield Astley, who consigned just about everything of worth to the auctioneer in 1817. Thomas Winstanley conducted a seven-day sale on the premises, which revealed once again how English gentlemen of discriminating eye benefited from the decline of the famous aristocratic families of Europe and the disruptions of Napoleon. Highlighted in the catalogue were an elegantly bound set of the works of Piranesi; Cornelis Bloemart's 'St. John preaching in the Wilderness', a canvas from the celebrated Orleans collection; an idyllic Italian landscape by Jan Both; a masterpiece of Titian, 'The Woman taken in Adultery'; and another example of Venetian art, Giorgione's 'The Judgement of Paris'.[2]

Less known was the collection of paintings belonging to John Lowe at Shepley Hall, which was also on the banks of the Tame. Early in the eighteenth century this estate came into the possession of John Shepley, a merchant of Stockport, and 'by that ascendancy which manufacturing opulence has in this part of the country gained over all other interests'[3] had passed to the Lowes, successful calico printers. In 1828 Agnew and Zanetti, appreciating John Lowe's connoisseurship and, no doubt, his purchases as well, engraved on a plate, a romantic view of the interior of the Collegiate Church, Manchester: 'To John Lowe, of Shepley Hall, Esq. An Admirer and Patron of the Fine Arts This Plate is inscribed with sentiments of respect and esteem.'[4] The following year a descriptive catalogue of his principal paintings appeared, a simple survey of the treasures of a proud possessor.

In 1827, William Ford, the bookseller and print dealer, drew up portraits, not always flattering, of the leading collectors of Manchester, taking particular note of their Old Master paintings. He took almost malicious delight in emphasising that some of the

---

Sold by Auction by Messrs. Winstanley and Taylor, of Liverpool, at the large room in the Exchange, Manchester. On Monday the 31st of October, 1814, and the nine following days (Manchester, 1814).

[1] Aikin, p. 452.

[2] *A Catalogue of the Valuable and Select Library, Splendid Books of Prints, the extensive and well-known Collection of Pictures, Prints and Drawings; ... The Property of Francis Dukinfield Astley, Esq.; ...* (Manchester, 1817).

[3] Edward Baines, *History of the County Palatine and Duchy of Lancaster* (London, 1836), II, 556.

[4] S. Hibbert, *The History of the College and Collegiate Church, Manchester, Founded by Thomas, Lord de la Warre* (Edinburgh, 1830), II, between pp. 246–7.

shrewdest businessmen had been duped by 'Picture Jockeys'. Perhaps their failure to consult him is the reason for this. Richard J. D. Ashworth, a barrister,

One of our most zealous collectors, . . . has suffered probably more than any other through the Rascally Conduct of that class of the profession, very justly denominated Picture Jockeys. He is an exception to the old adage 'burnt child dreads the fire' for his zeal and love for the Arts are nothing diminished and he the third time renews the pursuit with redoubled ardour and vigour, but with increased caution and judgment, . . . and his collection though not numerous, is as may be supposed, genuine and of fine quality, a credit to his taste as well as his judgment.[1]

Another victim was William Townsend:

This Gentleman has long been known as one of our most spirited collectors, and unfortunately also as one of those who have suffered most by the rascally part of the profession: . . . He unquestionably possesses some very fine and first rate productions, but mixed with others of an inferior quality which he long since ought to have discarded . . . his Collection may be considered one of the finest in Town as well as one of those most worthy the attention of the Amateur. . . . His head of Christ crowned with thorns, by Guido, and his Figure of Christ by Carlo Dolci have long been the admiration of all true connoisseurs.[2]

One who was not led astray by 'Picture Jockeys' was an unnamed gentleman who

has amused himself with the formation of a small Collection of Pictures in which the merit of the productions is more conspicuous than great names. . . .
   Here are no Raffaelles, Titians, Rubens, Claudes, and other great names to mislead the judgment and surprise the ignorant, but there are several which will please the Amateur of pleasing pictures, selected for their merit only.[3]

Other collectors were speculators, dealing in art as they would cotton and wool. Ford is rather hard on David Holt, a cotton spinner: 'It was rather been a love of gain, than a love of art which has made him a collector, consequently, his collection, having been formed with this interested view, exhibits a motley assemblage of all sorts, good, bad, and indifferent, classed indiscriminately one by the other, so that it may be compared to a picture which has some good parts, but in which the bad predominates. . . .'[4] Good pictures were 'Birds of Passage' soon taking flight, tempted by golden bait.[5]

Ford was complimentary, on the whole, in his remarks about the collections of the following. Edward Baxter, a dry-salter, was the possessor of a variety of pictures 'that will give greater pleasure to

---

[1] Ford, p. 8. William Carey admired greatly a painting of Christ washing the feet of his disciples, supposedly by Leonardo da Vinci, in this collection. *Letter to I . . . A . . .*, p. 30.
[2] *Ibid.*, p. 28.
[3] *Ibid.*, p. 56.   [4] *Ibid.*, p. 30.   [5] *Ibid.*

the tasteful amateur'.[1] Samuel Barton, Esq., a surgeon, was forming a small collection of choice pictures, though he 'possesses one large and fine picture of the Mother and Child by Schiavone which deserves mention here, because it is equal to any in this town or Neighbourhood as a specimen of the highest style of Art'.[2] Hardman, a manufacturer and one of the oldest collectors of Manchester, owned a collection that contained 'many good, if not many fine, pictures and is well worth the notice of the Connoisseur'.[3] John W. Barton, influenced by an enthusiastic friend, had built up another satisfactory collection, 'without apparently having taken much pains to do so and without possessing probably much feeling for the pursuit. . . .'[4] The collection of James Beardoe, a merchant, was selected with caution and good taste by a connoisseur who readily admitted visitors, and thus 'largely reaps that noble gratification of giving the greatest pleasure to others which he can. . . .'[5] John Dawson, a cotton manufacturer and the possessor of a relatively small collection, had one picture that was 'a Collection of itself, it has however this unfortunate quality that it throws all his other pictures into the background and renders them of less consideration than they really merit. This picture is the Holy Family, . . . from a design by Michael Angelo. . . .'[6]

These collections were not particularly memorable because they were often filled with fakery. 'Picture Jockeys' continued to fleece in early Victorian Manchester, Mr. Pateshall of London announced in 1840 to the connoisseurs of Manchester that he had arrived with his 'private COLLECTION of Pictures intending them for private sale. They are about forty in number, many of the highest class, all good subjects and in excellent condition.'[7] Among them were two works of del Sarto, a Berchem, the 'celebrated' 'Ecce Homo' by Correggio, and works by Titian, Rubens, Ribera, Albano, Panini, Maas, Wynants, Canaletto, and Moucheron. The whole group was Pateshall's own property, 'not gathered for the purpose of sale. . .'[8] When such treasures were lent to the exhibitions, now they were often examined in a very harsh light. 'An exhibition of Works of Ancient Masters (so-called) is now open in Manchester',[9] reported *The Art Union* in 1847:

It is a lamentable display of mistakes; take away ten out of two hundred, and the one hundred and ninety are not worth half the value of the frames in which they are contained. We earnestly hope the manufacturers of Manchester—enterprising, liberal and wealthy as they are—will not here-after be the victims of vagabond picture dealers, as they have been. In this assemblage are many works of which we could tell singular stories [about

[1] *Ibid.*, p. 16.   [2] *Ibid.*, p. 20.   [3] *Ibid.*, p. 24.
[4] *Ibid.*, p. 25.   [5] *Ibid.*, p. 24.   [6] *Ibid.*, p. 25.
[7] *Manchester Guardian*, 2nd September 1840, p. 1.
[8] *Ibid.*
[9] *The Art Union*, 1st April 1847, p. 139.

faking]. . . . But the eyes of buyers of ancient masters have been opened of late years; he who is now cheated, deserves to be so. . . . On the other hand, there are plenty of pictures by British Artists in Manchester, worth three times their original cost.[1]

Because S. C. Hall, the editor of *The Art Union*, worked diligently to point out fraudulent works, the evil grew less. The wealthier were more and more disposed to buy not only what they understood but also what they knew to be genuine.

The previously described collections of Old Masters were typical of the period when the classical tradition prevailed throughout England. There were fakes, copies, original works of less important artists, and, perhaps, one or two really good paintings by the masters of the sixteenth and seventeenth centuries. Few of these Northern collections—Roscoe's was a notable exception—reflected a system or plan, but rather the desire of banker, manufacturer, and merchant to own great works of art, the possession of which would indicate taste and refinement. Whether genuine or fraudulent, these Northern collections must be looked upon as examples of the prevailing taste of the period and not ridiculed. Without the time to travel extensively on the continent, and without the great fortunes of the fashionable noble collectors, certain Lancashire collectors had gathered together some good, if not excellent, works of art, and they very generously shared these with the local artists and the community at large, most notably when there were local exhibitions of Old Masters.

III. COLLECTORS OF THE ENGLISH SCHOOL

The lovers of English art, filled with strong nationalist sentiments, sought in various ways to achieve a high standard of painting in their country. Men of Lancashire visited the exhibitions and studios of the artists in London; they made purchases at the local exhibitions and from local dealers with a stock of English art; and they extended their personal patronage to artists of the region.

In the late eighteenth century, there was frequent communication between Liverpool patrons and London art circles. From London in 1779 Daniel Daulby wrote: 'Mr. Vernon has shown me uncommon Civilities and we have been often together, we visited West, Romney, Carter, and Angelica has many fine pieces in the Exhibition, she with Cipriani and the late Mortimer stand in the first rank in my opinion, I have seen some good pieces of West's but like Mortimer's better, I have a catalogue for you and shall make up the poverty of this by being as particular as you please when we next meet. . . .'[2]

---

[1] *The Art Union*, 1st April 1847, p. 139.
[2] Daniel Daulby, Lewes, 2nd June 1779, letter to Matthew Gregson, Gregson Correspondence, Vol. 18, No. 1, Liverpool Record Office.

On a London visit in 1782 Taylor, the friend of John Leigh Philips, 'was delighted beyond measure with West and so fortunate to visit his rooms when they were commonly well fill'd. . . .'[1] He saw many works by Reynolds but definitely preferred the efforts of Romney. Because Roscoe and his friends often visited Fuseli's studio in London, a special relationship grew up between the artist and Liverpool collectors. Roscoe and Fuseli were on particularly intimate terms, and it was Roscoe's generosity and support that allowed Fuseli to open the Milton Gallery in London, an undertaking inspired by the noble poet and the success of Boydell's Shakespeare Gallery.[2]

While Fuseli was creating the canvases for the Milton Gallery, Roscoe aided in solving financial problems. From 1795 to 1800 Roscoe took many pictures for himself, as well as others that he attempted to sell to his friends. Roscoe genuinely liked Fuseli's work for its literary quality, and at one time he owned a considerable number of Fuselis, displaying many in the dining room of Allerton Hall. Fuseli, familiar with the circle of connoisseurs in Liverpool, constantly reminded his friend of possible purchasers. On one occasion, he asked if Gregson would take a pendant to his 'Hamlet' and on another if Benjamin Arthur Heywood would take a companion to his 'Theseus'. In December 1795 he suggested that Philips or some other Manchester connoissur, such as Hardman, might buy the 'Creation of Eve' and 'Robin Goodfellow'. At one time or another, the following had Fuseli's works in their collections, largely through Roscoe's influence: Edward Rogers, Daniel Daulby, Benjamin Arthur Heywood, Matthew Gregson, William Earle, William Clarke, and the Rev. William Shepherd. These men did not all necessarily come forward with great enthusiasm to support Fuseli. Roscoe once described the marketing of Fuseli's work in the North as 'the experiment of Liverpool'.[3]

Daniel Daulby was a patron and close friend of Joseph Wright of Derby in the artist's last years. This lawyer and banker, a man of considerable culture, brought together in the late eighteenth century a large collection of books, prints and drawings and an interesting selection of works by Old Masters and contemporary artists. Both artist and connoisseur were lovers of Dutch art and Daulby's collections, rich in this area, were a centre of study and inspiration for Wright. In his Liverpool home Daulby placed many landscapes and genre pieces by Wright of more than ordinary interest: 'Julia in the Cavern', 'A Girl blowing on a charcoal stick',

---

[1] 'Correspondence of J. L. Philips', p. 16.
[2] This printseller commissioned more than one hundred and fifty pictures from leading English artists, exhibited the paintings in London and then sold engravings after them.
[3] Hugh MacAndrew, 'Henry Fuseli and William Roscoe', *The Liverpool Bulletin*, VII (1959–60), p. 52.

a lake scene between Rome and Florence, a 'Neptune's Grotto', a fiery 'Girandola', and a moonlight 'Vesuvius'. Daulby bought from Wright quite regularly from the late 1770s to the late 1780s.

In the late eighteenth and early nineteenth centuries, novice and seasoned artists, usually London-based, attracted by the wealth of the provinces, regularly sent pictures to the exhibitions and now and again made personal appearances in the hope that additional commissions or sales would be forthcoming. A pioneer outward voyager was Faithful Christopher Pack, an important member of Liverpool's first Academy. Many years later he wrote:

Forty-three years I think have passed away since I was in Manchester in a professional Character. I had then been only two years under the kind tutorage of Sir J. Reynolds, and was then only in my 19th year. The intensity of my application to study—not only of Painting but Surgery and Physic so impaired my constitution that a remove to the country was deemed necessary and Mr. T. Johnston of Manchester invited me down to paint his Portrait and some others. During my short abode to Dr. Barnes, Mr. Henry and others I was much indebted for kind attentions. To Mr. Ralph Kershaw and Mr. Lee Philips, I was much attached and they were enthusiastic lovers like myself of the Fine Arts—Mr. Kershaw introduced me to the Philosophical Society and stimulated by him I commenced a series of lectures on Painting, the first of which I delivered at the Liverpool Society in [1781]. . . . I am not informed if any of these gentlemen are now alive. Having recovered from my indisposition I returned to Sir J. Reynolds. . . .[1]

The short visit was favoured in the nineteenth century. In 1835, Etty paid a visit to Manchester, viewed the exhibition, and made the acquaintance of Daniel Grant, a manufacturer, from whom he received a commission to paint a hundred-quinea picture. In the subsequent dealings between artists and manufacturer, the laws of the market place prevailed. In 1837, again in Manchester, Etty was entertained at dinner by Daniel Grant who asked him to name a price for the vast 'Sirens' and the smaller 'Samson and Delilah', which had been shown both at the Royal Academy and at Manchester without finding a purchaser. Surprised by the offer to purchase them, Etty, who had previously refused £100 for 'Delilah', and had set a price of £300 on the 'Sirens' alone, went to the lowest sum, £300, in order to tempt Grant. Grant, although complaining like the other manufacturers of losses in the thousands, had taken £300 with him that morning to the Heaton Park races and had returned with only £25 less. Grant threw down £200 and when Etty hesitated, £50 more. After much heart-searching, the painter reluctantly accepted that sum. The episode was somewhat typical of the new patronage: on the one hand there was Grant, the wealthy,

---

[1] Faithful Christopher Pack, London, 21st February 1824, letter to G. F. Bury, Royal Manchester Institution Letters, 1823–32, p. 11. Central Reference Library, Manchester.

speculative industrialist: on the other, Etty, not the wisest of businessmen, anxious to move his paintings onto the market and always mindful of Haydon's precarious financial position. Daniel Grant had briefly examined the 'Sampson' and had not even seen the 'Sirens' before purchasing both pictures.[1]

In the early nineteenth century, a leading dealer, Thomas Vernon, of Liverpool, did much to bring the works of the English School to the attention of the wealthy collectors of Lancashire. Vernon 'for many years attempted to convince his countrymen of the excellence of modern and living artists; and procured of their works, for which he always paid liberally, celebrated their merits to the utmost, and was, sometimes perhaps, too enthusiastic in the cause. His townsmen were convinced and furnished themselves with the most beautiful productions of Morland, Anderson, Wheatley, and others.'[2]

Vernon made frequent visits to London. In 1806, he asked Farington, the artist, 'to look at a picture by Wilson which he is going to send to Manchester to be looked at'.[3] He told the artist that he had recently bought Wright's picture of the 'Destruction of the Floating Batteries' at the sale of the collection of John Mills for 68 guineas, and he hoped to sell it for 300 guineas where the name of Wright was still revered. Vernon also knew Samuel Rogers, the poet and banker, whose house in St. James's was the meeting place of all the intelligentsia of London, the most exclusive and most artistically influential salon of the first half of the nineteenth century. Rogers represented the new self-made class in London society, but at the same time he achieved recognition as the arbiter of refinement. In this celebrated home, Vernon saw the finest work of Flaxman, Stothard, and Chantrey and, 'no doubt, had ample opportunity to meet established and aspiring artists.[4] The dealer and connoisseur on occasion discussed the art market. At one point, Rogers informed Vernon that the aged Mr. Booth of the Adelphi 'had 80 pictures by Wilson, which when they are brought to sale, from their numbers,

---

[1] A. Gilchrist, *Life of William Etty* (London, 1855), II, 65-7. William Grant presented 'Ulysses and the Sirens' to the Royal Manchester Institution in 1838. J. E. Phythian, *City of Manchester Art Gallery: Handbook of Paintings* (Manchester 1908), p. 14.

[2] 'Early Art in Liverpool', The Mayer Papers, III, 43, Liverpool Record Office.

[3] Farington, III, 262.

[4] P. W. Clayden, *The Early Life of Samuel Rogers* (Boston, 1888); P. W. Clayden, *Rogers and His Contemporaries* (London, 1889), and Samuel Rogers, *Recollections* (Boston, 1859) are helpful. J. R. Hale in his introduction to *The Italian Journal of Samuel Rogers* (London, 1956) sums it all up nicely. 'Among the men of genius Rogers helped were Sheridan, Campbell, Wordsworth, and Moore, Chantrey, John Gibson, the sculptor, and Lawrence—to name only the most famous. He helped his friends not only with money but advice on how to make the most out of their works; he reconciled their quarrels and introduced them to people who might be of more use than he could be.' (p. 32.) Another formidable taste maker was Thomas Hope, interestingly presented in Sandor Baumgarten, *Le Crépuscule néo-classique: Thomas Hope* (Paris, 1958).

will lower the price of Wilson's pictures'.[1] Through such a dealer's efforts, Manchester and Liverpool were linked to London's art market.

In early Victorian England, at Manchester, John Clowes Grundy, John Rowbotham, and the Agnews were important in the life of the artist, for rich, successful businessmen, needing numerous pictures for a new mansion, often turned to these dealers. Grundy was one of the best judges of engravings in the country and one of the first to appreciate the talents of David Cox, Samuel Prout and Henry Liverseege.[2] A Manchester Pre-Raphaelite described Rowbotham as 'a man of sterling worth and simplicity of character' and his elder daughter as 'a trusted friend', who spoke 'in my interests with the wealthy buyers who frequented the shop'.[3] The Agnews more and more emphasised the acquisition and sale of modern art.

Much of the beneficial changes we have ourselves witnessed in the huge centres of manufactures must be traced to the enterprise and energy of Mr. Thomas Agnew. When we knew him and Lancashire first, it was a rare event to find the purchaser of any work of modern art; cart loads of trash under the pretence of being ancient masters, were annually sold in the north of England, works with the names of 'Rubens' or 'Raphael' or 'Titian' found ready buyers; but pictures by British artists had little or no chance of sale; the 'old' must be worth money, the 'new' worth nothing. . . . It was against this delusion, Mr. Agnew took arms, and Lancashire and Manchester especially, owe him a debt. . . .[4]

The economic conditions of an artist might improve greatly if he met the requirements of a dealer such as Agnew. In his last years, Etty was favoured, his friend and fellow-artist, Thomas Uwins, tells us:

He was taken up by the dealers and they can make a man's fortune. The dealers can no longer get a market for their Raphaels, Correggios and stuff, manufactured in their back shops, and smoked into the appearance of antiquity. The old nobility and landed proprietors are gone out. Their place is supplied by railroad speculators, iron mine men, and grinders from Sheffield, etc., Liverpool and Manchester merchants and traders. This class of men are as much in the hands of dealers as the old collectors were formerly. But they do not love darkness and therefore will deal only with their con-temporaries. The voluptuous character of Etty's work suits the degree of moral and mental intelligence of these people, and therefore his success.[5]

The last sentence is somewhat off the mark because there were far more works of earnest than of voluptuous character produced in this period.

[1] Farington, III, 262.
[2] 'John Clowes Grundy', *Dictionary of National Biography*, XXIII, 312.
[3] Ernestine Mills, *The Life and Letters of Frederic Shields* (London, 1912), p. 74.
[4] *The Art Journal*, 1st June 1871, p. 183.
[5] Quoted in Dennis Farr, *William Etty* (London, 1958), p. 95.

When the professional dealers banded together to support the national school, prices tended to rise. Dealers had enough capital to hold out for their own prices, and there were fewer scenes like that between Etty and Grant, when the manufacturer ultimately forced the artist to accept a cut-rate price for his work. The higher prices benefited the artists on the whole as did more rapid sales. Not all artists were completely happy with the more business-like methods. At one point, Haydon complained.

Finished my Romeo and Juliet, and now my Employer (a Hull dealer) won't pay me my balance, £45, till I deliver the work, and I won't deliver it till I get my balance. How unlike the Nobility. Everything with Lords Mulgrave, Egremont, Sutherland, Grey, Peel and all of the class honour and faith. All paid me before the work was home. I told this noodle it must dry before I glazed it, or it would crack; and for this bit of honesty he won't pay first. A bill of 39. 10 due 28. I can't pay and now begin again illegal interest and all the distractions of pecuniary want. The Liverpool men are twice as liberal and the Leeds [men] too; but at Hull they are a fierce democratic race, which makes them mistrust their own fathers.[1]

An artist satisfied with the new relationships was Frith, unimpressed with the businessman's knowledge of art:

The patron is often a strange creature; he places, very justly, but little reliance on his own judgement. He knows what he likes, but whether the object of his liking is worthy of that distinction or not, is a matter about which he is alarmingly uncertain. It too often happens that until a picture has received the 'hallmark' of the picture dealer, the collector is not satisfied, but after that, he is often ready to pay for his ignorant incredulity in the form of a great advance on the price for which he might have acquired the work.[2]

Often 'one of the merchant princes of Manchester', when visiting an artist's studio, attempted to bargain for works, while the dealer paid the artist's price.

It was at the end of the eighteenth century that the collectors of Manchester began, somewhat timidly, to introduce into their collections the works of the English school. Some were inspired by a love of nature and the spirit of nationalism; others merely followed fashion's dictates. Taylor's 'contemptible opinion' for old prints and etchings and his praise of Bright's etchings from Mortimer's designs is but one example of the new emphasis. Everywhere it was said that the English school had achieved much and much more could be expected from Britannia's artists.

John Leigh Philips focused on the works of Wright of Derby. His collection contained several of Wright's Italian scenes, including 'An Eruption of Vesuvius', one of the artist's favourite themes. 'The

[1] *Diary*, IV, 632.
[2] Frith, I, 140.

Bridge and Waterfall, at Rydal in Westmorland' was one of the artist's contributions to English landscape painting: 'A charming scene represented with great exactness; the stones, seen at the bottom of the water, give an effect to the picture at once curious and natural.'[1] Here as in so many of his views, the countryside was seen under unusual conditions of sunlight or moonlight. In his later years, Wright was more interested in subject pictures, and literature, rather than history, was the source of his themes. Philips owned 'The Old Peasant bewailing the Death of his Ass', from Sterne and his masterpiece in this genre, 'The Dead Soldier', a subject from Langhorne's poems, which was popularized by an engraving and according to contemporary letters brought tears to the eyes of the viewers. The age of romantic sensibility had arrived, and Wright's picture, shown at the Academy, of 1787, was one of the finest of its early examples: 'This acknowledged "chef d'oeuvre" . . . proves the assertion of Mr. Fuseli, in his biographical notice of Mr. Wright, that "he once eminently succeeded in the Pathetic".'[2]

William Hardman was another Manchester collector who favoured the works of Wright of Derby. In 1807 Farington learned from Hardman that there were many collections of pictures at Manchester: 'Wm. Hardman has about 70 pictures. He noticed Prince Hoare having mentioned him as a Collector of modern art.'[3] By 1827 Ford considered that the collection had declined in value.

The Collection had once the reputation of being one of the first and finest in the town both for number and value but 'tempora mutantur' but we are afraid that we cannot add 'sed non mutamus in ille' . . . so that from being the first and finest of its kind, it has fallen by others rising above it, which places it much lower in the scale. Pictures are no longer estimated by personal consideration to their Authors, posterity will appreciate their works and assign them their proper rank, according to the just standard of their merit—hence Wright of Derby is not now considered a Classic in the Art, and his works no longer fetch the ridiculous prices which they once did in the town and neighbourhood tho' never in London.[4]

Manchester men showed increasing interest in English art in the early nineteenth century. In 1809, Wilkie noted, 'had a call from Mr. Philips (now Sir George), who commissioned me to paint him a picture, for he was making a collection of the English School; he resides in Lancashire'.[5] William Collins later found Philips, another member of the textile clan, a generous patron.[6] In 1827 Ford noted

[1] *A Catalogue of the Valuable Collection of Paintings and Drawings, Prints and Etchings, Cabinet of Inserts, &c.,* p. 6.

[2] *Ibid.,* p. 7.

[3] Farington, V, 97. Prince Hoare linked Hardman's name with that of Sir Thomas Bernard. *An Inquiry . . . ,* p. 231.

[4] Ford, p. 5.

[5] Allan Cunningham, *The Life of Sir David Wilkie,* I, 295.

[6] W. Wilkie Collins, *Memoirs of the Life of William Collins* (London, 1848), II, Appendix.

that John Greaves, a magistrate, was collecting the works of George Morland, those nicely executed genre scenes so similar to the work of Teniers and always popular with men of wealth. Unfortunately he was ill-equipped for the task of developing a Morland gallery, for he knew little about art, 'or as much (which you please) as a "Cow does of a new Shilling".'[1] Ford praised the banker, B. A. Heywood, for his devotion to the English school, but he felt his collection lacked a point of view. 'His collection is a mere assemblage of all the schools tho' principally English, so far good, without any regular connected series of Art, such as would have been worthy of his good fame and Fortune. Still he has been through life a warm Friend of Art and few have shown a more convincing proof of it.'[2] Ford also commended Thomas Appleby, who possessed a small collection: 'The bent of his taste seems to run in preference to the productions of the modern school, though his collection comprises several of the Old Masters. . . .'[3]

By the forties, Lancashire was famed for her collections of English art. In 1840, *The Art Union* noted that

No collection of pictures in the North has been more talked of than Mr. Marsland's of Manchester. When we heard the sale of them announced by Messrs. Christie and Manson, we expected to find a more extensive collection than the Catalogue exhibited. Though small in extent, consisting of only forty-four pictures, they showed much taste in the selection, particularly in the collection possessing some of the best works of the late lamented Liverseege . . .[4]

There were two Boningtons, a Morland, and Wilkie's 'Alfred in the Neatherd's Cottage'. When Benjamin Hick of Bolton died in 1842, *The Art Union* declared that 'Mr. Hick was a patron of Art in the true sense of the word; encouraging genius and artistic worth wherever he found it; and his loss will be much felt by a number of artists of the present day, with whom he was on terms of intimacy.'[5] His collection was particularly rich in the works of Liverseege. The five most admired pictures in his sale, besides those of Liverseege, were 'a beautiful sunny landscape', by A. W. Callcott; a sketch on panel by Wilkie of 'John Knox administering the Sacrament at Calder House'; Linton's 'Return of a Greek Armament'; and Martin's extraordinary companion pictures 'The Rivers of Bliss' and 'Pandemonium' (six feet wide by four in height). There were drawings by Liverseege, Cattermole, Wilkie, Austin, and T. S. Cooper in the collection.

Seven outstanding Lancashire collections of English art in the fifties were those of Thomas Miller of Preston, Henry Cooke of

---

[1] Ford, p. 9.   [2] *Ibid.*, p. 40.
[3] *Ibid.*, p. 54.
[4] *The Art Union*, 15th June 1840, p. 99.
[5] *The Art Union*, 1st January 1843, p. 10.

Manchester, William Bashall of Farington, Samuel Ashton and John Chapman, near Manchester, and John Naylor and John Miller of Liverpool.

Horrocks and Miller's 'Long Cloth' is known, I believe, through-out the world. An intimacy such as frequently exists between artist and patron, arose between Mr. Miller and me. I spent many happy hours with him at Preston. He was one of the truest gentlemen and the warmest friend of art for art's sake, that I have ever known. He died long ago, while comparatively a young man, leaving his collection intact in the possession of his widow.[1]

Out of friendship, Frith descended to painting a public house sign, 'or, to speak more correctly, I assisted in doing so: for Egg worked one side of it, whilst I attended to the other. . . . This work of art was a present to our friend Miller, who had just then purchased an estate in Lancashire for which he was said to have paid a fabulous sum—as in addition to many hundreds or thousands of acres, a whole village and the public house were part of the bargain.'[2]

Miller's collection consisted entirely of works of the English school and were displayed in a gallery adjoining his house. Among the outstanding paintings were 'Hunt the Slipper' by Maclise; 'Van Tromp at the Mouth of the Scheldt' and 'Quilleboeuf' by Turner. *The Art Journal* considered the latter the most sublime of Turner's sublimest essays. 'The water and the sky are passages of the most subtle enchantment, and the light and colour of the work have no parallel in Art.'[3] There were seven Friths, including a small replica of 'Ramsgate Sands', five Etty's with 'The Coral Finders' perhaps the most important. Anecdote was piled on anecdote in the works of Leslie, Webster, Elmore, Egg, and Cope. One of Landseer's best productions, 'Highland Game' with its grouse, blackcock, ptarmigan, woodcock, snipe, and partridge was here. One of David Robert's magnificent church interiors and quiet works of Linnell also found their place, while there were a few watercolours—the most important perhaps was 'Cader Idris' by Turner.

Both Dr. Waagen and *The Art Journal* considered Henry Cooke's collection of watercolours outstanding. 'It is not numerous, but the quality of the Art evidences much refinement and elegance of taste; there are but few drawings in the catalogue that are not by artists now living, and they are in the very best spirit of the painters.'[4] The collection was hung in the dining and drawing rooms of Cooke's home in Burlington Street. There were five Turners: 'Windsor Castle', 'Carlise', 'Ghent', 'At Chelmsford', and 'Rolandseck on the Rhine'. The latter was the *chef-d'œuvre*; the viewer looks up the Rhine, and the cliffs decline until they are lost in the grey distance. In the foreground floating down the stream are some barges: 'And mark the masterstroke of the magician; the golden wealth of the

---

[1] Frith, I, 155.
[2] *Ibid.*, p. 264.
[3] *The Art Journal*, 1857, p. 41.
[4] *Ibid.*, p. 42.

drawing resides in the sunny cliffs and that mellow, respirable atmosphere. . . .'[1] There was no romantic water party in gilded barges. 'At a glance, the drawing looks slight and easy, but it is a result of a succession of the most careful washes, conducted in such a way as to render the paper itself all but transparent. In the cunning of his art, Turner has never outdone this drawing.'[2] The freshly painted achievements of Goodall, Topham, W. Wylde, Herbert, Cattermole, T. S. Cooper, Copley Fielding, Louis Haghe, D. Roberts, S. Prout, and D. Cox were also here. Dr. Waagen particularly admired 'The Harvest Waggon' and 'The Erection of the Maypole' by Goodall; Cattermole's 'Lady Macbeth putting the daggers in Duncan's Bedroom'; 'Monks giving drink to Pilgrims' by Louis Haghe, and the heads of two greyhounds in profile by Sir Edwin Landseer—'Of extraordinary truth and broad and masterly treatment.'[3]

William Bashall, a founder and partner of the textile firm of Bashall and Boardman at Farington,[4] was a collector of 'taste and discrimination' and possessed many works of the English school which he had commissioned or purchased from the artists themselves, not waiting for the dealer's sign of approval. His collection was hung in the lower rooms of a mansion 'well-lighted; insomuch that many of the pictures look more fresh than when exhibited'.[5] There were many historical and anecdotal essays here by Maclise, Goodall, Hilton, E. M. Ward, Poole, Frith, and Egg. *The Art Journal* particularly praised Goodall's 'An Episode of the Happier Days of Charles I', 'Josephine Signing the Articles of her Divorce' by E. M. Ward, 'Pericles, Prince of Tyre', one of the major works of P. F. Poole, and 'The New Dress' by Thomas Faed, 'One of those scenes in humble life, in the delineation of which this artist has signalised himself.'[6] There were many landscape and architectural studies by D. Roberts, C. Stanfield, W. Muller, F. R. Lee, and W. Linnell. No English collection was complete without animal studies, and Bashall possessed Ansdell's 'Sheep-washing in the Isle of Skye' and 'Red Deer' by Sir E. Landseer. 'This is a large picture, presenting a family group of three of these animals—a stag, a hind, and a fawn. The expression and attitude of the older animals are that of alarm from the approach of some enemy, human or canine. The fixed attention and startled "pose", especially of the vigilant stag, is a most happy passage of nature.'[7]

When Dr. Waagen visited the estate near Manchester of Samuel Ashton, a merchant, fustian manufacturer, spinner and dyer, he found paintings and watercolours of the English school and 'some

[1] *Ibid.*, p. 43.
[2] *Ibid.*
[3] G. F. Waagen, *Treasures of Art*, III, 415.
[4] Christopher Townson, *The History of Farington* (1893), p. 30.
[5] *The Art Journal*, 1857, p. 206.   [6] *Ibid.*, p. 208.   [7] *Ibid.*

pleasing specimens of the modern French school'.[1] In a small room were several watercolours including Sir David Wilkie's 'Tam O'Shanter'. On the staircase was one of Constable's chief works, a large landscape, with a rainbow, and figures crossing a ford in a boat, in the background the cathedral of Salisbury. In the library was another view of Salisbury executed by Muller. In the drawing room were oils by Egg, Elmore, Calcott, and Turner. The last artist's painting was a study of trees beside a stretch of water. 'In the style of Hobbema. Of airy warmth, but somewhat indistinct.'[2] In the dining room English and French achievements were intermixed. Poole, Stanfield, Collins, Webster, and T. S. Cooper were represented with studies from nature. Dr. Waagen liked them all. He marked T. S. Cooper's 'Three Cows', 'true, powerful, and clear'.[3]

Near Manchester, Dr. Waagen also examined the collection of John Chapman, the majority of whose pictures were of the English and early Dutch schools. The *chef-d'oeuvre* of the dining room was Sir David Wilkie's 'The Rent Day'. 'As regards refinement of motive, individuality of expression, clearness and power of colouring, and solid execution and rendering of forms, this picture, painted in 1809, is the finest I know by the master.'[4] Chapman had paid about £2,000 for it. There were also works by Mulready, Eastlake, Stanfield, Linnell, Landseer, Lee, Webster, Creswick, and Redgrave. A van de Velde, a Steen and a Teniers also found places. Waagen particularly admired Linnell's 'Landscape with Cattle' and two Landseers. The first was 'A black dog, the size of life, watching packages.' 'Signed, and dated 1821, and therefore painted in his nineteenth year. The truth, extraordinary power, and careful execution in a good impasto, show how early the powers of this painter were developed.'[5] The second canvas was a study of three dogs watching a ferret who was unearthing a weasel. Another ferret was in a cage with an iron grating. 'Of the most delicate observation of nature, especially the white dog. . . .'[6] In the drawing room were works by Callcott, Maclise, Webster, Herbert, and Turner. The Turners were 'Fishmarket on the Shore' and a landscape 'in which he has borrowed the lovely scenery of Sicily. High mountains of fine lines and a waterfall, with the Rape of Proserpine, very cleverly introduced. The whole conception is grand, the lighting and warm evening sky splendid, and the execution very fine,'[7] although the whole effect is somewhat busy.

John Naylor, a partner in the banking firm of Leyland and Bullins, over the years amassed a fine collection of oil paintings and drawings, which were hung at Leighton Hall, Welshpool, Montgomeryshire. Dr. Waagen particularly admired Sir Charles Eastlake's

---

[1] Waagen, *Treasures of Art*, III, 415.
[2] *Ibid.*, p. 416. [3] *Ibid.*, p. 417. [4] *Ibid.*
[5] *Ibid.*, p. 418. [6] *Ibid.*, p. 419. [7] *Ibid.*, pp. 419–20.

study of Christ weeping over Jerusalem; two works of Turner: a view of Venice and a mist-enshrouded harbour; 'A Circassian Slave-market' by Sir William Allan, and three awe-inspiring canvases by John Martin: 'The Feast of Belshazzar', 'Joshua with his Host', and 'The Flight into Egypt', with their wild rocky landscapes, huge architecture, and threatening clouds. The banker also owned works by Landseer, Cooper, Wilkie, Collins, Leslie, and Ansdell,[1] which he generously shared with his fellow citizens of Liverpool on such an occasion as the *soirée*, given by the Mayor and Mrs. Lloyd in the Town Hall, in September 1854 which Hawthorne and his wife attended. 'It was quite brilliant; the public rooms being really magnificent; and adorned . . . with a large collection of pictures belonging to Mr. Naylor. They were mostly (I believe entirely) of modern artists,—of Turner, Wilkie, Landseer, and others of the best English painters. Turner's seemed too airy to have been done by mortal hands.'[2]

John Miller of Liverpool, 'the most open-handed of merchants; and the most loveable of Scotchmen and picture collectors'[3] appears in all studies of the Pre-Raphaelite movement. Many fine paintings of Millais were to be found at one time or another in his possession, and Millais, Holman Hunt, and Madox Brown were all occasional visitors at his house. He took considerable interest in the Pre-Raphaelite artists and their careers apart from Liverpool. Thus he did yeoman service in collecting and lending pictures for the exhibition of their works at Russell Place in 1858, or was, as Madox Brown put it, 'an indefatigable recruiting sergeant'. As a judge of the sort of pictures he liked, he had few equals, and his criticisms, quite as much as his patronage, must have been of considerable value to the artists with whom he was on intimate terms. Ford Madox Brown, in his diary of 1856, gives the following description of Mr. Miller and his house:

This Miller is a jolly, kind old man with streaming white hair, fine features, and a beautiful keen eye like Mulready's; a rich brogue, a pipe of cavendish, and a smart rejoinder, with a pleasant word for every man, woman, and child he meets, are characteristics of him. . . . His house is full of pictures, even to the kitchen. Many pictures he has at all his friends' houses, and his house at Bute is also filled with the inferior ones. Many splendid Linnells, a fine Turner, and a good Constable, are among the most marked of his collection, plus a host of good pictures by Liverpool artists—Davis, Tonge, and Windus chiefly.[4]

The immediate helpful result of this Liverpool visit for Brown was

---

[1] *Ibid.*, pp. 241–2.
[2] Hawthorne, p. 127. John Naylor's younger brother, Richard, a partner in the same firm, also accumulated a valuable collection of pictures and *objets d'art*, which he arranged at Hooton Hall, Cheshire.
[3] William Michael Rossetti, *Some Reminiscences* (London, 1906), I, 226.
[4] F. M. Hueffer, *Ford Madox Brown* (London, 1896), pp. 136–7.

Miller's purchase of his 'English Fireside' for 80 guineas from the Academy's exhibition. Miller had begun acquiring Pre-Raphaelite works earlier in the fifties. He had bought Deverell's 'As You Like It' in 1854 and earlier had given Rossetti some hopes of patronage. He had several pictures by Millais: 'Wedding Cards', 'The Blind Girl', 'Autumn Leaves', and two early works, 'Cymon and Iphigenia' and 'Capture of the Inca of Peru'. He also had Henry Wallis's 'Fireside Reverie'. In 1857, Miller lent 'The Blind Girl' to the Liverpool Academy exhibition where it gained the prize. Every year since 1851, the prize had gone to one of the Pre-Raphaelites or an artist who showed their influences in his work.[1] This time it proved too much for a rival faction within the academy, which under W. G. Herdman, set up an opposition organization that held annual exhibitions for several years and in doing so undermined the Academy, which ceased to hold exhibitions after 1867. Miller sold his pictures at Christie's in May 1858. His place as a vigorous supporter of the Pre-Raphaelites was taken by George Rae of Birkenhead who was very active in the sixties and seventies.[2]

God's word, nature's beauties, and the nation's history drew responses from 'Manchester men' and 'Liverpool gentlemen' and influenced their choice of art. The collection of Disraeli's Millbank reflected these influences and was in many ways typical of those made by the men of the North in the forties and fifties. Millbank's dining room walls were covered with pictures of the modern English school. He

understand no other he was wont to say, and he found that many of his friends who did, bought a great many pleasing pictures that were copies, and many originals that were displeasing. He loved a fine landscape by Lee, that gives him the broad plains, the green lands and running streams of his own land, a group of animals by Landseer, as full of speech and sentiment as if they were designed by Aesop, above all he delighted in the household humour and homely pathos by Wilkie. And if a higher tone of imitation pleased him, he could gratify it without difficulty among his favourite masters. He possessed some fine specimens of Etty worthy of Venice when it was alive; he could muse amid the twilight ruins of ancient cities raised by the enigmatic pen of Danby, or accompany a group of fair Neapolitans to a festival by the genial aid of Uwins.[3]

Lancashire collectors often made particular efforts to place the local artists in their homes. Early in the nineteenth century, Roscoe and his friends not only aided Gibson but they also encouraged Crouchley, a sculptor of lesser talents. Samuel Austin, the landscape artist, was well acquainted with Roscoe, the Rathbones, the

---

[1] Mary Bennett, 'A Checklist of Pre-Raphaelite Pictures exhibited at Liverpool 1846–67, and some of their Northern Collectors', *Burlington Magazine*, CV (November, 1963), p. 489.

[2] See Appendix for a description of the collections of a lesser known enthusiast.

[3] Benjamin Disraeli, *Coningsby* (New York, 1962), p. 188.

Lawrences, the Custs of Leasowe and other well-known families of or near Liverpool. The venerable Roscoe wrote the following impromptu epigram for the artist, in an album dated 30th March 1830, a year before his (Roscoe's) death:

> Tho faint the line that flows with sable stream,
> And frail the paper that receives my name,
> Yet may they still preserve their worthless trust,
> When this still frailer hand returns to dust.[1]

Although in Victorian Liverpool there were many collectors of the works of local artists, perhaps the outstanding name was Miller, who favoured Davis, Tonge, and Windus. He encouraged Davis to abandon figure painting and to devote himself to landscape. He was among the first and most enthusiastic supporters of Windus, Liverpool's interesting Pre-Raphaelite, encouraging him to go up to London in order to broaden his experience. While there, Windus saw Millais's 'Carpenter's Shop', and became a warm friend of the Brotherhood. Holman Hunt's 'Two Gentlemen of Verona', seen shortly afterwards, completed the conversion which also embraced Davis and other Liverpool artists. It was from this period and under these circumstances, that the Liverpool Academy began to invite the exhibition of Pre-Raphaelite works, and to allot them the annual prize.

A few artists found support in Manchester at the end of the eighteenth century. The paintings of Joseph Parry, better known as 'old Parry' and traditionally considered the father of art in the area, appealed to such businessmen as Otho Hulme, Horatio Barton, and David Holt. Parry's best pictures were familiar incidents, romanticised: country wakes, fairs, and gypsy groups, though he went beyond his depth when he occasionally attempted large historical canvases in the manner of West. John Ralston, the son of an engraver to calico printers and a pupil of Parry, did landscapes in a Wilsonesque manner, while he also made many copies from Dutch pictures for his early and liberal patron, John Astley, the portrait painter, friend of Reynolds, husband of wealthy women, and master of Dukinfield Lodge in Cheshire. Ralston thoroughly mastered the details of marine architecture, and his vessels were well drawn and firmly placed upon the water. Joshua Shaw, believed to be a native of Manchester, specialised in landscapes, excelling in effects of light and shadow. He gained the patronage of David Holt and his work gradually arose in public estimation, until at length he received 50 or 60 guineas for a medium-size canvas. Daniel Stringer of Knutsford, a portrait and historical painter, occasionally resided in Manchester, where he received encouragement from Thomas Kershaw, among others, who introduced the artist to Northcote and

---

[1] H. M. Marillier, *The Liverpool School of Painters* (London, 1904), p. 58.

also to Hazlitt, who mentions him in one of his essays as 'Poor Dan Stringer' and goes on to lament that 'Cheshire Ale and the company of Cheshire Squires'[1] robbed the world of one of its finest geniuses.

Farington, ever on the watch for new artists and new patrons, noted in 1797, '[Charles] Towne is much employed at Manchester, has six months' work bespoke—improved much from seeing last Exhibition, never was in London before—was with Loutherbourg and saw him paint—surprised at his exhibition painting—was originally with a coach painter, Towne is a man of coarse, debased manners and conversation—paints cows.'[2] Farington's evaluation is somewhat harsh. As a portrayer of pedigree dogs, horses, and cattle, Towne must be placed among those artists who did very useful work in the provinces. His landscapes are minutely studied and have a Dutch mannerism; animals and figures are put in with diligent and affectionate care.

Certain Manchester men appreciated the caricatures of the 'Lancashire Hogarth', John Collier, a student of folk dialect who worked under the pseudonym of Tim Bobbin and whose chief published work was the engravings of *The Passions Delineated* (1773). He was 'a small schoolmaster, a provincial, entirely popular artist and sign painter'.[3] Ford had only contempt for Peter Turner who was making a collection of his works. 'This Gentleman is remarkable for his refined taste in collecting, being a great admirer of the genuine works of an Artist of low humour and little merit . . . which he purchases—having a long purse—at any price that he can obtain them. . . .'[4]

The patronage of Liverseege was truly a Lancashire project in the eighteen thirties. He exhibited three small pictures of banditti at the first exhibition of the Royal Manchester Institution, but did not find instant acclaim. Only after those zealous patrons of the English school, Vernon and Wells, had commissioned works, did Manchester men become enthusiastic patrons. Benjamin Hick of Bolton bought 'The Inquiry' from the easel and

he immediately appreciated the man, became his warm supporter, and not only bought his pictures himself, but induced his friends to do the same. 'He is my best friend', said the grateful Artist with emotion. . . .

Give honour where honour is due, and Bolton has the undoubted honour of supporting the genius of Liverseege and of rendering the path towards fame comparatively an easy and pleasant one. Mr. Hick bought his next Picture, 'The Black Dwarf', also from the easel, and 'Captain Macheath', from the exhibition of the Royal Manchester Institution where it had hung in company with the 'The Betrothed' until nearly the close of the Exhibition without a purchaser, Mr. Hick's friend, Mr. Dobson of Bolton buying the

---

[1] Quoted in *Catalogue of the First Exhibition of the Works of Local Artists* (*Living and Deceased*), (Manchester, 1857), pp. 7-8.

[2] Farington, I, 211.

[3] Antal, p. 183.

[4] Ford, p. 47.

latter, and at the same time commissioning a portrait group. Peter Rothwell, Esq. (Mr. Hick's partner in business) became the owner by commission of the 'Othello and Desdemona' and 'The Gravediggers'.[1]

IV. A TRIUMPH FOR LANCASHIRE

In the fifties, the majority of the leading patrons of Lancashire continued to believe that a knowledge of art and the development of taste began with the Old Masters. They wished to view the supreme achievements of the artists of earlier periods, but they no longer wanted to be ridiculed as collectors of forgeries. Their better taste and judgment is revealed in the planning and execution of the Art Treasures Exhibition of 1857 in Manchester. Drawing its inspiration from the Paris International Exhibition of 1855, the Manchester endeavour was a supplement to the Great Exhibition of 1851.[2]

When an inaugural meeting was held under civic auspices early in 1856 the mayor of Manchester became chairman of a council formed of more than 700 patrons, who underwrote the endeavour, and by May royal patronage had been successfully obtained. Then an executive committee, which the Royal Manchester Institution asked to carry out the scheme, was appointed and the work of organisation began. Lord Ellesmere, the chairman, and after his death, Lord Overstone, were assisted by Thomas Fairbairn, Thomas Ashton, William Entwisle, Joseph Heron, Edmund Potter, and Sigismund J. Stern, leading members of the business community.[3]

Arrangements were made for the construction of a tremendous set of exhibition buildings, designed by Francis Fowke, on the large cricket ground of Sir Humphrey de Trafford at Old Trafford, and the committee and its assistants began seeking the finest works of art. They were given substantial aid by the Prince Consort, who was generous with loans from the royal collections and who helped with the initial approaches to private owners for particular works. In a letter to Lord Ellesmere, intended for publication, Prince Albert emphasised that a purposeful educational plan would elicit the greatest response.

In my opinion the solution will be found in the satisfactory proof of the usefulness of the undertaking. The mere gratification of public curiosity, & the giving an intellectual entertainment to the dense population of a particular locality, would be praiseworthy in itself, but hardly sufficient to convince the owners of works of art that it is their duty at a certain risk and inconvenience, to send their choicest Treasures to Manchester for Exhibition.

---

[1] *Catalogue of the Exhibition of the Works of Local Artist* (*Living and Deceased*) (Manchester, 1857), p. 7. A list of proud possessors of the forties precedes *Engravings from the works of Henry Liverseege* (London, n.d.).

[2] S. D. Cleveland, 'Introduction', *Art Treasures Centenary: European Old Masters* (Manchester, 1957), p. vii.

[3] *The Art Journal*, 1st June 1857, p. 185.

That national usefulness might however be found in the *Educational direction* which may be given to the whole scheme.—No country invests a larger amount of Capital in works of art of all Kinds, than England, & in none, almost, is so little done for art Education! If the collection you propose to form were made to illustrate the History of Art in a chronological & systematic arrangement, it would speak powerfully to the Public mind, & enable in a practical way the most uneducated eye to gather the lessons which ages of though & scientific research have attempted to abstract. . . .

As far as Painting is concerned, I enclose a Catalogue exhibiting all the different schools. . . .[1]

If such a Catalogue for instance, were to be filled up with the specimens of the best paintings by the different Masters enumerated in it, which exist in this country, I feel certain that the committee would come with very different powers of persuasion & a very different claim to attention to their owners, than when the demand for the loan of certain of their pictures were apparently dependent upon mere accident or Caprice.—A person who would not otherwise be inclined to part with a picture would probably shrink from refusing it, if he knew that his doing so tended to mar the realisation of a great national object.[2]

The Committee accepted this good advice, using such guides as Dr. Waagen's *Treasures of Art in Great Britain*. George Scharf, who later became the first director of the National Portrait Gallery, as art secretary, assumed the responsibility for the organisation of the Old Master's section and wrote the materials for the catalogue.[3] The paintings were representative of both the old and the new taste, for there were not only the works of the long-praised masters of the sixteenth and seventeenth centuries, but also a representative group of primitives, admired now by many, including the Prince Consort.[4] The great collectors were generous lenders: Queen Victoria and her husband; the Dukes of Portland, Richmond, Newcastle, Manchester, and Bedford; the Earls of Marlborough, Spencer, Stamford, Warwick, Derby, Ellesmere, Carlisle, Darnley, and Pembroke; and Lords Ward, Lyttleton, Overstone, de Tabley, and Northwick. The Marquess of Hertford made a contribution which filled one gallery. Manchester revealed her devotion to the English achievement by organising a British portrait gallery and a comprehensive display of British painting and sculpture. There were fifty Reynoldses and a great many Hogarths.[5] Townsmen took particular pride in a

[1] This was a copy of the list of schools and masters of painting which Prince Albert, Eastlake, and others had made up for the National Gallery.
[2] Prince Albert, London, 3rd July 1856, Letter to Lord Ellesmere, MA 1907, The Pierpont Morgan Library.
[3] Watercolours and prints were selected by Edward Holmes, and J. M. Kemble chose the Celtic and Anglo-Saxon antiquities.
[4] Outstanding were the Wilton Diptych, 'The Agony in the Garden' by both Mantegna and Bellini, the Rokeby Venus by Velasquez, Titian's 'The Rape of Europa', Rubens's 'Prometheus', Raphael's 'Three Graces', and works by Botticelli, Michelangelo, Mabuse, Rembrandt, and Van Dyck.
[5] All the great English watercolourists, led by Turner, were here.

comprehensive exhibit of the work of Manchester artists that was mounted in the new wing of the Peel Park Museum in Salford.[1] 'On the whole it was a superb exhibition, and the first really great general exhibition of works of art.'[2]

Some visitors, such as Hawthorne, examined the treasures with great care: 'I must go again and again, many times more, and will take each day some one department, and so endeavour to get some real use and improvement out of what I see.'[3] He questioned, however, the seriousness of the majority of the crowd: 'They were nearly all middling-class people; the Exhibition, I think, does not reach the lower classes at all; in fact, it could not reach them, nor their betters either, without a great deal of study to help it out.'[4]

One who did benefit from this exhibition was the young artist, Frederic Shields, struggling in Manchester against a grim background of poverty, for, here, he made his first acquaintance with what he described as 'a marvellous unparalleled gathering'[5] of pictures, the art of the Pre-Raphaelites. Holman Hunt's 'Hireling Shepherd' and 'Strayed Sheep', some of Millais' best work, including 'Autumn Leaves', and Arthur Hughes' 'April Love' were discovered and were a strong influence upon his subsequent artistic development. Here, also, Shields studied 'Christ Washing Peter's Feet', by the artist who later became his close friend, Ford Madox Brown. About this time Shields began those exquisite water-colour drawings of country life, such as 'The Holly Gatherers', which appealed to the collector of careful studies of nature. In the early sixties appeared the two great works that established his reputation as an important Pre-Raphaelite illustrator, Bunyan's *Pilgrim's Progress* and Defoe's *Journal of the Plague Year*. Later came the major efforts in oil and fresco, religious in theme, so close to Holman Hunt's pietistic studies. So much that was important in his later career stemmed from the formative influence of the Great Exhibition of 1857.

APPENDIX

A curious little book by H.S.G. (Henry Steinthal Gibbs, 1829–94), *Autobiography of a Manchester Cotton Manufacturer; or Thirty Years'*

---

[1] *Catalogue of the First Exhibition of the Works of Local Artists (Living and Deceased)* (Manchester, 1857). Sir James Kay-Shuttleworth wanted to have an exhibition at Burnley in the same year to illustrate the history of Lancashire. 'His scheme was of a very comprehensive character, and included a pictorial illustration of Lancashire. . . . All the mechanical inventions that have enriched Lancashire would also have been represented.' Sir James attempted to induce Philip G. Hamerton to act as his chief lieutenant. The young artist refused and the project came to nothing. Philip Gilbert Hamerton, *Autobiography and Memoir* (Boston, 1896), pp. 186–7.

[2] Winslow Ames, *Prince Albert and Victorian Taste* (New York, 1968), pp. 150–1.

[3] Hawthorne, p. 549.

[4] *Ibid.*, p. 551.   [5] Mills, p. 42.

Experience of Manchester,[1] cast in a semi-fictional form, contains interesting references to the art interests and the art acquisitions of a less celebrated Lancashire collector. While a young man at Kearsley, learning the fundamentals of the cotton trade, H.S.G. began a modest collection of watercolours. Many evenings were spent with an older friend, the manager of a chemical plant, who enjoyed literature, music, and old engravings, his portfolio containing many fine impressions of Wille, William Woollet, and Raphael Morghan.

Expensive works of art were beyond the reach of H.S.G., but the search for choice prints of fine quality became 'one of the keenest pursuits of my leisure moments'. Many hours were spent with 'Mr. Rareworthy', a Manchester printseller,[2] discussing the merits and defects of prints and drawings. Among favourite purchases from this dealer 'who had a discriminating love of the beautiful' were a folio of engravings from the works of Reynolds and 'the first David Cox drawing I ever possessed, of course for a small sum. I paid him three pounds for it, and kept it for nearly thirty years. The subject was called "Rowsley".'[3]

After collecting for sixteen years and crowding his walls with drawings and pictures, H.S.G. decided a sale was in order, if he were to continue collecting. Christie and Manson handled the transaction:

I did not regard the sale as a particularly good one, although some of the drawings brought moderately high figures. A little drawing of Corsica, by J. M. W. Turner, measuring about seven inches by five, which had once belonged to the late Canon Kingsley, realized 100 guineas, and was bought by Messrs. Agnew, from whom I had purchased it. This was a lovely little drawing, depicting the shore of the Mediterranean, and high up was the evening star, reflected in the ripples of the water. . . . A Meadow Scene, with Cattle, by that prince of painters, David Cox, brought 140 guineas, three of Sam Prout's architectural subjects sold for £256. Two of Fred Taylor's figure compositions for £213; and a very small drawing, exquisitely painted by George Cattermole obtained 80 guineas, and another by the same artist £111. One of Clarkson Stanfield's highly finished drawings sold for 105 guineas. The subject was Mount St. Michael, Cornwall, and it was considered to be one of the most perfect specimens of Stanfield's work. I purchased it, with a vast number of other fine drawings, from the late W. Smith, of Messrs. Grundy and Smith.

In this sale there was a remarkable drawing, by De Wint, of a hayfield, with figures resting. It had all the appearance of a highly-finished work, but in reality was made up of broad washes. . . . Many drawings brought considerably more money than I gave for them, whilst others did not fare

---

[1] Manchester, 1887. He died in Melbourne, Australia (*Textile Manufacturer*, May 1894, p. 204).

[2] This is probably John Rowbotham, the dealer friend of many artists and collectors.

[3] H.S.G., p. 128.

so well. The collection contained a hundred works, the whole of which were by good men, and included thirty-nine drawings by David Cox, five beautiful specimens of De Wint, seven of Samuel Prout's architectural subjects, eight fine drawings by George Cattermole, and four of George Barrett's classical compositions.[1]

Several times afterwards H.S.G. parted with collections with varied results. Occasionally he sold works privately; once a transaction with a well-known firm brought several thousand pounds. He accumulated fine old and contemporary prints, which were also sent to the auction rooms. Included in these lots were fine early impressions of Sir Joshua Reynolds' works, practically all of the engravings of Sir Edwin Landseer's works, and the famous reproductions by Charles Turner, Willmore, Lupton and Le Keux of J. M. W. Turner:

The thirteen cartoons by F. J. Shields, representing the 'Triumph of Faith', which I bought from that artist, were put into this sale, and were bought in. Subsequently I sold them to some gentlemen of spirit in the city, who presented them to the Royal Institution in Mosley Street, where they now hang.[2]

The disastrous downturn of trade in the late seventies forced H.S.G. to sell the collection of his mature judgment; then, to liquidate his firm Turnbull and Gibbs, manufacturers of domestic cloth; and finally, to seek a new life in Australia. Agnew's was so impressed with this collection that a combination of exhibition and sale was arranged, opening in March 1878. 'Such an exhibition, with a view of sale on the part of the client, was a departure from the rules of the eminent firm who conducted it.'[3]

Among the 122 works forming the collection, the landscape artists were predominant. Thirty-seven paintings of David Cox; ten, of Peter De Wint; seven, of George Barrett and George Cattermole; five, of Copley Fielding, David Roberts, and William Hunt; four, of Samuel Prout, three, of F. Taylor; and one, of J. M. W. Turner were hung. The collection also contained works by Briton Riviere, Luke Fildes, Francis Danby and Frederic Shields.

When the depressed condition of the Lancashire industry of 1878 is taken into consideration, the exhibition was a success. In its earlier stage there was a rush of visitors and customers. It was only when the great strike of the Preston cotton spinners occurred that a check was put to the business which commenced so auspiciously.[4]

---

[1] *Ibid.*, pp. 187–8.   [2] *Ibid.*, p. 189.
[3] *Ibid.*, p. 208.   [4] *Ibid.*, p. 209.

L

CHAPTER VIII

THE INFLUENCE OF THE PROVINCES

By the middle of the nineteenth century, the many elements that foster art patronage were present in Lancashire. Entrepreneurs such as Sir John Gladstone, Benjamin Hick, and Thomas Miller had accumulated sizeable fortunes, that provided surplus capital for the purchase of paintings, sculpture, and other works of art. The population of Liverpool and Manchester, as well as the adjoining cities and towns, constantly increasing, was large enough to support art programmes and institutions, and the railway easily brought people from the outlying areas to the cultural centres.[1] After the distress of the forties, the industries of Lancashire expanded and civic-minded leaders of the North, confident that economic growth, would continue, felt challenged to attempt greatness in other areas, public libraries, museums and art galleries. The social mobility of Lancashire society also created a favourable setting for the arts. In the largely Philistine world of the middle class, much given to good, if not gracious, living, there were some who were intent on moving as quickly as possible to the upper strata of society, and they believed that there was no quicker way than by supporting artists and forming collections of art.[2]

Old Masters of dubious lineage were definitely out; the men of the North favoured English art. Leading periodicals such as *The Art Journal* praised the collections of Henry Cooke, Thomas Miller, and Benjamin Hick as lavishly as they did the collections of Old Masters of the nobility. This trio, serious collectors, were joined by other men who collected only for fashion's sake. Nevertheless, their expenditure was generous, *The Art Journal* declaring that Lancashire was a district rich in English art and that painters were receiving more than liberal support from the neighbourhood of Preston and Manchester.[3] Scattered throughout other areas of provincial England were keen patrons of the national school of art. 'The real leadership in patronage of living British artists had passed at about the time of Thomas Lawrence's death [1830] to "unheard-of" provincial collectors such as Vernon and Sheepshanks—and this in the end was good for the nation.'[4]

---

[1] See 'The Impact of Railways on Society' in Michael Robbins, *The Railway Age in Britain and Its Impact on the World* (London, 1965).

[2] A commonplace idea, discussed in many works, such as those of Thorstein Veblen, Thomas Ashcroft, and E. W. Bovill, *English Country Life* (Oxford, 1962), p. 76.

[3] *The Art Journal*, 1857, p. 206.   [4] Ames, p. 173. See also Appendix.

The collectors of the North particularly appreciated works of art that portrayed nature in her many aspects. For them, the painting that captured characteristic features of the country's rivers, vales, and shores revealed the deepest truths, the idealism and morality of the English way of life. Often an artist was asked to repeat a work because it was considered such a fresh and truthful depiction of an aspect of nature. For example, F. R. Lee painted several versions of 'The Avenue', a landscape in which a line of forest trees 'retire in perspective, the road here and there lighted by flakes of sunshine with admirable truth'.[1] The highest compliment that artist and collector could receive was that the work was 'true to nature'. Time and again, the phrase is found in the pages of *The Art Journal*, the volumes of Dr. Waagen, and other Victorian studies. For Reynolds and the artists and connoisseurs of the eighteenth century, thought was shown in the artist's interpretation of subject. To Ruskin it was revealed in the anlysis of nature. This prophet often stated that the pale sheet of a perceptive watercolourist, such as Turner,[2] might reveal greater truth and beauty than the most highly finished canvas. Ruskin's ideas, infused with a sense of religious morality, influenced the taste of many English collectors.

To many patrons, the most important aspect of a work of art was its moral tone. The moral qualities of the paintings of the Roman Nazarenes, Peter Cornelius, Joseph Fuhrich, Frederick Overbeck, Franz Pforr, and Schnorr von Carolsfeld, had a profound effect on British opinion in the thirties and forties. That element in society that can be labelled 'Young England' wanted a style of painting that was heroic, chaste, and devout. Pugin, 'the apostle of Gothic principles in architecture',[3] considered Overbeck a 'prince of Christian painters,'[4] and zealots like him favoured the establishment of an English Nazarene school. John Rogers Herbert was one of the few English artists who came near to the Teutonic style, though, undoubtedly, the most purely Nazarene was William Dyce, 'a kind of Puseyite Pugin, a chief advisor in things artistic to the ecclesiologists and Young Oxford'.[5] Rossetti's painting of the 'Girlhood of the Virgin Mary', the earliest picture to be exhibited with the initials P.R.B., had something of the flatness and light colours of the Nazarenes and Dyce, and the public from the first associated the mysterious initials with medievalism and the German school.[6]

Often the pictures that were most heartily praised at the London and provincial exhibitions were those that expressed 'earnestness',

[1] *The Art Journal*, 1857, p. 208.

[2] Ruskin's activities as a collector of Turner's works are interestingly presented in Luke Hermann, *Ruskin and Turner* (New York, 1969).

[3] Peter Kidson, Peter Murray, and Paul Thompson, *A History of English Architecture* (Harmondsworth, 1965), p. 289.

[4] Quoted in Keith Andrews, *The Nazarenes* (Oxford, 1964), p. 78.

[5] Quentin Bell, *Victorian Artists* (Cambridge, Mass., 1967), p. 23.

[6] Boase, p. 280.

'passion', and 'feelings'. Everywhere critics and patrons pleaded loudly and vigorously for the moral in art. 'The art that has no relevancy to actual life, the passing of God's truth and the facts of man's nature as if they had no existence, the art that does not serve to ennoble and purify and help us in our life-long struggle with sin and evil, however beautiful, however serene and majestic, is false and poor and contemptible.'[1] When Edward Lear exhibited his large picture 'Cedars of Lebanon' in Liverpool in 1861 a critic there wrote: 'Mr. Lear has in this great picture not only achieved a professional success, but he has also conferred an obligation of the highest order on the whole Christian world.'[2] Thomas Plint of Leeds, stockbroker, Nonconformist leader and art patron, commissioned Ford Madox Brown in 1856 to complete his canvas 'Work', stipulating that he introduce 'Both Carlyle and Kingsley and change one of the four fashionable young ladies into a quiet, earnest, holy-looking one holding a book or two, and tracts. I want this put in, for I am much interested in this work myself, and know those who are.'[3]

Many less famous works in the great Northern collections were moral lessons on canvas. Vivid examples in the Thomas Miller collection were: 'L'Enfant du Regiment' by Millais with its wounded child covered by a soldier's coat, resting on a tomb; 'Jacob and Rachael' by Dyce based on the beautiful line, 'And Jacob kissed Rachael, and lifted up his voice and wept' and Herbert's 'Sir Thomas More in Prison, visited by his Daughter'.[4] Henry Cooke's collection of watercolours contained Herbert's drawing of 'Doge Donaldo and his Family', where the warrior-ruler shows the armour in which he bravely fought; 'The Mother's Blessing' and 'The Mother's Pride' by Topham, hymns of sentimentality.[5] William Bashall's collection was filled with such moral essays as: Sant's 'The Child Timothy' and 'The Infant Samuel'; Eastlake's 'Gaston de Foix taking leave of his wife before the battle of Ravenna'; 'The Cruel Sister' by Faed; and Herbert's 'The Crusader's Wife'.[6]

The thousands who flocked to the annual exhibitions in Liverpool and Manchester are testimony that there was great interest in the achievements of English artists. These provincial exhibitions not only provided the middle class with an opportunity of viewing the works of the leading artists, but also deepened their knowledge and appreciation of art. Artists were given opportunities both to extend their reputations and to increase sales. The cultivated looked with

---

[1] T. D. Coleridge writing in the *Christian Remembrancer*, April 1854, quoted in W. L. Burn, *The Age of Equipoise* (London, 1964), p. 40. For a complete review of the subject, see Henry Ladd, *Victorian Morality of Art* (New York, 1932).
[2] Quoted in Vivien Noakes, *Edward Lear: The Life of a Wanderer* (Boston, Mass., 1969), p. 188.
[3] Hueffer, pp. 111–12.   [4] *The Art Journal*, 1857, p. 41.
[5] *Ibid.*, p. 43.   [6] *Ibid.*, pp. 206–8.

respect upon those artists who had won the Academy's prize at Liverpool or one of the Heywood medals at Manchester, while time and again, *The Art Union* emphasised that the Northern market was a lucrative one, in which good pictures never failed to move. In 1840, this journal noted that at Liverpool such established artists as Thomas Webster, Copley Fielding, T. S. Cooper, F. R. Lee, George Lance, A. Cooper, and J. Stark had sold works.[1] In each succeeding year, the English artist was assisted by private sales or purchases made by the art unions. Paintings that were poorly placed at the exhibition at the Royal Academy often 'emerged' at the provincial exhibits. When Frith found no purchaser for one early work, a scene from the 'Merry Wives of Windsor', he 'sent it to Liverpool, where it must have been seen, for it found a purchaser for a hundred pounds.'[2]

After the quality of the exhibitions had improved at Manchester, the *Art Union* in 1845 disclosed that 'the Exhibition has been largely aided by contributions from London, . . . with many we have already formed an acquaintance, and we are induced to believe—not only from the number marked "sold", but from the rightly-directed spirit in the "rich town"—that a large portion of them will be retained in Manchester. . . .'[3] In 1847 the same journal noted that Liverpool was a safe and sane market for works of art and that the merchants of that vast emporium spent money liberally on the purchase of objects of elegance and refinement, revealing much taste and discrimination in their selections.[4] The artists of Lancashire were also given ample opportunities to obtain the patronage of the public at these exhibitions. The local newspapers and *The Art Union* often made it a point in their reviews of the exhibitions to single out the best works of local artists.

The men of the North usually bought pictures at the exhibitions or from such influential dealers as Agnews, although the more serious might commission pictures. Miller of Preston liked to buy paintings from the artist's studio,[5] and Miller of Liverpool gave many commissions to artists, including the Liverpool artists, Davis, Tonge, and Windus. While the number of men such as Sheepshanks, Vernon, and the Millers who collected art because they loved it was relatively small, there were many who were interested in English art and with so much money and so many new homes in the North needing pictures, high and low motives blended to bring vigorous patronage to artists. Ruskin emphasised that low motives predominated. 'Enormous sums are spent annually by this country in what is called patronage of art, but in what is for the most part

[1] *The Art Union*, 15th January 1840, p. 6.
[2] Frith, I, 100.
[3] *The Art Union*, 1st August 1845, p. 266.
[4] *Ibid.*, 1st October 1847.   [5] Frith, I, 261.

merely buying what strikes our fancies. True and judicious patronage there is indeed; many a work of art is bought by those who do not care for its possession, to assist the struggling artist, or relieve the unsuccessful one. But for the most part, I fear we are too much in the habit of buying simply what we like best, wholly irrespective of any good to be done, either to the artist or to the schools of the country.'[1]

Many of the educated public of Lancashire were faithful supporters of the exhibitions and lectures on the arts at the Royal Institution, the literary and philosophical societies and the mechanics' institutes because of their conception of taste. In the eighteenth century problems of taste were one aspect of the study of philosophy and writers on this subject declared time and again that their ultimate aim was to assist in the development of more moral behaviour. The influence of such writers as Shaftesbury and Reynolds appeared in the doctrine of morality in art preached powerfully by Pugin and Ruskin. The former proclaimed that Gothic architecture was a means of grace, a way to salvation;[2] while the latter intoned, 'Taste is not only a part and index of morality; it is the only morality.'[3]

Shaftesbury and those who followed him did not doubt that there was a standard of taste that was applicable for all areas of the arts and a true beauty for which an appreciation could be developed once the general rules were learned. Correct taste could be taught by various media: books, exhibitions, lectures, and discussions. Since the ultimate goal of such an educational programme was greater refinement for both the individual and the state, the problems of taste were directly related to the problems of the healthy social fabric of the state. The nation's art, which was the basis for the development of taste, had to be permeated with moral and spiritual truths if a sound taste was to develop.

In the nineteenth century, Ruskin time and again returned to the subject of art and morality in his lectures and writings. In conjunction with the Art Treasures Exhibition of 1857, he delivered at the Manchester Athenaeum the pair of lectures that he called *The Political Economy of Art*. Before a large and fashionable audience, he discussed the problem of discovering and cultivating artistic genius. The patron should give praise, monies, and above all moral direction to the artist. The ultimate aim was 'to make, in the noble sense of the word, gentlemen of them; that is to say, to take care that their minds receive such training that in all they paint they shall see and

[1] John Ruskin, *Lectures on Architecture and Painting, Delivered at Edinburgh, in November, 1853*, Vol. XII of *The Works of Ruskin* (London, 1904), p. 68.

[2] Augustus Welby Northmore Pugin, *Contrasts, or a Parallel between the Noble Edifices of the Fourteenth and Fifteenth Centuries and Similar buildings of the present day* (London, 1836).

[3] Quoted in J. H. Buckley, *The Victorian Temper* (London, 1951), p. viii. Mr. Buckley does not give the source of this quotation.

feel the noblest things.'[1] He went on to denounce unbridled competition and invited the governing classes to pay greater attention to the social and economic needs of the governed in order that art might flourish in a healthy national environment. In the most moving passages of the lectures, he asked the men of the North to look beyond their well-kept homes and to contribute to the restoration of those art treasures of Italy which were ravished by decay, gateways built by the greatest sculptors and drawing rooms decorated by Titian and Veronese that now housed rats.

In the early eighteenth century, only the few had opportunities to study and enjoy great works of art. As the century unfolded, the *philosophes* emphasised that art should instruct the many as well as the few and their influence was felt. The Imperial Gallery of Austria, when it was re-opened in the Belvedere Palace, was arranged (to quote from the catalogue of 1783) 'so that it should be as far as possible a source of Instruction and a visual History of Art'.[2] Roscoe and other civic leaders of the North believed that collections of art in their cities could help men develop a connoisseurship that would to a certain degree equal that of the *virtuosi*, who had travelled to Italy, compared the work of the Florentines and the Venetians, and had many other opportunities to examine great works of the ancient and Renaissance cultures. In Roscoe's last years, there were even some who were such enthusiasts for the achievements of English art that they did not believe it was necessary to be deeply involved with the art of past ages.

The leaders of provincial cultural institutions believed that exhibitions of works of art that reflected the finest aspects of nature and emphasised moral truths in a simple and direct way would hasten the development of a finer taste in the working classes. *The Art Union* was enthusiastic when the Liverpool Academy in 1845 extended the exhibition, allowing admission to adults at 2d. each and children for 1d.: 'We trust the experiment will fully answer the expectations and hopes of its wise and generous projectors; this is indeed making Art a teacher of the millions!'[3] The exhibitions, organised at first as money-making devices at the mechanics' institutes, came to be regarded by such patrons as Benjamin Heywood as an important contribution to the creation of 'a new and nobler taste':[4]

It is impossible to say whether their influence was so great as their organizers claimed for them, but their early popularity was almost overwhelming Tens of thousands visited the exhibitions at Manchester and elsewhere and the directors were deeply impressed by the character of the public response. The philanthropists felt that at last something had been done to bring the

---

[1] John Ruskin, '*A Joy For Ever*' (*The Political Economy of Art*), Vol. XVI of *The Works of Ruskin* (London, 1905), p. 34.   [2] Compton, p. 29.
[3] *The Art Union*, January 1846, p. 16.   [4] Tylecote, p. 275.

working classes into touch with their cultural heritage and to stimulate their imagination.[1]

One afternoon at the Art Treasures Exhibition, Hawthorne observed the people who came into the hall after two o'clock when the admission price was 6p: 'The Exhibition was thronged with a class of people who do not usually come in such large numbers. It was both pleasant and touching to see how earnestly some of them sought to get instruction from what they beheld. The English are a good and simple people and take life in earnest.'[2]

When Ruskin testified in 1860 before the Parliamentary Committee investigating the possibility of opening public galleries in the evenings to encourage 'the healthful recreation and improvement of the people',[3] he emphasised that the full appreciation of the treasures of art galleries and museums could come to the working class only with better working conditions, shorter hours, and less competition.

The governing committees of the Royal Institutions, the mechanics' institutes, and the School of Design in Manchester believed that the classes in the fine and applied arts that the institutions sponsored were hastening the development of a finer taste among the managerial and the working classes. Exhibitions of examples of the best products of industry such as that sponsored by the School of Design in Manchester were considered very effective for the development of taste and appreciation, and of moral value, inspiring a sense of self-respect.

Those who were in the forefront of these endeavours, men of wealth and education who insisted on the importance of culture for their communities, often maintained these enterprises against great odds. William Roscoe had shown these men that Renaissance patronage of art and architecture had developed as a result of economic and political forces as well as the enlarged tastes and desires of powerful rulers, merchants, and bankers, while generous patronage had brought benefits to artists, princely houses, and the city-states in the Italy of the Renaissance. Roscoe gave to the men of the North great inspiration. His great justification is to be found in the words of Ramsay Muir, 'that he kept alive other longings of men's minds than that for wealth'.[4] Benjamin Arthur Heywood, Sir John Tobin, Sir John Gladstone, and other civic leaders came to feel a particular kinship with the merchants and bankers of the Italian Renaissance. These men of Lancashire believed, as Roscoe had believed, in the cultural mission of the fine arts and in the responsibility of the educated for bringing men closer to the great traditions of Western art.

---

[1] Tylecote, p. 275. [2] Hawthorne, p. 557.
[3] John D. Rosenberg, *The Darkening Glass: A Portrait of Ruskin's Genius* (New York, 1961), p- 104. [4] *A History of Liverpool* (London, 1907,) p. 17.

APPENDIX

It is interesting to note how many fine Turners were in Lancashire collections. Henry M'Connel (1801–1871), of the great spinning firm of M'Connel & Kennedy,[1] owned one of Turner's most magnificent essays, 'Keelmen heaving in Coals by Night'. 'Commissioned at my special suggestion'[2] by the textile manufacturer as a pendant to his 'Venice' (the 'Venice: Dogana and San Giovanni Maggiore' shown at the Royal Academy in 1834), M'Connel most likely wished the artist to contrast the timeless calm of Venice with the industrial bustle of the river Tyne. Turner responded with a masterpiece, welcoming an industrial landscape 'for its pictorial possibilities, using it to depict the contrast of moonlight and artificial light that had fascinated him in his first exhibited oil'.[3] M'Connel, who sold the two canvases to John Naylor[4] of Welshpool in 1849 before going to America on a business trip, attempted to buy back the 'Moonlight' after his return. 'But his letter in which he asks the new owner "are you irresistibly determined not to part with the Moonlight?" seems to expect the answer that it got.'[5]

John Naylor also possessed 'Cologne—the Arrival of a Packetboat (Evening)', 'Pas de Calais', 'Dutch Fishing Boats', 'Mercury and Argus', and 'Rockets and Blue Lights'.[6]

Walter Thornbury was not only familiar with the Naylor collection, but he also appended to his biography of Turner a careful description by John Hugh of Manchester of his collection of drawings, engravings and oils, which included 'The Grand Canal at Venice', well known by its engraving.[7] In this appendix is also found a list of memorable Turner sales. In 1858 the marvellous collection of watercolours and oils which John Miller of Liverpool had collected was sold at Christie, Manson, & Woods.[8] Another auctioneer sold the interesting collection of Mr. A. Fairrie of Liverpool, which included 'Five Turners; one on Italian subject, an early drawing, and Litchfield and Rochester, both early works; also the "View of Stamford", one of the very best of his watercolours, which was engraved by Miller for the "England and Wales"; and Lucerne, a later drawing, which also has been engraved, but which is as different as possible from the Lucerne at

---

[1] 'In the factory returns of 1833 M'Connel & Co. were employing 1,553 people, over 200 more than any other spinning firm.' C. H. Lee, *A Cotton Enterprise 1795–1840: a history of M'Connel & Kennedy, fine cotton spinners* (Manchester, 1972), p. 152.

[2] *Turner, 1775–1851* (London, 1974), p. 143. This is the catalogue of the massive retrospective of Turner's work held at the Royal Academy.

[3] John Rothenstein and Martin Butlin, *Turner* (New York, 1964), p. 54.

[4] The Turner catalogue refers to 'John Taylor' but this should be John Naylor. See Walter Thornbury, *The Life of J. M. W. Turner, R.A.* (London, 1862), II, 400.

[5] Evelyn Joll, 'Indisputably the first Landscape Painter in Europe', *The Times*, 16th November 1974, p. 11.

[6] Thornbury, p. 400.   [7] *Ibid.*, pp. 398–9.   [8] *Ibid.*, pp. 404–5.

Farnley Hall—one of the most tender and poetical of Turner's poetical works. There is more colour, and greater feeling of atmosphere, in this Lucerne, but there is more exquisite repose and positive beauty about that of Farnley Hall.'[1]

[1] Thornbury, p. 407.

BIBLIOGRAPHY

I. MANUSCRIPTS AND MANUSCRIPT COLLECTIONS

Crozier, Robert. 'Reminiscence of the Manchester School of Design.' Central Reference Library, Manchester.

Ford, William. 'Character of the Different Picture Collectors, in and about Manchester, faithfully and impartially Delineated.' Central Reference Library, Manchester, *circa* 1827.

Gregson Correspondence. Liverpool Record Office.

Holt and Gregson Papers. Liverpool Record Office.

Liverpool Academy of Arts. Council Minute Book. 1830–60. Liverpool Record Office.

Liverpool Literary and Philosophical Society. A bound collection of 30 unpublished papers read before the Society. 1812–27. University of Liverpool Library.

Liverpool Royal Institution. Index to Minute Book. 1822–42. University of Liverpool Library.

Liverpool Royal Institution. Letters concerning gifts and deposits. 1817–51. University of Liverpool Library.

Liverpool Royal Institution. Minute Book of Gallery Committee. 1840–5. University of Liverpool Library.

The Mayer Papers. Liverpool Record Office.

Roscoe Papers. Liverpool Record Office.

Royal Manchester Institution Association for the Patronage of the Fine Arts. Minute Book. Central Reference Library, Manchester.

Royal Manchester Institution. Correspondence. Central Reference Library, Manchester.

Royal Manchester Institution. Council Minute Book. 1823–35. Central Reference Library, Manchester.

Royal Manchester Institution. Council Minute Book. 1835–48. Central Reference Library, Manchester.

Royal Manchester Institution. Exhibition Committee Minute Book. 1832–46. Central Reference Library, Manchester.

Royal Manchester Institution. Lecture Committee Minute Book. 1832–43. Central Reference Library, Manchester.

Royal Manchester Institution. Letters. 1823–32. Central Reference Library, Manchester.

Royal Manchester Institution. Proceedings of the General Meetings. 1823–35. Central Reference Library, Manchester.

Royal Manchester Institution. Proceedings of the General Meetings. 1835–1907. Central Reference Library, Manchester.

II. WORKS WRITTEN IN OR BEFORE 1870

Periodicals and Newspapers:

The Academic. Liverpool, 1821.
The Albion. Liverpool, 1827–8.

Annals of the Fine Arts. 1817–20.
The Architectural Magazine. 1834.
The Artist. 1807–9.
The Art Union: A Monthly Journal of the Fine Arts . . . 1839–48. Continued as
    The Art Journal. 1849–1912.
The Builder. 1843–50.
The Edinburgh Review. 1803–50.
The Exhibition Gazette (Manchester), first series (April–June 1840); second
    series (December 1842–April 1843); third series (December 1844–
    March 1845).
Fraser's Magazine for Town and Country. 1844.
The Gentleman's Magazine. 1780–1833.
The Hermes. 1822–3.
Kaleidoscope. Liverpool, 1818–20.
The Liverpool Magazine. 1816.
The Liverpool Mercury, 1811–50.
The Liverpool and Manchester Quarterly Magazine. 1819.
Manchester Guardian. 1812–50.
Memoirs and Proceedings of the Manchester Literary and Philosophical Society.
    1785– .
The North British Review. 1857.
The Quarterly Review. 1809–50.
The Westminster Review. 1844.

Addresses, Catalogues, and Books:

An Account of the Liverpool Mechanics' and Apprentices' Library . . . Liverpool,
    1824.
*An Account of the Statutes, Busts, Bass-Relieves, Funery Urns and Other Ancient
    Marbles at Ince.* Collected by H.B. Liverpool, 1803.
Aikin, John. *A Description of the Country from Thirty to Forty Miles Round
    Manchester.* London, 1795.
Alison, Archibald. *Essays on the Nature and Principles of Taste.* New York,
    1830.
Baines, Thomas, *History of the Commerce and Town of Liverpool.* 2 vols. London,
    1852.
Ballantine, James. *The Life of David Roberts, R.A.* Edinburgh, 1866.
Barry, Rev. Alfred. *Memoir of the Life and Works of Sir Charles Barry, Architect.*
    London, 1867.
Byng, John (later Fifth Viscount Torrington). *The Torrington Diaries.*
    Edited by C. Bruyn Andrews. London, 1954.
Carey, William. *Cursory Thoughts on the Present State of the Fine Arts; occasioned
    by the founding of the Liverpool Academy; respectfully addressed to Thomas
    Walker, Esq. of Leeds, President of the Northern Society for the Encouragement
    of Arts.* Liverpool, 1810.
Catalogue of the Casts in the Statue Gallery of the Liverpool Royal Institution.
    Liverpool, 1823.
Catalogue of . . . Drawings and Pictures, the Property of William Roscoe, Esq., . . .
    Liverpool, 1816.
Catalogue of the First Exhibition of the Works of Local Artists (Living and Deceased).
    Manchester, 1857.
Catalogue of the Library of the Manchester Athenaeum. Manchester, 1847.

Catalogue of the Library of William Roscoe, Esq., . . . Liverpool, 1816.

Catalogue of the Pictures, Casts from the Antique, &c. in the Liverpool Royal Institution. Liverpool, 1836.

A Catalogue of the Present Collection of Books in the Liverpool Library, to which is prefixed a Copy of the Laws and a List of the Subscribers. Liverpool, 1760.

Catalogue of . . . Prints . . . the Property of William Roscoe, Esq., . . . Liverpool, 1816.

A Catalogue of the Valuable Collection of Paintings and Drawings, Prints and Etchings, Cabinets of Inserts, &c. (The Property of the late John Leigh Philips, Esq.). Manchester, 1814.

A Collection of Prints, from pictures painted for the purpose of illustrating the dramatic works of Shakespeare by the Artists of Great Britain. 2 vols. London, 1803.

Collins, W. Wilkie. *Memoirs of the Life of William Collins, esq., R.A.* London, 1848.

A Companion to Mr. Bullock's Museum. Liverpool, 1808 and 1810.

Cooper, Antony Ashley, 3rd Earl of Shaftesbury. *Second Characteristics on the Language of Forms.* Edited by Benjamin Rand. Cambridge, 1914.

Cunningham, Allan. *The Lives of the most eminent British Painters, Sculptors and Architects.* Edited by Mrs. Heaton. 3 vols. London, 1879–80.

—— *The Life of Sir David Wilkie.* 2 vols. London. 1843.

Daulby, Daniel. *A Descriptive Catalogue of the Works of Rembrandt, and of his Scholars, Bol, Lievens and van Vliet.* Liverpool, 1796.

Descriptive and Historical Catalogue of the Pictures, Drawings and Casts in the Gallery of Art of the Royal Institution. Liverpool, 1859.

Disraeli, Benjamin. *Coningsby or The New Generation.* New York, 1962.

Eastlake, Sir Charles L. *Contributions to the Literature of the Fine Arts.* 2nd series, with a Memoir by Lady Eastlake. London, 1870.

—— *A History of the Gothic Revival.* London, 1872.

Eastlake, Lady Elizabeth. *Journals and Correspondence.* Edited by C. E. Smith. 2 Vols. London, 1895.

—— *Life of John Gibson, R.A., Sculptor.* London, 1870.

Engravings from the Works of Henry Liverseege. London, n.d.

Farington, Joseph. *The Farington Diary.* Edited by James Greig. 8 vols. London, 1923–8.

Gibbs, Henry Steinthall. *Autobiography of a Manchester Cotton Manufacturer; or Thirty Years' Experience of Manchester.* Manchester, 1887.

Gilchrist, Alexander. *Life of William Etty, R.A.* 2 vols. London, 1855.

Hall, Samuel Carter (ed.), *The Vernon Gallery of British Art.* 3 vols. London, 1854.

Hawthorne, Nathaniel. *The English Notebooks.* Edited by Randall Stewart. New York, 1962.

Haydon, Benjamin Robert. *Correspondence and Table Talk.* 2 vols. Boston, 1877.

—— *The Diary of Benjamin Robert Haydon.* Edited by Willard Bissell Pope. 5 vols. Cambridge, Mass., 1960–3.

Hazlitt, William. *Criticisms on Art: and Sketches of the Picture Galleries of England.* Edited by his son. London, 1843.

Heywood, Benjamin Arthur. *Addresses delivered at the Meetings of the Proprietors of the Liverpool Royal Institution, on the 17th February 1822 and 13th February, 1824.* Liverpool, 1824.

Heywood, Sir Benjamin. *Addresses delivered at the Manchester Mechanics' Institution.* London, 1843.

Heywood, James. *Address to the Members of the Manchester Athenaeum.* Manchester, 1836.

Hoare, Prince. *An Inquiry into the Requisite Cultivation and Present State of the Arts of Design in England.* London, 1806.

Hogarth, William. *The Analysis of Beauty. With the Rejected Passages from the Manuscript Drafts and Autobiographical Notes.* Edited by Joseph Burke. Oxford, 1955.

Jackson, George. *Two Essays on a School of Design for the Useful Arts.* Manchester, 1837.

Knight, Richard Payne. *The Landscape.* London, 1794.

—— *Analytical Inquiry into the Principles of Taste.* 4th ed. London, 1808.

Knowles, John. *The Life and Writings of Henry Fuseli.* 3 vols. London, 1831.

Leslie, Charles Robert. *Autobiographical Recollections.* Edited by Tom Taylor. London, 1860.

Liverpool Academy. *Catalogues.* 1810–14; 1822–5; 1827–32; 1834–50.

Liverpool Mechanics' Institution. *Catalogues.* 1840, 1841, 1842.

Liverpool Mechanics' School of Arts. *Address delivered by Thos. Stewart Traill* . . . *and Resolutions, adopted at a General Meeting* . . . Liverpool, 1825.

Liverpool Mechanics' School of Arts. Annual Reports. 1825, 1828, 1833, 1836, 1842.

Manchester Athenaeum. Annual Reports. 1837–47, 1849.

Manchester Association for the Promotion of Fine Arts. Annual Reports. 1840–50.

Manchester Mechanics' Institution. Annual Reports. 1828, 1829, 1831, 1832, 1834, 1835–49.

Manchester Mechanics' Institution. *Catalogues.* 1839 and 1844.

Manchester School of Design. Annual Reports. 1844–51.

Meteyard, Eliza. *The Life of Josiah Wedgwood.* 2 vols. London, 1865–6.

Palgrave, Francis Turner. *Essays on Art.* London. 1866.

Price, Uvedale. *An Essay on the Picturesque as Compared with the Sublime and the Beautiful.* London, 1794.

Pye, John. *Patronage of British Art.* London, 1845.

Raimbach, Abraham. *Memoirs and Recollections of the late Abraham Raimbach, Esq., Engraver.* London, 1843.

Redgrave, Richard and Samuel. *A Century of Painters of the English School.* 2 vols. London, 1866.

Resolutions, Reports and Bye-Laws of the Liverpool Royal Institution, March, 1822. Liverpool, 1822.

Reynolds, Sir Joshua. *Discourses on Art.* Edited by Robert R. Wark. San Marino, 1959.

Rickman, Thomas. *Attempt to Discriminate the Styles of English Architecture, from the Conquest to the Reformation.* 2nd ed. London, 1819.

Romney, John. *Memoirs of the Life and Works of George Romney.* London, 1830.

Roscoe, Henry. *The Life of William Roscoe.* 2 vols. London, 1833.

Roscoe, William. *Catalogue of a Series of Pictures, Illustrating the Rise and Early Progress of the Art of Painting in Italy, Germany, etc.* Liverpool, 1819.

—— *The Life and Pontificate of Leo the Tenth.* London, 1846.

—— *The Life of Lorenzo de Medici, called the Magnificent.* 7th ed. Revised by his son, Thomas Roscoe. London, 1846.

—— *On the Origin and Vicissitudes of Literature, Science and Art, and their influence on the present State of Society.* Liverpool, 1817.

Royal Manchester Institution. *Catalogues.* 1827–50.

Shepherd, William. *A Selection from the Early Letters of the late Rev. William Shepherd.* Liverpool, 1855.

Smith, J. T. *Nollekens and His Times.* London, 1929.

Smithers, H. *Liverpool, its Commerce, Statistics, and Institutions; with A History of the Cotton Trade.* Liverpool, 1825.

Society for Promoting Painting and Design in Liverpool. *Catalogues.* 1784 and 1787.

Syllabuses of lectures, programs of entertainments, notices of meetings, and lists of classes and lectures. (Found with annual reports or in other volumes of various societies.)

de Tocqueville, Alexis. *Journeys to England and Ireland.* Edited by J. P. Mayer. New Haven, 1958.

Traill, Thomas Stewart. *Address delivered in February, 1828, at the General Meeting of the Members of the Liverpool Institution.* Liverpool, 1828.

—— *Address delivered in February, 1829, at the General Meeting of the Members of the Liverpool Institution.* Liverpool, 1829.

Waagen, G. F. *Works of Art and Artists in England.* Translated by H. E. Lloyd. 3 vols. London, 1838.

—— *Treasures of Art in Great Britain.* Translated by Lady Eastlake. 4 vols. London, 1854–7.

Wallis, George. *Introductory Address, . . . to the Students of the Manchester, School of Design.* Manchester, 1844.

Walpole, Horace. *Anecdotes of Painting in England.* With additions by Rev. James Dallaway. 5 vols. London, 1828.

Waring, J. B. (ed.). *Art Treasures of the United Kingdom.* London, 1858.

Wheeler, James. *Manchester: Its Political, Social and Commercial History, Ancient and Modern.* London, 1836.

Williams, D. E. *The Life and Correspondence of Sir Thomas Lawrence, Kt.* 2 vols. London, 1831.

Winckelmann, J. J. *History of Ancient Art.* 3 vols. Boston, 1880.

Winstanley, Thomas. *Observations on the Arts.* Liverpool, 1828.

III. WORKS WRITTEN AFTER 1870

Periodicals:

The Architectural Review. 1896– .
Burlington Magazine. 1903– .
Economic History Review. 1927– .
The Liverpool Bulletin. 1951– .
The Times Literary Supplement. 1902– .
Transactions of the Historic Society of Lancashire and Cheshire. 1849– .
Victorian Studies. 1957– .
Warburg Institute Journal. 1937– .

Addresses, Catalogues, Articles and Books:

Ames, Winslow. *Prince Albert and Victorian Taste.* New York, 1968.
Anderson. M. S. *Eighteenth Century Europe 1713–1789.* London, 1966.
Antal, Frederick. *Fuseli Studies.* London, 1956.
—— *Hogarth and His Place in European Art.* New Tork, 1962.
Art Treasures Centenary: European Old Masters. Manchester, 1957.

The Arts Council of Great Britain. *Early Conversation Pieces of the Eighteenth Century*. Illustrated Catalogue. London, 1946.

—— *The Romantic Movement*. Catalogue of the Exhibition. London, 1959.

Ashcroft, Thomas. *English Art and English Society*. London, 1936.

Ashton, T. S. *An Economic History of England: The Eighteenth Century*. New York, 1959.

Axon, W. E. A. (ed.). *The Annals of Manchester*. Manchester, 1886.

Bate, Walter Jackson. *From Classic to Romantic: Premises of Taste in Eighteenth Century England*. New Tork, 1961.

Beard, Miriam. *A History of Business: From Babylon to the Monopolists*. Ann Arbor, 1962.

de Beer, G. R. *Sir Hans Sloane and the British Museum*. Oxford, 1953.

Bell, Quentin. *The Schools of Design*. London, 1963.

Bemrose, William. *The Life and Works of Joseph Wright, A.R.A., commonly called 'Wright of Derby'*. London, 1885.

Berry, Henry F. *A History of the Royal Dublin Society*. London, 1914.

Binyon, Laurence. *English Water-Colours*. London, 1933.

Boase, T. S. R. *English Art: 1800–1870*. Vol. X of *The Oxford History of English Art*. Oxford, 1959.

Bolton, Arthur. *The Architecture of Robert and James Adam 1758–1794*. 2 vols. London, 1922.

Boney, Knowles. *Liverpool Porcelain of the Eighteenth Century and its Makers*. London, 1957.

Bovill, E. W. *English Country Life*. Oxford, 1962.

Bowden, Witt. *Industrial Society in England Towards the End of the Eighteenth Century*. 2nd ed. New York, 1965.

Briggs, Asa. *The Age of Improvement*. London, 1962.

—— *Victorian Cities*. London, 1964.

Briggs, M. S. *Men of Taste, from Pharaoh to Ruskin*. London, 1947.

Brindley, W. H. 'The Manchester Literary and Philosophical Society', *Journal of the Royal Institute of Chemistry* (February 1955).

—— (ed.). *The Soul of Manchester*. Manchester, 1929.

Brown, A. T. *How Gothic Came Back to Liverpool: a paper read to the Literary and Philosophical Society*. London, 1937.

Burn, W. L. *The Age of Equipoise; A Study of the Mid-Victorian Generation*. London, 1964.

Cameron, Rondo, *et al*. *Banking in the Early Stages of Industrialisation: A Study in Comparative Economic History*. New York, 1967.

Chaloner, W. H. 'Manchester in the Latter Half of the Eighteenth Century', *Bulletin of the John Rylands Library*, XLII, No. 1 (September, 1959).

Chandler, George. *William Roscoe of Liverpool 1753–1831*. London, 1953.

Checkland, S. G. *The Rise of Industrial Society in England: 1815–1885*, London, 1964.

Clark, Sir Kenneth. *The Gothic Revival: A Study in the History of Taste*. London, 1950.

Clayton, Ellen C. *English Female Artists*. 2 vols. London, 1876.

Cleveland, S. D. *Guide to the Manchester Art Galleries*. Manchester, 1956.

—— *The Manchester Royal Institution to 1882*. Manchester, 1931.

Clifford, James L. (ed.). *Man Versus Society in 18th Century Britain: Six Points of View*. Cambridge, 1968.

Conway, William Martin. *The Gallery of Art of the Royal Institution, Liverpool.* Liverpool, 1884.

Crook, J. Mordaunt. 'Sir Robert Peel: Patron of the Arts', *History Today* (January 1966).

Davis, Frank. *Victorian Patrons of the Arts: Twelve Famous Collections and Their Owners.* London, 1963.

Davis, Ralph. *The Rise of the English Shipping Industry in the Seventeenth and Eighteenth Centuries.* London, 1962.

Deane, Phyllis and Cole, W. A. *British Economic Growth, 1688–1959: Trends and Structure.* Cambridge, 1962.

Dibdin, E. Rimbault. 'Liverpool Art and Artists in the Eighteenth Century", *Transactions of the Walpole Society* (1917–18).

Dickinson, H. W. *Matthew Boulton.* Cambridge, 1937.

Dodds, John W. *The Age of Paradox: A Biography of England 1841–1851.* New York, 1952.

Dyall, Charles. *Descriptive Catalogue of the Permanent Collection of Pictures: Walker Art Gallery.* Liverpool, 1886.

Evans, Joan. *A History of the Society of Antiquaries.* Oxford, 1956.

—— *John Ruskin.* New York, 1954.

Farr, Dennis. *William Etty.* London, 1958.

Finberg, A. J. *The Life of J. M. W. Turner, R.A.* 2nd ed. Revised and with a supplement by Hilda F. Finberg. Oxford, 1961.

Fitton, R. S., and Wadsworth, A. P. *The Strutts and Arkwrights, 1758–1830; a Study of the Early Factory System.* Manchester, 1958.

Fleming, John. *Robert Adam and His Circle, in Edinburgh and Rome.* Cambridge, Mass., 1962.

Frankl, Paul. *The Gothic: Literary Sources and Interpretations through Eight Centuries.* Princeton, 1960.

Frith, W. P. *My Autobiography and Reminiscences.* 3 vols. London, 1887–8.

Garlick, Kenneth. *Sir Thomas Lawrence.* London, 1954.

Gash, Norman. *Mr. Secretary Peel.* Cambridge, Mass., 1961.

Goodyear, William H. 'Winckelmann's Place in Modern History', *Brooklyn Museum Quarterly* (July 1917).

Greaves, Margaret. *Regency Patron: Sir George Beaumont.* London, 1966.

Grindley, B. H. *History and Work of the Liverpool Academy of Arts.* Liverpool, 1875.

Grindon, Leo H. *Manchester Banks and Bankers: Historical, Biographical and Anecdotal.* 2nd ed. Manchester, 1878.

Gwynne, Stephen. *Memorials of an Eighteenth Century Painter* (James Northcote). London, 1898.

Handlin, Oscar (ed.). *The Historian and the City.* Cambridge, Mass., 1963.

Haskell, Francis. *Patrons and Painters; A Study in the Relations between Italian Art and Society in the Age of the Baroque.* New York, 1963.

Hauser, Arnold. *Rococo, Classicism, Romanticism,* Vol. III of the Vintage Edition of *The Social History of Art.* New York, 1958.

Hueffer, Ford Madox. *Ford Madox Brown.* London, 1896.

Hitchcock, Henry-Russell. *Early Victorian Architecture in Britain.* 2 vols. New Haven, 1954.

Hudson, O. and Luckhurst, K. W. *The Royal Society of Arts: 1754–1954.* London, 1954.

Hughes, John. *Liverpool Banks and Bankers: 1760–1837.* Liverpool, 1906.

Hussey, Christopher. *The Picturesque: Studies in a Point of View.* New York, 1927.

Ironside, Robin. *Pre-Raphaelite Painters. With a Descriptive Catalogue by John Gere.* London, 1948.

Jenkins, Frank. *Architect and Patron.* London, 1961.

Jordan, Robert Furneaux. *Victorian Architecture.* Harmondsworth, Middlesex, 1966.

Kaufman, Paul. 'The Community Library: A Chapter in English Social History', *Transactions of the American Philosophical Society*, new series, Vol. LVII. Philadelphia, 1967.

Kelly, Thomas. *A History of Adult Education in Great Britain.* Liverpool, 1962.

Kitson Clark, G. *The Making of Victorian England.* Cambridge, 1962.

Klingender, F. D. *Art and the Industrial Revolution.* London, 1947.

Kohn, Hans. *The Idea of Nationalism: A Study in its Origins and Background.* New York, 1961.

Luckhurst, Kenneth W. *The Story of Exhibitions.* London, 1951.

MacKenna, R. W. *The Athenaeum.* Liverpool, 1928.

Manchester Art Gallery. *Handbook to the Permanent Collection.* Compiled by J. E. Phythian. Manchester, 1910.

Manchester and its Region: A Survey prepared for the British Association. Manchester, 1962.

Manson, James A. *Sir Edwin Landseer.* London, 1902.

Mantoux, Paul. *The Industrial Revolution in the Eighteenth Century.* rev. ed. London, 1931.

Marillier, H. C. *The Liverpool School of Painters.* London, 1904.

Marshall, Dorothy. *English People in the Eighteenth Century.* London, 1962.

Marshall, Leon S. *The Development of Public Opinion in Manchester.* Syracuse, 1946.

Mayer, Joseph. *Early Exhibitions of Art in Liverpool.* Liverpool, 1876.

McLachlan, H. *Warrington Academy: Its History and Influence.* London, 1943.

Mingay, G. E. *English Landed Society in the Eighteenth Century.* Toronto, 1963.

Mitchell, B. R., with the collaboration of Phyllis Deane. *Abstract of British Historical Statistics.* Cambridge, 1962.

Morton, G. H. *Museums of the Past, the Present and the Future.* Liverpool, 1894.

Muir, J. R. *A History of Liverpool.* 2nd ed. London, 1907.

Mumford, Lewis. *The City in History: Its Origins, its Transformations, and its Prospects.* New York, 1961.

Munford, W. A. *William Ewart, M.P., 1798–1869; Portrait of a Radical.* London, 1960.

Nicolson, Benedict. *Joseph Wright of Derby: Painter of Light.* 2 vols. London, 1958.

Olney, Clarke. *Benjamin Robert Haydon: Historical Painter.* Athens, Ga., 1952.

Ormerod, Henry A. *The Liverpool Royal Institution.* Liverpool, 1953.

Owen, David. *English Philanthropy 1660–1960.* Cambridge, Mass., 1964.

Paviere, Sidney H. *The Devis Family of Painters.* Leigh-on-Sea, 1950.

Peardon, Thomas Preston. *The Transition in English Historical Writing 1760–1830.* New York, 1933.

Pevsner, Nikolaus. *Academies of Art, Past and Present.* Cambridge, 1940.

—— *The Englishness of English Art.* New York, 1956.

Picton, J. A. *Memorials of Liverpool, Historical and Topographical, including a History of the Dock Estate.* 2nd ed. 2 vols. London, 1875.

Pictures from Ince Blundell Hall. Manchester, 1960.

Pilcher, Donald. *The Regency Style, 1800 to 1830.* London, 1947.

Pratt, Tinsley, *The Portico Liberary of Manchester: Its History and Associations 1802–1922.* Manchester, 1922.

Pressnell, L. S. *Country Banking in the Industrial Revolution.* Oxford, 1956.

Rathbone, Eleanor F. *William Rathbone: a Memoir.* London, 1905.

Read, Donald. *The English Provinces, c. 1760–1960: A Study in Influence.* New York, 1964.

Redford, A., and Russell I. S. *History of Local Government in Manchester.* 3 vols. London, 1939–40.

Reitlinger, G. R. *The Economics of Taste: the Rise and Fall of Picture Prices, 1760–1960.* London, 1961.

Reynolds, Graham. *Painters of the Victorian Scene.* London, 1953.

Romantic Art in Britain: Paintings and Drawings, 1760–1860. Philadelphia, 1968.

Rosenberg, John D. *The Darkening Glass: A Portrait of Ruskin's Genius.* New York, 1961.

Rossetti, William Michael. *Pre-Raphaelite Diaries and Letters.* London, 1900.

Ruskin, John. *The Works of John Ruskin.* Edited by E. T. Cook and Alexander Wedderburn. 39 vols. London, 1903–12.

Schofield, Robert E. *The Lunar Society of Birmingham.* Oxford, 1963.

Shapiro, Seymour. *Capital and the Cotton Industry in the Industrial Revolution.* Ithaca, 1967.

Simon, Brian. *Studies in the History of Education, 1780–1870.* London, 1960.

Smart, Alastair. *The Life and Art of Allan Ramsay.* London, 1952.

Sparrow, Walter Shaw. *British Sporting Artists from Barlow to Herring.* London, 1922.

Steegman, John. *The Rule of Taste from George I to George IV.* London, 1936.

—— *Consort of Taste, 1830–1870.* London, 1950.

Stewart, Cecil. *A Short History of the Manchester College of Art.* Manchester, 1953.

—— *The Stones of Manchester.* London, 1956.

Summerson, John. *Architecture in Britain 1530 to 1830.* Harmondsworth, Middlesex, 1958.

—— *Heavenly Mansions.* New York, 1963.

Swindells, T. *Manchester Streets and Manchester Men.* 5 vols. Manchester, 1906–08.

Tietze, Hans. *Treasures of the Great National Galleries.* New York, 1954.

Turberville, A. S. (ed.). *Johnson's England: An Account of the Life and Manners of his Age.* 2 vols. Oxford, 1952.

Twenty Pictures by Liverpool Artists. Liverpool, 1951.

Tylecote, Mabel. *The Mechanics Institutes of Lancashire and Yorkshire Before 1851.* Manchester, 1957.

Wadsworth, A. P., and Mann, J. L. *The Cotton Trade and Industrial Lancashire, 1600–1780.* Manchester, 1931.

Waterhouse, Ellis. *Painting in Britain: 1530 to 1790.* 2nd ed. Baltimore, 1962.

Watson, J. Steven. *The Reign of George III, 1760–1815.* Vol. XII of *The Oxford History of England.* Edited by Sir George Clark. Oxford, 1960.

Watson, Robert Spence. *The History of the Literary and Philosophical Society of Newcastle-Upon-Tyne 1793–1896.* London, 1897.

Webb, R. K. *Modern England: From the Eighteenth Century to the Present*. New York, 1968.

Whitley, William T. *Artists and Their Friends in England 1700 to 1799*. 2 vols. London, 1928.

—— *Art in England, 1800–1820*. Cambridge, 1928.

—— *Art in England, 1821–1837*. Cambridge, 1930.

Williams, Raymond. *Culture and Society, 1780–1950*. London, 1958.

Wittkower, Rudolph and Margaret. *Born Under Saturn, The Character and Conduct of Artists: A Documented History from Antiquity to the French Revolution*. London, 1963.

Woodward, E. L. *The Age of Reform, 1815–1870*. 2nd ed., Oxford, 1962.

Yates, S. A. T. *Memorials of the Family of Rev. John Yates*. Liverpool, 1890.

Young, G. M. (ed.). *Early Victorian Enland 1830–1865*. 2 vols. Oxford, 1951.

Reference Works:

Bryan, M. *Dictionary of Painters and Engravers*. 1st ed., 1816. Revised by G. Stanley, 1849, and G. C. Williamson, 1903–04. 5 vols. London, 1913.

Colvin, H. M. *A Biographical Dictionary of English Architects 1660–1840*. London, 1954.

Dictionary of National Biography. Edited by Leslie Stephen and Sidney Lee. 22 vols. London, 1908–09.

Encyclopedia of World Art. 15 vols. London, 1959–68.

INDEX

Academies of art, 14–15; in Liverpool, 25 f., 33 f., 44–5, 47 f., 52 f.; in Manchester, 76–7
Adam, Robert, 24
Agnew, Thomas, 110, 129
Agnew and Zanetti, 101, 129, 133
Agnews, 140, 159
Albert of Saxe-Coburg, Prince Consort, 151–2
Alison, Archibald, 38
Allnutt, Mr., of Clapham Common, 16
Ansdell, Richard, 54, 76, 145
Appleby, Thomas, 143
Architecture: in Liverpool, 13, 33, 102; in Manchester, 11–12, 67, 103–4; in Salford, 11
Aristocracy as patrons of art, 1–3, 15–16, 123–4, 152, 156
Art academies, see Academies of art
Art society in eighteenth-century Liverpool, see Liverpool Academy
Art Treasures Exhibition of 1857, 151–3
Art Unions: goals, 80, 81, 82; in Germany 80–1; in Scotland, 81–82; London Art Union, 82, 89; in Liverpool, 82 f.; in Manchester, 85 f.; in Dublin, 91; influence of, 91 f.
Ashton, John, 24
Ashton, Mrs. John, 24
Ashton, Nicholas, 24
Ashton, Samuel, 144, 145, 146
Ashworth, Richard J. D., 134
Astley, Francis Dukinfield, 133
Astley, John, 133
Atheneum, 22
Atkinson, William, 38
Austin, Samuel, 49, 54, 70, 149

Bachelier, Jean Jacques, 28
Banking, 10–11
Banks, Joseph, 17
Barber, Charles, 49
Barker, Charles, 70
Barnes, John, 25
Barnes, Dr. Thomas, 21, 96–7

Barry, Sir Charles, 67
Barton, John, W., 135
Barton, Samuel, 70, 135
Bashall, William, 144, 145, 158
Baxter, Edward, 134
Beaconsfield, see Disraeli
Beardoe, James, 70, 135
Beaumont, Sir George, 15, 16
Bell, John Zephaniah, 114
Bent, Edward, 110
Bentley, Thomas, 21, 22
Bird, John, 39
Blundell, Henry, 2–3, 30, 36, 37
Bond, Richard, 56
Bonington, Richard Parkes, 143
Botanic garden of Liverpool, 22–3
Boydell, John, 17
Bradley, William, 65, 74
Britton, John, 69
Brotherton, Joseph, 63, 119
Brougham, Henry, Baron Brougham and Vaux, 5, 105
Brown, Ford Madox, 79, 147
Brown, Mather, 65
Broxall, William, 52
Brunswick Buildings, Liverpool, 102
Bullock, George, 40
Bullock, William, 118
Bulwer-Lytton, see Lytton
Burdett, P. P., 25, 26, 28, 29
Burns, William Henry, 39
Buss, Robert William, 106
Byers, James, 2
Byng, John, fifth Viscount Torrington, 11

Caddick, Richard, 25, 26, 27, 29, 30
Callcott, Augustus Wall, 16, 48, 70, 143
Calvert, Charles, 65, 66, 70, 74, 106
Carey, William, 33, 34, 126
Carrington Bowles, publishers, 17
Cary, George, 16
Cattermole, George, 145, 154
Chaffers, Richard, 8
Chamberly, Mr., 16
Chapman, John, 144, 146
Chetham's Hospital, Manchester, 12

Chubbard, Thomas, 25, 28, 29, 30, 32
Clarke, William, 10, 137
Clarke, William, & Co., 11, 60
Clayton, Mrs. Sarah, 24
Cobden, Richard, 63, 103
Cockerell, Charles Robert, 45, 102
Collections of English art in Lancashire, 136 f., 158
Collectors of Old Masters in Lancashire, 124 f.
Collier, John, 150
Collins, William, 18, 38, 72
Comenius, 21
Commercial Room, Manchester, 12
Common Council of Liverpool, 51
Constable, John, 15, 146
Cooke, Henry, 143, 144, 156, 158
Cooper, Abraham, 70
Cooper, Anthony Ashley, see Shaftesbury
Cope, Charles West, 53
Copley, John Singleton, 15
Cotman, John Sell, 86
Coventry, Lord, 16
Cox, David, 70, 154
Craig, William Marshall, 65
Creswick, Thomas, 86
Cross Street Chapel, Manchester, 12, 21
Currie, Dr. James, 22

Daniell, Thomas, 36
Daniell, William, 36
Daulby, Daniel, 4, 28, 29, 31, 32, 130, 136, 137
Davidson, Alexander, 15
Davis, William, 149
Dawson, Henry, 56
Dawson, John, 135
De Quincey, Thomas, 94
Derby, James Stanley, tenth Earl of, 3
Derrick, Samuel, 8
Design, see Schools of design
Devis, Arthur, 14–15
De Wint, Peter, 38, 70, 154
Disraeli, Benjamin, first Earl of Beaconsfield, 148
Dissenting academies, 20–1
Dodd, William, 64, 65, 66, 128
Dodgson, George, 56
Duff, William, 131
Duval, Charles Allen, 77
Dyce, William, 157, 158

Earle, William, 137
Eastlake, Sir Charles, 92, 110, 146, 158
Eastlake, Lady Elizabeth, 91, 123
Economic growth: in Lancashire, 7; in Liverpool, 7–9, 33; in Manchester, 9–10, 63–4
Educational institutions, 20–1, 42–3, 96–7; see also Academies of art
Egerton, see Ellesmere
Ellesmere, Francis Egerton, first Earl of, 151
Elmes, Harvey Lonsdale, 102
Engels, Friedrich, 11
English art: collections of, in Lancashire, 136 f., 158
Enlightenment: influence on merchants and manufacturers, 20
Etty, William, 38, 73, 75, 79, 138, 140, 141, 144
Everard, William, 21, 25, 26, 29
Ewart, William, 80, 120
Exhibitions of art: Royal Academy, 15; Liverpool Academy, 27–8, 30–3, 36 f., 47 f.; Liverpool Autumn Exhibitions, 57–8; Royal Manchester Institution, 69 f.; Mechanics' Institutes, 109 f.; Manchester School of Design, 115–17; Art Treasures Exhibition, 151–3
Eyes, Charles, 25, 29
Eyes, John, 25

Faed, Thomas, 145, 158
Fairbairn, William, 113, 114
Farington, Joseph, 34, 139, 150
Faulkner, Benjamin, 74
Faulkner, Joshua Wilson, 39
Fawkes, Walter, 16
Fielding, Copley, 49, 70
Finch, John, 3
Fletcher, Jacob, 131, 132
Ford, William, 128, 133–5, 142
Foster, John, 39, 40, 45, 100
Fowke, Francis, 151
Francia, Louis, 38
Fraser, James, 112
Frith, William Powell, 84, 92, 141, 144, 159
Fuseli, Henry, 31, 32, 40, 137

Gainsborough, Thomas, 16, 32
Gallery of British Painters, 15
Gandy, Joseph Michael, 34, 37
Gentry as patrons of art, 1–3

George III, 15
George IV, 37, 45, 67
Gibbs, Henry Steinthal, 153-5
Gibson, John, 40, 148
Gibson, Solomon, 100
Gilpin, Sir William, 38
Gladstone, Sir John, 13, 49, 50, 51, 52, 60, 131, 132, 148, 156
Glover, John, 38, 70
Godwin, George, 106
Goodall, Frederick, 145
Goore family, 24, 25
Grant, Daniel, 110, 138
Graves, Henry, 18
Greaves, John, 143
Greg, Samuel, 64
Gregson, Matthew, 3, 4, 28, 29-30, 39, 137
Grosvenor, Robert, second Earl, 16
Grundy, John Clowes, 89, 140

Haghe, Louis, 145
Hall, Samuel Carter, 136
Hammersley, James A., 78, 115
Hancock, Charles, 73
Hardman, Mrs. James, 70
Hardman, William, 142
Hargreaves, Richard, 70
Hargreaves, Thomas, 39
Harrison, Mary, 54
Harrison, Thomas, 12, 39
Havell, William, 70
Hawthorne, Nathaniel, 77, 129-30, 147, 153, 162
Haydon, Benjamin Robert, 15, 39, 45, 61, 69, 72-3, 102, 106, 108, 112, 113, 141
Hazlitt, William, 65
Heaphy, Thomas, 16, 38
Hearne, Thomas, 31
Henry, Dr. Thomas, 95, 97
Herbert, John Rogers, 53, 157, 158
Herdman, William Gawin, 53, 148
Hesketh, Fleetwood, 24
Heywood, Arthur, 21
Heywood, Sir Benjamin, 105, 108, 109, 111, 112, 113, 114, 161
Heywood, Benjamin, 21
Heywood, Benjamin Arthur, 43, 44, 46, 60, 67, 68, 105, 137, 143
Heywood, Richard, 30
Hick, Benjamin, 84, 143, 150, 156
Hills, Robert, 16
Hindley, Robert, 129
Hoare, Sir Richard Colt, 15-16
Hofland, Thomas Christopher, 36, 70

Hogarth, William, 16
Holland, Peter, 32
Holt, David, 134
Holt, John, 32
Howard, Henry, 36, 49, 50, 51
Hugford, Ignazio Enrico, 2
Huggins, William, 55
Hulme, Dr. Davenport, 68
Hunt, William Holman, 54, 147

Illidge, Thomas Henry, 65, 70, 74, 100
Industrial Revolution, 1, 7, 63-4
Italian art: influence of, 2-3

Jackson, Samuel, 64
Jackson, W., 32
Jenkins, Thomas, 2
Jones, Loyd & Co., 11
Jordan, Francis, 131

Kauffmann, Angelica, see Zucchi
Kay-Shuttleworth, Sir James Phillips, 64
Keeling, William Knight, 77

Labruzzi, 60
Landseer, Sir Edwin, 18, 110, 144, 145, 146
Lawrence, Sir Thomas, 38, 51, 68
Lear, Edward, 158
Learned societies, see Literary and philosophical societies
Lee, Frederick Richard, 72, 157
Leeds: Northern Society, 34
Leicester, Sir John, 16, 67
Lever, Sir Ashton, 118
Leveson-Gower, see Stafford
Leyland, Bullins & Co., 11
Linnell, John, 86, 146
Linton, William, 56, 70, 72, 143
Literary and philosophical societies: goals, 95; Liverpool Philosophical and Literary Society, 23, 29; Liverpool Literary and Philosophical Society, 98-100; Manchester Literary and Philosophical Society, 95-8
Littledale, Arthur, 45
Liverpool, 1, 4, 7, 8, 9, 13, 20, 21-3, 33, 102-3; Society of Amateurs of, 52, 53
Liverpool Academy, 25 f., 33 f., 44-45, 47 f., 52 f.
Liverpool Autumn Exhibitions, 57-58

Liverpool Common Council, 51
Liverpool Library, 21-2
Liverpool Literary and Philosophical Society, 98-100; papers on art and architecture, 99-100
Liverpool Mechanics' Institute, 104 f., 119
Liverpool Philosophical and Literary Society, 23, 29
Liverpool Royal Institution, 42-4; lecture programme, 45-6; collection of paintings, 58 f.; permanent gallery, 61
Liverpool Society for Promoting the Study of Architecture and Engineering, 101
Liverseege, Henry, 70, 74-5, 143, 150
Locke, John, 21
London: influence on provinces, 12-13, 23
Lowe, John, 133
Loyd, Edward, 70
Lytton, Edward George Bulwer-, first Baron Lytton, 40

Macartney, George, first Earl, 17
M'Connel, Henry, 110, 163-4
Maclise, Daniel, 144
McMorland, Patrick, 30, 32
Manchester, 1, 7, 9, 10, 11-12, 13, 20, 62-3, 103-4
Manchester Academy of Art, 76-7
Manchester Architectural Society, 101-2
Manchester College of Arts and Science, 21, 96-7
Manchester Institution, Royal, 66 f.
Manchester Literary and Philosophical Society, 23, 42, 63, 95-8
Manchester Mechanics' Institute, 105, 106, 109-11, 119
Manchester School of Design, 109, 112-17
Marsland, Mr., 143
Martin, John, 18, 143, 147
Mechanics' Institutes, 104 f.
Memoirs of the Literary and Philosophical Society of Manchester: papers on art and archaeology, 97-8
Middle classes as patrons of art, 1, 3-5, 12-13, 14, 17-19, 23-4, 51-2, 65-6, 80, 83, 93-4, 122 f.
Millais, Sir John Everett, 54, 147, 148, 158
Miller, John, 144, 149, 159, 163

Miller, Thomas, 143, 144, 156, 158, 159
Morland, George, 143
Mulgrave, Henry Phipps, first Earl of, 16
Mulready, William, 16
Myall, A. T., 74

Naylor, John, 144, 146, 147, 163-4
Nazarenes, 157
Northcote, James, 15, 16, 17, 70, 75
Northern Society of Leeds, 34

Oakes, John Wright, 55
Old Masters, *see* Collectors
Orme, Daniel, 65

Pack, Christopher, 29, 30, 137
Palmer, James, 84
Parker of Newcastle, 110
Parry, Joseph, 32, 149
Pateshall, Mr., 135
Pelham, James, II, 57
Pennington, John, 56
Percival, Thomas, 65, 94
Perigal, Arthur, 70
Philipe, Thomas, 126
Philips, Sir George, 142
Philips, John Leigh, 29, 125, 132 141
Philips, Robert, 64
Phipps, Sir Henry, *see* Mulgrave
Pickersgill, Henry, 49
Plint, Thomas, 158
Poole, Paul Falconer, 145
Potter, Sir Thomas, 64
Pre-Raphaelites, 54, 57, 147-8, 149, 153
Preston, Thomas, 64
Price, Sir Uvedale, 38, 122
Print society of Liverpool, 4
Prints and print sellers, 17-19, 31, 64, 82, 84-5, 87, 128-9
Prout, Samuel, 70, 155
Public Libraries Act of 1850, 120
Public museums in Lancashire: early history, 117 f.
Pugin, Augustus Welby Northmore, 157, 160

Rae, George, 148
Ralston, John, 149
Rathbone, John, 65
Redgrave, Richard, 91-2
Redgrave, Samuel, 91-2
Renshaw, Thomas, 64

Renwick, Michael, 25, 26
Repton, Humphry, 122
Reynolds, Sir Joshua, 3, 14–15, 27, 28, 30, 31, 32, 38, 47, 122, 124, 157, 160
Richardson, Mr., Liverpool picture dealer, 56
Rickman, Thomas, 36, 38, 99, 100
Roberts, David, 124, 144
Roebuck, John Arthur, 5
Rogers, Edward, 130, 137
Rogers, Samuel, 139
Romantic art: subjects, 78
Rome, 2, 3
Romney, George, 23
Romney, Peter, 23, 65
Roscoe, William, 10–11, 24, 28, 31, 35; as cultural leader, 3–4, 22, 23, 25, 36, 42; philosophy of art, 26–7, 35–6, 40, 58–60, 161; as patron of art and promoter of patronage, 34, 36, 37–8, 137, 162; collection of art, 58–60, 125–7
Rowbotham, John, 140
Royal Academy, 14–15, 19, 25, 28, 30, 31, 33
Royal Institution of London, 42
Royal Manchester Institution, 66 f.
Royal Society of Arts, London, 12, 23
Ruskin, John, 54, 79, 123, 157, 159, 160, 162

St. George's Hall, Liverpool, 102
St. Paul's Church, Liverpool, 9
St. Peter's Church, Manchester, 12
Salford, 10, 11
Sandby, Paul, 17, 30
Sandby, Thomas, 31
Scharf, George, 152
Scholes, George, 70
Schools of design: Gregson advocacy of, 28, 39; in Manchester, 109, 112 f.
Schwanfelder, Charles Henry, 70
Scientific societies, see Literary and philosophical societies
Select Committee on Art Unions, 90
Semper, George, 117
Shaftesbury, Anthony Ashley Cooper, third Earl of, 27, 160
Shaw, Joshua, 65, 149
Shepherd, Rev. William, 137
Shields, Frederick, 153, 155
Shuttleworth, see Kay-Shuttleworth

Smeaton, John, 1
Smirke, Robert, 15
Smith, Adam, 20
Society of Amateurs of Liverpool, 52, 53
Society for Promoting the Arts in Liverpool, 28–9
Stafford, Granville Leveson-Gower, first Marquis of, 16
Stanfield, Clarkson, 154
Staniforth, Thomas, 24
Stanley, James, tenth Earl of Derby, 3
Stephenson, James, 78
Stothard, Thomas, 18 n., 31
Stringer, Daniel, 149
Subjects of paintings, 32–3, 78, 157–158
Subscription libraries, 21–2, 25
Swinburne, Sir John, 16

Tate, Richard, 23, 25, 31
Tate, William, 29, 30, 32
Taylor, Frederick, 154
Taylor, John Edward, 64
Taylor, Thomas, 29, 30, 31, 32, 125, 137
Tennant, John, 73
Thackeray, William Makepeace, 18
Thomas, Richard, 64
Thomson, James, of Clitheroe, 114, 116
Thorpe, John, 2
Tobin, Sir John, 131
de Tocqueville, Alexis, 2 n., 63
Topham, Francis William, 158
Torrington, see Byng
Towne, Charles, 37, 39, 70, 150
Townley, Charles, 2
Townsend, William, 70, 134
Trafford, T. J., 70
Traill, Dr. Thomas Stewart, 36, 42, 51, 105
Tresham, Henry, 15
Turmeau, John, 39
Turner, Joseph Mallord William, 16, 37, 38, 144, 145, 146, 154, 163–4
Turner, Dr. Matthew, 25, 26, 29

Uwins, Thomas, 140

Varley, John, 70
Vernon, Thomas, 127, 139
Voltaire, 20

Waagen, Gustave, 80–1, 125, 131, 132, 145, 146, 152
Walker, Thomas, 13
Walker Art Gallery, 62
Wallis, George, 106, 115, 117
Walters, Edward, 103
Ward, Edward Matthew, 145
Ward, James, 37, 38, 67, 70
Warehouses of Manchester, 103–4
Warrington Academy, 21
Watts, George Frederick, 87
Webster, Thomas, 53
Wedgwood, Josiah, 21, 25, 28 n.
West, Sir Benjamin, 15, 17, 36, 38
Westall, Richard, 15, 37, 47, 48, 50, 70
Wheatley, Francis, 32
Wheeler, Mr., 16
Wilkie, Sir David, 15, 18, 142, 143, 146
Williams family, painters, 49
Williamson, Daniel, 37, 39
Williamson, John, 30, 32, 39
Williamson, Samuel, 38, 39, 70
Wilson, Richard, 3, 16, 17

Windus, William, 149
Winstanley, Hamlet, 3
Winstanley, James T., 60
Winstanley, Peter, 3
Winstanley, Thomas, 36, 49, 51, 52, 60, 61, 62, 100, 127–8
Wood, George William, 64
Wood of Bath, John, 8, 24
Woodforde, Samuel, 16, 37
Wordsworth, William, 38
Wornum, Ralph Nicholson, 106
Wright of Derby, Joseph, 23–4, 25, 26, 29 n., 30, 31, 32, 47, 137, 141–2
Wyatt, Henry, 65
Wyatt, James, 12
Wycke, John, 25

Yates, John Ashton, 60, 125, 131
Yates, Joseph Brooks, 60, 130–1

Zanetti brothers, carvers and gilders, 129
Zoffany, John, 2 n., 4, 30
Zucchi, Angelica Kauffmann, 32